Secrets of

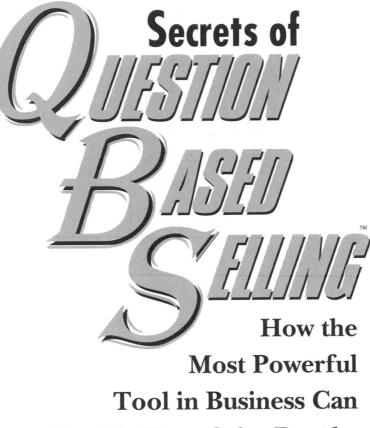

QUESTION BASED SELLING ™

How the
Most Powerful
Tool in Business Can
Double Your Sales Results

Thomas A. Freese

sourcebooks

Copyright © 2000, 2013 by Thomas A. Freese
Cover and internal design © 2013 by Sourcebooks, Inc.

Sourcebooks and the colophon are registered trademarks of Sourcebooks, Inc.

All rights reserved. No part of this book may be reproduced in any form or by any electronic or mechanical means including information storage and retrieval systems—except in the case of brief quotations embodied in critical articles or reviews—without permission in writing from its publisher, Sourcebooks, Inc.

This publication is designed to provide accurate and authoritative information in regard to the subject matter covered. It is sold with the understanding that the publisher is not engaged in rendering legal, accounting, or other professional service. If legal advice or other expert assistance is required, the services of a competent professional person should be sought. —*From a Declaration of Principles Jointly Adopted by a Committee of the American Bar Association and a Committee of Publishers and Associations*

All brand names and product names used in this book are trademarks, registered trademarks, or trade names of their respective holders. Sourcebooks, Inc., is not associated with any product or vendor in this book.

Published by Sourcebooks, Inc.
P.O. Box 4410, Naperville, Illinois 60567-4410
(630) 961-3900
Fax: (630) 961-2168
www.sourcebooks.com

Library of Congress Cataloging-in-Publication data is on file with the publisher.

Printed and bound in the United States of America.
VP 19 18 17 16 15 14 13 12 11

This book is dedicated to
my three miracles: my wife Laura,
and our daughters Sarah and Mary Claire.

Contents

THE BEST SALES EXPERIENCE I HOPE YOU NEVER HAVE

On Monday, August 22, 1994, our dreams were shattered when my wife Laura was diagnosed with cancer. Sensing the gravity of the situation, Dr. George Cierny carefully placed a box of Kleenex on the adjoining table before telling us that a grapefruit-sized tumor had been discovered in Laura's hip. She had lymphoma, and we were both devastated.

In the blink of an eye, life as we knew it had changed. With a bouncing baby girl, two thriving professional careers, and a nice home in the suburbs, we had been living out the American Dream. Now, we were faced with the challenge of chemotherapy, the loss of Laura's mobility, and a 60/40 chance of survival. Laura's career was halted and she would probably lose fertility. On top of that, Dr. Cierny, as if he was looking down the barrel of a loaded gun, added, "We probably won't have to amputate…but we'll see."

Unless you have actually been there, it's hard to imagine the emotional impact of this news. It was like being hit in the face with a brick. The grief on my wife's face was daunting. I remember thinking, "This can't be happening!"

Success in my business life suddenly seemed unimportant. The fact that sales were booming was insignificant. Though I had achieved top sales honors for several consecutive years, these accomplishments now paled in comparison to the new challenges that lay ahead. It was a helpless feeling. After all, what difference does success make when everything else is falling apart?

After we grieved over this news for several days, life found a way to slap us back into reality. The daily routine took over. There were chores to do and mouths to feed, and our two-year-old daughter needed our love and attention now more than ever. Self-pity was fruitless. Instead, we dug in—knowing that we were engaged in a battle that would yield only one winner.

Laura underwent chemotherapy treatments for six long months. When she wasn't in the hospital with complications, she was at home—struggling to maintain her strength. I continued to work, but mostly for therapeutic reasons.

Selling was a release of sorts, one that helped distance me from the uncertainty of her medical condition. The usual seventy-hour workweek shrank dramatically, so it was safe to assume that my sales would suffer as a result. Selling was still a passion, but it was no longer a priority.

This adversity caused my perspective to change dramatically. With respect to my selling career, it was as if a great burden had been lifted, where all the stress, anxiety, and pressures that usually exist in a competitive business situation were suddenly gone. No more nervous butterflies before key presentations. No more agonizing over things that were out of my control. While I still wanted to do a good job, I didn't have the time or the emotional energy to worry. As a result, I relaxed and focused on those things that were most important.

Ironically, this change in perspective placed me in a unique position of strength. Because I was no longer intimidated by the threat of losing a sale, it was easy to ask the "hard" questions without fearing how customers might respond. It was also easy to differentiate important action items from things that were unnecessary. Those action items that were beneficial for the customer, my company, and me got done. Anything that was unreasonable, superfluous, or unnecessary didn't. It was that simple.

Everyone (including me) expected my sales results to drop off considerably, but that didn't happen. Devastation gave way to new resolve, and any lingering trepidation regarding a sale was quickly replaced by a new sense of clarity and purpose. In fact, during the six-month period that Laura was sick, I worked less and sold more. But not just a little more. I sold *twice as much* as I ever had. Twice as much! I couldn't believe it. The significance of this eclipsed anything else that I had ever accomplished.

Through a strange twist of fate, Laura's illness had actually created an opportunity. It had given me a chance to view the sales process from a completely different perspective. When new priorities took over, I no longer had anything to lose, and when the traditional risks of failure disappeared, my effectiveness soared. It was horrifying and enlightening at the same time—which is why I call it *the best sales experience I hope you never have.*

With the efforts, prayers, and support of countless people, Laura's cancer was reversed into full remission. She had been to the edge and back—and when the battle was over, she emerged the winner. Laura reclaimed her energy, but she never lost her spirit. Several months later, thanks to the miracle of modern medicine, her hip was replaced and her mobility was fully restored. She was back.

Almost two years after Laura was diagnosed, tears flowed once again as the city of Atlanta was getting ready to host the Twenty-Sixth Summer Olympic

Games. When the organizers for the Olympics heard about Laura's story, they recognized she had faced the ultimate personal challenge and had won. Because it was clear that her victory over cancer was as great as anything that would be achieved on the athletic field, she was given the honor of carrying the Olympic Torch.

On July 19, 1996, friends and family joined an enthusiastic crowd of 50,000 people who lined the streets of Atlanta to cheer the Olympic torch relay as it passed by on the way to the opening ceremonies. Whether they knew it or not, they were cheering for Laura too as she hoisted the Olympic Flame—a symbol that reflected her own personal accomplishment. In fact, if you look closely, you can see the Gold Medal tears in her eyes.

While adversity didn't actually teach me how to sell, it did inspire me to complete my dream, which you are now holding in your hands. The original *Secrets of Question Based Selling* and this updated version are the result of many years of extensive research, coupled with some good old-fashioned trial and error. As a sales methodology, QBS has already endured the test of time, and it has also proven itself in many different industries.

Nineteen years later, Laura is back to full strength and is very healthy, to the point where you would think she's never had a common cold. We were also very fortunate to be in the very small fraction of best-case scenarios where Laura was able to regain her fertility and we were able to have our second daughter (our miracle child) in 1998. Hooray!

My sincere hope is that this book will inspire you as much as it has me, and the many others whom I have had the opportunity to instruct. Life is short, and success is *definitely* within reach. May your own experiences in sales, and in life, build on the premise that faith, commitment, and hard work will always persevere. Always!

Acknowledgments

Three long and wonderful years were invested into bringing my initial book (*Secrets of Question Based Selling*) to fruition. At the beginning of the project, it was easy to fill pages with words. Ideas were flying onto the paper. As the project matured, however, it became clear that crafting my ideas about selling into a comprehensive and cohesive message was going to be an enormous challenge. But somehow it happened—and I could not have done it without the encouragement, loyalty, and support of a tremendous team of professionals and friends, whom I have thanked, acknowledged, and congratulated time and time again.

This book, the "new" *Secrets of Question Based Selling*, is a revised and updated version of the original work. I have learned so much over the last thirteen years of training salespeople and sales organizations, and I just had to share all of that with you.

Much appreciation goes out to Todd Stocke and Jenna Skwarek of Sourcebooks for pulling this project together. I am especially grateful to Todd for championing *Question Based Selling*'s run of having outsold itself for thirteen years straight. I wish to thank Emily Gilreath for her editing contributions in making this material more readable by removing my wayward commas and undangling my participles.

I am grateful also to Scott Whitney for his contributions. In addition to creating a killer website for QBS Research, Inc., Scott's input was integral to the organization and development of the QBS sales training programs that are now being delivered all over the world. He is a true professional.

Special thanks go out to my sales mentors whom I have had the privilege to work with and learn from over the years. In no particular order, I wish to acknowledge Alan Rohrer, Tom Flynn, Barry Gillman, Chris Andrews, Evan Steiner, Al Zuckerman, Greg Ablett, Mitch Little, Mike Wilhelm, and Julija Noskova.

Emotional support played a far greater role in the creation of this book than I could have imagined, and I can honestly say that this project would not have succeeded without the motivation and encouragement from the following talented and caring people: Richard Sites, Joe Monday, Leslie Elliott, Chip Graddy, Steve Johnson, Matt Ure, and Mark Reed. I would like to add a special note of thanks to the men in my Bible study group, who offered encouragement on a weekly basis since the original project began.

I must also thank all my clients over the years, as well as all the people who recommended Question Based Selling to their respective sales organizations, especially those people who were willing to take a chance on the QBS methodology before it took off.

Last but certainly not least, I wish to thank my wife and daughters for keeping the noise down to a dull roar while dad was downstairs writing.

THE "NEW" QUESTION BASED SELLING

Selling has become increasingly more difficult. Prospects have less time…yet decision makers are on the receiving end of more sales calls than ever before. With a boom in the number of products being offered, "No" has become the standard customer response, and the vast majority of these calls end in rejection.

This creates an interesting dilemma for salespeople and managers. When the risk of rejection is high, sales productivity tends to be very low. QBS reverses this trend by showing salespeople that the best way to increase their probability of success is to decrease their risk of failure.

Since I published my first book (*Secrets of Questions Based Selling*) some thirteen years ago, the selling environment has changed—in some ways dramatically, while other changes are very subtle. That's the difference between my original book and this updated version, the new *Secrets of Question Based Selling*. Now that I have trained hundreds of sales teams over the last fifteen years, I've discovered the QBS methodology has evolved significantly from my first work. Not surprisingly, many of the base concepts still apply—things like the need to establish credibility, pique the customer's interest, and minimize your risk of failure—all of which are indeed timeless. But, my intention with this updated version of the book was to enhance those concepts by including many of the metaphors, anecdotes, and syllogisms that have made Question Based Selling the top-rated sales course that our clients have ever experienced.

Ultimately, selling is a creative act—one that requires salespeople to go out into their respective markets and create business opportunities that otherwise wouldn't exist. This means knocking on unfamiliar doors. It also means picking up the telephone and calling new prospect accounts. Of course, once you get in, the focus changes from engagement to further developing the opportunity. This includes uncovering prospect needs, building value around your solutions, and securing the prospect's commitment to move forward.

Sounds easy, doesn't it?

It isn't. In fact, for most salespeople it's becoming increasingly difficult to secure a precious slice of the customer's time and attention, not to mention cracking into new prospect opportunities.

I am perhaps the only author/trainer who is willing to come right out and state that there is a problem in the world of sales training—where it has become very unclear which sales programs are the most effective given all of the conflicting information floating around the marketplace.

The positioning of different sales training courses is crazy! While one program touts the value of "Getting to Yes," another program focuses on the value of "Getting to the No." So which is it? Should we be shooting for a "yes," or "no"? Similarly, consultative selling has become a common buzzword in training circles for some time now, but the interpretations of what "consultative selling" is runs the gamut from SPIN Selling, to Power Base Selling, Solution Selling, Target Account Selling, and Strategic Selling, each of which contradicts the next in one way or another. Trust me, I've been through all of these programs (and more) during my years as a sales rep and also as a manager. Knowing where to turn for success can be very confusing.

The truth is, most of the sales training that has been delivered over the past twenty years has been process oriented. Don't get me wrong. Defining the steps of the sales process and having some sense of organizational consistency is important and necessary. Formalizing a sales process was particularly faddish back in the 1990s, which is when many of these programs really took off.

What process training attempts to do, however, is define the steps of the sales process. For example, I just read an article written by an entrepreneur espousing the value of the five-step model that he learned while at Procter & Gamble. Step 1: Summarize the Situation. Step 2: State the Idea. Step 3: Explain It. Step 4: Discuss. Step 5: Close. The author of this article refers to this five-step regimented sales process as "brilliant."

Other companies promote a slightly different sales process, where Step 1 is: "Identifying New Opportunities," followed by Step 2: "Qualify," Step 3: "Uncover Needs," Step 4: "Propose Solutions" …and so on.

Whichever model you settle on is immaterial from the QBS point of view. I say this because the steps are irrelevant. If you looked more closely at the reps using the Procter & Gamble model, you would very quickly notice that some of them were successful, while others continually struggled to keep their heads above water. If they are all using the same process model, why are their sales results so different?

The difference between success and failure at most companies is not related to the brilliance of whoever outlined the steps of the sales process. The difference between success and failure is more closely related to the execution of the steps within the sales process. Therefore, instead of just redefining the sales process, what salespeople and managers really want to know is something else. They want to know *how* to identify more new opportunities? *How* to be more effective at qualifying new opportunities? *How* do you uncover more needs in order to give yourself an opportunity to provide more value? And, *how* can you close more sales faster?

Question Based Selling very specifically focuses on sales effectiveness—identifying those strategies and techniques that will increase the salesperson's probability of success, while at the same time discarding whatever may reduce your risk of rejection. To me, success is about execution. Simply put, salespeople who are killing it are doing so because of their ability to successfully *execute* the various steps of the sales process. On the flip side, sellers who are not executing effectively face a significant disadvantage.

It's worth noting that the actual steps of the sales process are pretty consistent from company to company. Thus, just identifying the steps of the sale does not afford you any advantage over your competitors who have a similarly formalized sales process in place.

How well are you executing each of these steps? That's a question only you can answer. But, I must tell you that I have yet to meet a salesperson who didn't want to take their game to the next level.

With regard to QBS methodology, ask yourself this question: *Why do companies all over the world spend millions of dollars telling salespeople what to say, but they invest almost nothing when it comes to teaching them what to ask?*

I still can't figure out why most of the sales training offered today is geared toward teaching people to sound the same as everyone else. Back when I was a fledgling salesperson, I tried to do everything in my power to differentiate myself from the competition, as opposed to commoditizing my company's value proposition with industry buzzwords.

Today, the effectiveness of the individual salesperson has become more important than the products they sell or the company they represent. All you have to do is glance around your industry and you will see that some salespeople are more significantly more effective than others, even though they are selling the same types of products to the same target audience.

Therefore, the real challenge sellers face is less about defining the steps of the sales process, and more to do with figuring out *how* to execute more effectively. Things like: *How* can you pique the prospect's interest to penetrate more new opportunities? *How* do you earn enough credibility to compete for mindshare from key decision makers within important target accounts? *How* can you create the sense of urgency needed to move deals forward? Or better still, *how* can you cause skeptical customers to "want to" share information with a salesperson they don't yet know or trust? As well as, *how* can you increase your "return on invested sales effort," enough to secure an "unfair" advantage over the competition? The goal of executing more effectively is ultimately about understanding *how* to close more deals, at higher margins, in reduced time, and with less effort.

> **Secret #1**   Effective execution is more important than just defining the steps of the sales process.

Unfortunately, the sales profession in general has responded poorly to recent business trends. As prospects and customers have had to become more judicious with their time, salespeople have started pushing even harder to get a foot in the door. How do prospects respond to being pushed? Most push back in some way. When sellers call, some prospects get frustrated and hang up immediately. Others program their phones to roll directly into a voice-mail system, or they use caller ID to hold salespeople at arm's length. Invariably, that means the next salesperson who calls on the account will have to work even harder than the last. It also means they inherit the negative baggage created by all the previous callers.

When you combine reluctant prospects with pushy salespeople, it's not surprising that the average success rate when contacting new prospects has declined significantly. Depending on which article you read, the average "hit rate" for engaging new prospects is between 2 and 5 percent. So, out of every one hundred sales calls, the average salesperson will uncover only a small handful of qualified opportunities. What if we could change that? What if this initial call number could be increased to as much as 70 or 80 percent? Would that help your selling efforts?

One of my goals when I first developed QBS was to simplify the sale. We accomplished this by identifying the activities, strategies, and actions that increase your probability of success, and then incorporated those things into the sales process. But, rather than ignore the negatives, we also sought to identify and avoid anything that would hinder our progress. Not every idea is a good one, and not every activity adds value.

The single most effective way to increase your probability of success in a sale is to decrease your risk of failure. It's one of the great secrets of consistent sales performance. Probability and risk share an inverse relationship in sales: when one goes up the other goes down. The greater your risk, the lower your probability of success. On the flip side, it's also true that lowering your risk of failure can significantly increase your probability of success.

This is an important point, because it's no longer enough for companies or sales execs to pat their salespeople on the back and send them out into a competitive marketplace, hoping for the best. Everything you say or do in the sales process will either move you closer to a successful sale or farther from it. For that reason, everything we do throughout the rest of this book is designed to increase your probability of success, and also to decrease your risk of failure. Not only will your hit rate increase when calling new prospect accounts, but you will also engage more prospects in more productive sales conversations. When the customer wins by consummating a transaction with your company, you win too. It's that simple.

> **Secret #2**   In order to achieve above-average sales results, one must first be open to thinking about above-average sales concepts.

My sincere hope is that a collaborative effort has occurred, where having trained thousands of salespeople over the years, many of whom were skeptics at first, has vetted the QBS methodology into a bulletproof recipe for success where you (the reader) are the ultimate winner. Congratulations for taking the first step in improving your results moving forward.

Come with me now and I'll show you *how*.

Part One

A Short Course on QBS Strategy

Salespeople have gotten a bad rap over the years. We've been labeled as pushy, conniving, and self-serving. Some of these reputations have been earned over the years, to be sure, dating all the way back to the days of the snake-oil salesmen who rode into town, flung open the backs of their wagons, and peddled everything from cigarettes to elixirs that they claimed would cure every ailment. Fortunately, we salespeople have come a long way from those days. QBS seeks to bring us along even further.

In short, Question Based Selling is ultimately about two things: helping people and communicating effectively. Asked strategically, questions are great tools for gathering information about the customer's needs. But strategic questions are also one of your best vehicles for differentiating your offerings, piquing the customer's interest, establishing your own credibility, creating a sense of urgency, and securing commitments throughout the sales process. Helping customers in all these ways is a significant departure from just asking questions to obtain information.

Part I of *Secrets of Question Based Selling* is a short course on QBS strategy. The first five chapters are intended to serve as building blocks for the QBS methodology, where you will learn how to expand your value proposition, and engage more prospects in more productive sales conversations. Once you understand the fundamentals, Parts Two and Three of the book then focus more specifically on how to maximize your effectiveness in every aspect of implementing and executing the QBS sale.

Chapter 1

SELLING INTANGIBLES

Do you sell products and services? Or, do you really sell the benefits of those products and services? Moreover, are the benefits you are attempting to convey to customers tangible or intangible?

Would it surprise you to know that most of the value you convey to prospective customers is highly intangible, yet most of your selling efforts tend to focus on creating value around tangible goods and services? Are you tangibly confused? Your customers sure will be, unless you bring some clarity to the real benefits contained in this highly intangible sales process.

I have noticed that life is a continuum of interesting paradoxes. Just when you think something should be one way, you discover it's completely the opposite. Have you ever noticed, for example, that some of the richest people in the world are also some of the unhappiest? Just check out the latest issue of *People* magazine at your local newsstand. Here's another example. Isn't it strange that we vaccinate humans against chronic diseases like polio and smallpox by injecting them with small doses of the actual disease?

Do you like sports? Have you ever wondered why deer hunters carefully dress in camouflaged clothing, but just before they go into the woods, they strap on a fluorescent orange vest and cap? If you play golf, you probably know that if you want to curve the ball to the right, then you must swing to the left. Of course, there are legitimate underlying reasons to support these behaviors. Since deer are color blind, for example, hunters know that wearing a bright orange vest doesn't expose them to their prey, but it does identify them to other hunters who may also be in the woods. In golf, swinging to the left creates clockwise rotation on the ball, which makes it curve to the right when the ball encounters normal air resistance.

I can keep going. Have you ever noticed that the more anxiously you look forward to Christmas, the slower it seems to come? Or, isn't it odd that parents who want to maintain close relationships with their children must be willing to let them move away and make some mistakes on their own?

These dichotomies are evident in sales as well. For example, don't you think it's strange that the introduction of sophisticated communication tools like voice mail, email, caller ID, and smartphones has actually made it more difficult for salespeople to get through to new prospects? There are many paradoxes in sales like that. Here's another example. Prospective buyers in today's business climate are more cautious and standoffish than ever before. But isn't it weird that many sellers have responded to this by being even more aggressive and tenacious? The result? Customers are retreating even further.

For years now, part of my mission has been to expose the fact that several of the mind-sets salespeople have been conditioned to accept over time are no longer valid. For example, sellers are often encouraged to be super-positive and highly enthusiastic. But you will find that top-performing salespeople in most companies are generally not the cheerleader types. In fact, top performers are oftentimes naturally analytical and quite introspective, always looking for strategic advantages or possible obstacles that could bolster a successful relationship, or undermine the sale. That's why one of the fundamental concepts I originally introduced as part of Question Based Selling was, "Always positive is not always most productive."

To illustrate, sellers have long been conditioned to ask questions with a positive, even hopeful, tone. Therefore, typical sales questions tend to sound optimistic, like: *Mr. Prospect, would next Tuesday work for a conference call?* Or: *Does your boss like our proposal?* Sometimes sellers ask: *Are we still in good shape to close this deal by the end of the month?* The salesperson in these examples is obviously hoping next Tuesday will work for a conference call, or hoping the boss likes the proposal, and that the deal is still in "good shape" to close by month-end. These positively dispositioned questions do not generate more positive results. In reality, just the opposite occurs. I will talk at length later in the book about the fact that positively dispositioned questions tend to cause customers to withhold, or give less accurate information, which is counterproductive to your selling efforts.

Possibly the most intriguing paradox in sales has to do with sellers and their attempts to communicate value. Companies are working harder than ever to create and communicate impactful messages about their respective value propositions, and salespeople are trying to be more and more emphatic about the value their products and services bring to the table. Yet these claims of greatness are quickly discarded by prospective customers. In fact, the more emphatic a salesperson is, the more skeptical prospects tend to become, which creates an interesting challenge for sellers who are desperately trying to differentiate themselves in the marketplace. They only end up commoditizing their respective value propositions.

> **Secret #3**   Sellers are desperately trying to differentiate themselves in the marketplace, only to end up commoditizing their respective value propositions.

The truth is we live in an increasingly cautious society, and people have grown increasingly skeptical with regard to accepting claims of greatness from a vendor at face value. Don't take my word for it. How many pieces of junk mail have you thrown away so far this year, even though they all claim to offer some phenomenal benefit *just for you*? For that matter, how many unsolicited emails have you deleted in the last few months that made raving claims about a product or service?

So, here's the paradox. To win in sales, you must be able to successfully communicate an impactful message about your product or service, and you must be able to differentiate yourself from the other competitive offerings in the marketplace. But, how can we accomplish these objectives if value propositions that all sound the same are ultimately falling on deaf ears?

The Intangible Nature of Perceived Value

Perhaps the biggest difference between the original book and the new *Secrets of Question Based Selling* is the realization that the intangible criteria being sought by the customer and the benefits being offered by the proposing vendors are more important that the product itself.

> **Secret #4**   The intangible criteria being sought by the customer and the benefits being offered by the proposing vendors are more important that the product itself.

Do you sell a tangible product or an intangible one? When asked this question, sellers tend to reflect on the product's technical specifications in comparison to the definition of tangibility. Can you touch it? If you can, then it must be a tangible product. Someone who sells laptop computers, for example, could easily conclude that their products are indeed tangible. Not only can you touch and feel a laptop computer, but you also can actually put it in your lap. The salesperson who distributes medical supplies could say the same thing about their new IV pumps. If you can bring one into an operating room and show it to a doctor, then it must be a tangible item.

Most service offerings are not tangible items, however. A salesperson cannot bring a dozen hours of consulting time into a sales call and hand it to a prospective customer. Other familiar products, like insurance, have a similar intangibility. I mean…how often do you roll over and take one last look at your life insurance policy just before going to sleep at night?

One could easily conclude that since customers cannot actually hold an intangible product in their hand, selling intangible items is more difficult than selling tangible goods. In fact, marketing an intangible item is much more of a conceptual sale, where you are actually selling the perception of value, as opposed to the value itself. And, with intangible items, if customers don't perceive high levels of value, your chances of making a sale are greatly reduced. Consequently, successfully selling intangibles is largely attributable to a sales-person's ability to communicate concepts that cause prospects to *perceive* high levels of value, as opposed to relying on the tangible nature of the product itself.

Secret #5	Even if the product you are selling is indeed tangible, the true value proposition of that product is not.

But, guess what? Even if the product you are selling is indeed tangible, the true value proposition of that product is not. That's because the value proposition of most tangible products is, in fact, intangible. Can you see the paradox? Even though you can physically hold a tangible product in your hand, you are still selling its perceived value. And, if potential buyers don't perceive significant value, then your chances of transacting a sale are greatly reduced.

Let me give you a simple example. A laptop computer is a tangible item, right? But you can't necessarily touch the real value of a laptop computer. In other words, why are laptop computers valuable? Different users have differ-ent requirements. But speaking for myself, a laptop computer offers increased productivity when I'm away from the office. It enables to me to connect to the Internet when I am traveling, stay in closer touch with clients, and communi-cate with other certified QBS trainers. It also puts me in closer touch with my family and friends. So, although a laptop computer is definitely a tangible item, I cannot touch the value of my increased productivity as a result of owning it. Other intangible benefits of a laptop include mobility, reliability, ease of use, cost effectiveness, and of course, the ability to play computer games on long flights. Priceless! All of these intangible benefits create perceived value, but you still can't hold mobility, reliability, ease of use, or cost effectiveness in your hand.

This same principle applies if you sell real estate, manufactured goods, cellular telephones, or medical supplies. Real estate, for example, is certainly a tangible item. You can touch the dirt, and even go inside the physical structures located on the property. But people don't buy real estate just for the dirt and structures. Instead, they buy because of perceived intangibles like location, usefulness, aesthetic beauty, spaciousness, growth potential, return on investment, quality of schools, and the view out the kitchen window. And, I can guarantee that if a potential buyer doesn't perceive some of these, or other equally intangible benefits as being valuable, they will not move forward with a purchase.

The value proposition of more sophisticated products like clinical IV pumps in medical sales is just as intangible. Although an IV pump is certainly tangible, physicians don't care about the pump's product specifications. They care about the intangible aspects of these products and their impact on things like ease of use, clinical efficacy, patient comfort, availability of product, cost effectiveness, possible exclusions or complications, reimbursement rates, legal liability, and seamless integration with other medical devices.

I would argue that even everyday products like toothbrushes, breakfast cereal, or a pair of Italian loafers are purchased based on value propositions that are highly intangible. How can you touch the value of having cleaner-feeling teeth, a healthier diet, or feeling stylish all the way to the ground? It's easy to conclude that the product is important. So is the company and the sales rep or whoever is representing your proposed solutions. The importance of each, however, isn't distributed equally as the traditional graphic above would have you believe.

Although this is rarely talked about in other sales programs, the inherent benefits of the products and services you offer are, in fact, intangible. And in order for prospective customers to make a purchase decision, those customers must first perceive enough value to create a sense of urgency for moving forward.

The Intangible Nature of the Entire Sale

So far, we have been talking about the intangible nature of the strategic sale in terms of the product. That's good, because the product certainly makes up some portion of the sale itself. But, as the graphic indicates, the product is not the only component that we should pay attention to.

Your company (hopefully) is loaded with intangible benefits like stability, references, innovation, and financial security. These benefits offered by your company are often very important aspects of the strategic sale, and should definitely be pointed out in some deliberate way during the sales process. Now you can see the bigger picture; the intangible nature of the product is important, the intangible nature of the company is important, and, guess what, so are the intangible benefits that come from you, the sales rep.

The wrinkle to this model is that the intangible benefits that come from your products, company, and yourself are not evenly distributed, as the previous graphic would have you believe. They are all important, to be sure, but the intangible value that you (the rep) bring to the table is far more important than your product or company. Therefore, the disbursement of value should look more like the updated graphic.

The salesperson somehow has to garner more value than the product or company, and not just in theory. I can prove it with one simple geometric postulate. Let's hold the product and company constant for the moment. At virtually every company, you will find that some reps are more successful than others selling the same basic products to very similar types of customers. It's not the product that's the differentiator. It's not the company either. It's the value conveyed by the rep. More specifically, it's the intangible value being conveyed by effective salespeople that makes them successful.

> **Secret #6** At virtually every company, you will find that some reps are more successful than others selling the same basic products to very similar types of customers.

Can you give us some examples of the intangible benefits being conveyed by a salesperson? Absolutely. Here's a partial list of some of the things you might bring to the table in a sale:

- Integrity
- Honesty
- Thought leadership
- Competence

- Confidence
- Capability
- Responsiveness
- Accountability
- Follow-through
- Comfort level
- Humility
- Attitude
- Vision
- Being forthright
- Humor
- Knowledge
- Experience
- Expertise
- Understanding
- Empathy
- Caring

…just to name a few. Of course, I can keep going. A successful rep is also hard-working, diligent, well prepared, credible, purposeful, professional, relevant, and customer focused, rather than self-serving.

Are these intangible benefits important in the strategic sales process? You bet they are! In fact, your ability to convey many of these qualities in a short period of time is likely to be the difference between gaining the customer's trust or losing the sale. The challenge for sellers is knowing how to convey this much intangible value without trying to personally claim it.

> **Secret #7**   A salesperson's ability to convey many of these qualities in a short period of time is likely to be the difference between gaining the customer's trust or losing the sale.

Imagine a salesperson saying to a customer: *"Mr. Customer, I am the most humble person in the world, with a track record of experience and expertise that is second to none. I am also the most professional sales rep you will ever meet, as I am hardworking, honest, forthright, competent, and capable. Essentially, Mr. Customer, you can trust me."*

Anyone who would actually come out with such outlandish claims of greatness sounds more like a jerk than a valuable resource. You see, credibility is not something that can be claimed; it must be earned. You can't just tell customers you have excellent vision and valuable thought leadership, you have to actually demonstrate those qualities in order to get credit for bringing them into the decision process.

So, how is a salesperson supposed to convey maximum personal value to customers within a short period of time? Great question! In fact, that's what the rest of this book is about. If you want to increase your probability of success and decrease your risk of failure, then you must learn how to leverage yourself as the biggest asset that could possibly be brought to the sale.

Corporate Messaging Has Become Convoluted

Now that we understand that the value propositions of the products and services you offer, your company, and the benefits you bring to the table are highly intangible, we need to put some thought into how best to communicate a strong sense of value from them to prospective customers.

Most salespeople have been taught that the best way to establish value in the eyes of a prospective customer is to simply explain all the wonderful advantages of their product or service. As a result, sellers tend to highlight the features of their proposed solutions, followed by an explanation of their corresponding benefits. Here's what that might sound like: *Mr. Prospect, our products are designed using high-density plastic to provide greater tensile strength when lifting heavy objects, which makes them more durable for a longer useful life.* This feature/benefit combination is fairly straightforward, to the point where a customer who was interested in durability, strength of product, or life expectancy would likely register significant value when hearing this pitch.

However, with the increasing competitive pressure of today's business environment, I have noticed that value propositions are becoming more and more difficult to understand. Have you seen any product brochures lately? Corporate marketing departments are really stretching their thesauruses. You might say they feel the need to *tailor vivid product descriptions that are both evocative and expressive, by applying verbiage that eloquently characterizes the gamut of intrinsic product value and by using words that combine urbane sophistication with erudite refinement.* Can you dig it? Of course not—it's just a bunch of gobbledygook!

Product descriptions have evolved to a point where the feature/benefit combinations that are now being positioned to customers, both in written form and in product presentations, have become so convoluted they actually erode your value proposition. To cite an example, check out the excerpt below from a recent product launch I found on the web. (Of course, I changed the name of the vendor and product to protect the innocent.)

"ABC Company's new X-1400 was designed to improve customer retention through personalized customer initiatives and increased communications, strengthen business partner relationships through increased collaboration and access to information, and improve employee productivity by connecting all the people, information, and applications employees need to do their job, organized in a format that allows them to be increasingly more efficient."

Whoever came up with this "blurb" linked together some fancy words and phrases, but what does this passage really mean? From my perspective, it doesn't pass the Layman's Terms Test, meaning the average person can't even tell what the product does, not to mention understand what its value would be to them.

I understand why corporate messages are now headed in this direction. Competitive pressures in the marketplace are not receding; rather, they are becoming more intense. If you turn the clock back to a simpler time thirty years ago, the corporate marketing function was almost an afterthought. Businesses wanted to be competitive, but they had nowhere near the market sophistication that exists today. Now, spin doctors in corporate marketing departments research what competitors are saying, and then create messages about their respective product or service that they feel are more impactful and have more punch. Of course, once their competitor gets wind of any new messaging, they immediately put the wheels in motion to create their next-generation message that will hopefully be even more impactful. Consequently, we have escalated ourselves into a vicious cycle of increasing complexity, where corporate marketers and salespeople are battling to "out-describe" each other.

Convoluted is a good word for this mess. Now value propositions have become so flamboyant and verbose that the actual benefits companies want to communicate are lost in the words. This creates yet another interesting paradox. As companies work harder and harder to communicate greater value, the messages being conveyed become less and less impactful.

Secret #8   As companies work harder and harder to communicate greater value, the messages being conveyed become less and less impactful.

This phenomenon of companies trying to out-describe each other is everywhere—even in your local grocery store. Have you noticed that it is no longer possible to buy regular dishwashing liquid? You can only buy *new and improved* dishwashing liquid, with the *advanced formula for extra strength*. But, if you look down the aisle, you will notice that everyone else claims to have a new and improved dishwashing formula, too. As a result, these claims of superiority are discounted by consumers because all the different products sound essentially the same.

If you want a dose of reality, check out the website of your top three competitors. Be warned that this can be an enlightening experience. I bet you will find that your competitors say they possess and provide many of the same capabilities listed on your website. I bet they are even saying that they do a better job than you! All these similar-sounding value messages present a problem from the customer's point of view. When customers invest the time to research vendor options, only to discover that everyone's value proposition sounds pretty much the same, it becomes very difficult for them to determine which option provides the best fit.

> **Secret #9**   When customers invest the time to research vendor options, only to discover that everyone's value proposition sounds pretty much the same, it becomes very difficult for them to determine which option provides the best fit.

What companies are attempting to do is differentiate themselves and cause customers to perceive greater value. The tendency, however, has been to try to communicate greater value by encouraging salespeople to be increasingly more emphatic about their offerings. But the difference between touting something as being *really great, incredibly great, unbelievably great,* or *phenomenally great* is negligible. Consumers today are extremely skeptical, and they are quick to commoditize a salesperson's declarations of superiority. Therefore, these claims of greatness are falling on deaf ears, meaning salespeople are left facing the challenge of how to differentiate their value propositions in an increasingly competitive marketplace.

At that point, you could take the salesperson out of the equation totally, and leave the sale to come down to whoever has the better product. But let me ask. Have you ever had the better product and still lost the sale? I have. Have you ever had a slightly inferior product and come out on top? I have been there too. The point is, it's not just the product or the company that will make or break the sale; it's also how you position your product and your company.

People Buy from People
People buy from people. It's true. Prospective buyers tend to gravitate toward salespersons who are not only knowledgeable about their products, but also

come across as straightforward in their dealings. They inspire a sense of confidence that makes customers feel comfortable. The reverse is also true. People also "sell" to people. And, those salespeople perceived by target customers as more capable and more professional than others calling on the same account create a more positive impression. Consequently, they tend to have greater sales success.

Most corporate executives would agree that the human element of a company is critically important, and can determine the success or failure of an organization. Yet the quality of the personnel on the sales team never appears on a company's balance sheet. That's probably because there is no good way to empirically quantify the quality of people in the sales organization. How do you put a numerical value on innovative ideas, strong leadership, commitment to excellence, and the desire to achieve, if not exceed, one's sales objectives? Nonetheless, these qualities represent the underlying cultural fabric of every company, and they will have an undeniable impact on the productivity of your sales organization.

Years ago, large companies invested heavily to develop and deliver their own sales competency programs internally. The goal was to preserve the overall culture of the company by making sure that everyone in the sales organization was on the same page relative to following the sales methodology. IBM, for example, was both diligent and purposeful in its efforts to instill and preserve a sales culture in the early days of technology that has become legendary among business historians. One of the reasons companies back then were set on developing their own training programs could be that there were relatively few other options for sales training back in the 1970s.

The Burroughs Corporation, for example, put newly hired salespeople through a twelve-month sales insertion program, where the first four to six months were spent in a classroom setting, followed by a "promotion" to a sales assistant role to complete the rookie year. General Electric used to put salespeople through a graduated eight- to twelve-week sales development program, depending on the division. Procter & Gamble, Honeywell, Eli Lilly, Unisys, Merrill Lynch, Digital Equipment Corporation, and Xerox all had very extensive internal sales development programs. Have you ever visited the Xerox training facility in Leesburg, Virginia? My wife, Laura, "graduated" from the Xerox sales school, and its facilities would rival the facilities of any college campus. In fact, they called it Xerox U.

In-house corporate training facilities like Xerox's were basically the sales schools of the 1970s and 1980s. The University of Florida, my alma mater, doesn't teach professional selling skills. When I attended the business school at

Florida, the choice was to major in either marketing, economics, accounting, or, in my case, finance. Selling was simply not considered to be an academic skill. If you wanted to be a salesperson, you took a job with IBM, Xerox, Burroughs, Merrill Lynch, Johnson & Johnson, or Honeywell, and after graduation they would teach you how to sell.

But guess what happened? The economy grew, and as businesses expanded so rapidly late in the twentieth century, these highly trained salespeople in large corporations became easy targets for other companies who needed to quickly build a sales organization. Smart managers figured out that it was significantly less expensive to lure experienced sales professionals away from other companies than to try to develop people from scratch. Consequently, up-and-coming companies began offering lucrative signing bonuses to sellers with IBM, Burroughs, or Honeywell experience who were willing to jump ship. In addition to saving the upfront cost of education, companies who hired these experienced salespeople could dramatically reduce the expected ramp-up time. Having salespeople who could hit the ground running meant realizing increased productivity much sooner. Anyone who was in sales back in the 1980s, for example, can attest that merely having the three letters "IBM" on one's résumé was extremely valuable in the job market.

As time went on, the larger corporations with extensive internal training programs started bleeding salespeople, and turnover became a real problem. Not surprisingly, the mentality started to shift regarding in-house skills development. It was no longer advantageous for the cultural giants to serve as the training ground for new salespeople, only to lose those people a few months later to smaller and leaner competitors who could reap the benefits without incurring the upfront development cost.

The talent pool for instructors has also evaporated over time. Back in the days of the large corporate sales schools, salespeople from the field were routinely rotated back into corporate positions to serve as internal sales trainers. In many organizations, it was an honor to be selected for this role, and it was a good career move too, since it often served as a stepping-stone into higher levels of management. That is seldom the case anymore. Companies who are fighting to survive in today's business environment want their best salespeople to remain in the field to maximize revenue. Talented salespeople prefer staying in the field anyway because they know they will make more money selling than training. The continuous push to cut back has also put corporate education departments on notice that overhead positions and expense budgets will be closely scrutinized. This sense of expendability has caused most of the really talented sales instructors to seek other opportunities.

As a result, very few companies offer extensive in-house, skills-based, sales development programs anymore. It's just not practical or feasible to fund the investment that's required for companies to maintain these in-house development efforts, and remain competitive in today's business environment. Therefore, the practice of investing heavily in the sales culture of a company has basically ended, and most of the corporate sales schools that served as the initial training ground for so many salespeople have long since closed their doors, and the "old school" of selling is officially dead. That leaves us wondering, where do those companies who want to have strong sales organizations find good people?

In Search of Top Performers

One could argue that the most sensible thing companies could do is make it a practice to hire experienced salespeople—proven professionals who already have a track record of success. Simply go out and find the top 5 to 10 percent of the salespeople in your respective industry, the ones who have already demonstrated they are capable of overachieving their sales goals, and bring them aboard. By hiring salespeople who have already proven themselves, you would significantly reduce your ramp-up times because your sales staff would hit the ground running, right?

Unfortunately, targeting the highest echelon of top performing salespeople has a downside. Let's start with the fact that everyone else in your industry is trying to identify and hire those same top salespeople. When I was consistently exceeding my numbers as a salesperson, I received dozens of calls from headhunters and recruiters. It got to the point where fending them off started to feel like a part-time job. Finding out who the top performers are, of course, is only part of the battle. Then you also have to convince them to change the direction of their careers, knowing full well that their existing employers are probably very intent on retaining their services. Couple this with the fact that a top performing salesperson usually doesn't need another job. Being tops in their field means they are earning large sums of money already, so why risk making a change? It's also likely that many of the current top performers are very comfortable in their positions. It's rewarding to feel like a "big fish in a small pond," having earned the political capital that comes from having an established record of proven success. Top performers may also be reticent to walk away from meaningful business relationships that have been established over time, or groundwork that has been laid for future career advancement. Even when a top-performing salesperson does become available, they typically come with a healthy price tag, because they are in demand.

Identifying who the good salespeople are can be yet another challenge. I don't mean to overstate the obvious, but just because someone has a good-looking résumé doesn't necessarily mean they are a blue-chip performer. Lots of salespeople achieved their annual sales goals when the economy was strong, which certainly was the case in the 1990s and early 2000s. It was easy to sell lots of goods and services when everyone had money to spend! But the question moving forward is, how will these salespeople fare, especially since 2008, now that potential buyers are more cautious with their decision-making and more judicious with their budgets and spending than ever before?

> **Secret #10** Every successful salesperson started off as a diamond in the rough, looking for a manager or company to give them an opportunity to prove themselves.

Is it possible to find good salespeople without targeting only the top echelon of potential candidates? Absolutely! If you think about it, every successful salesperson started off as a diamond in the rough, looking for a manager or company to give them an opportunity to prove themselves. Some of these salespeople struggled at first, but after they got a few quarters under their belts, they started to blossom as professionals. The key is recognizing someone's potential early enough to have an opportunity to mold them into a true sales professional, which one might say is more of an art form than an exact science. With QBS, we recognize that it also requires sales managers to focus on developing the list of highly intangible qualities that lead to top performance in sales.

Good salespeople are a rare commodity indeed, but I should make the point up front that this chapter isn't about "finding" good salespeople. Rather, our discussion here is about selling intangibles and building high-performance sales teams, which has more to do with "developing" quality salespeople. I should also make the point that the sales profession in general has become more of a team sport, rather than an accumulation of individualized efforts. And the team concept changes the paradigm for small, medium-sized, and large corporations. While you still may want to hire strong individual performers, you also need to develop a corporate sales culture that rewards successful behavior, in order to duplicate these high-performance traits and qualities across the broader organization.

Experience Is a Double-Edged Sword

One might assume that having sales experience is a wonderful asset. In many cases, that's true. As I have said, an experienced salesperson can presumably hit the ground running and become more productive sooner. But experience is a double-edged sword, especially when your objective involves bringing together a team of people from a variety of different backgrounds. You still have to merge different experience levels together with a variety of selling styles and product knowledge into a cohesive organization.

I am not a "human resources guy" by experience, and my purpose here is not to scrutinize corporate hiring practices or assess the validity of corporate personnel strategies. Instead, I simply want to comment first on the human aspects of building a high-performance sales team, and then on what sales managers should look for when evaluating potential talent.

Like anyone else, salespeople are creatures of habit. As such, they tend to gravitate toward whatever is most familiar. You can ask salespeople, "Why are you doing such-and-such?" The response you will likely hear back is, "Because that's the way I have always done it."

The approach a salesperson "has always" taken may, in fact, be the most effective way of dealing with a certain situation. But, what are the chances that every salesperson in your company, who have all come from different selling backgrounds and had different experiences, will all gravitate to the same approach? The truth is, salespeople have their own way of doing things, which tends to leave the typical sales organization with a mishmash of tactics and strategies that may or may not be congruent with the overall business objectives of the company.

The best-case scenario for a sales team is to have everyone on the same page regarding the company's go-to-market strategy, and the execution of that strategy. Of course, the goal isn't to turn salespeople into robotic clones. Different people do have different strengths that can be leveraged. Rather, the goal when building a high-performance sales team is to develop a corporate culture that supports the varying styles of individuals on the team, but also achieves a certain level of continuity that will maximize the effectiveness of the broader sales organization.

Touting "Solutions" May Be the Problem

As with most paradoxes, there is a reason things are the way they are. As we discussed, the tendency for sellers is to communicate value in terms of the solutions they provide. Logic would therefore suggest that the more "wonderful" your product seems, the more valuable it will be in the eyes of prospective customers.

Can we agree that customers are much more interested in solving their own problems than they are in hearing a sales pitch? That leaves sellers in a precarious position—they are communicating value by touting the "wonderful-ness" of their proposed solutions, while potential buyers are much more interested in solving their own problems, issues, and concerns. Furthermore, when sellers try to communicate a value proposition that is based on intan-gible benefits, the tendency is to explain value in terms of the *presence* of their product or service, basically describing how satisfied customers will feel after the purchase. But with many solutions, it's difficult to characterize the value of an intangible benefit by describing it in material terms. Again, how many people go to bed at night thinking, "Boy, my car insurance policy really did a good job today"?

I am not suggesting that insurance is not valuable. Insurance is absolutely valuable, which explains why you and I both continue to purchase auto, home-owner's, health, and life insurance on a yearly basis. Nonetheless, it is difficult to describe the intrinsic value of insurance in terms of how wonderful it will feel once you own it. In fact, if you sat in on a sales call with a top life insurance salesperson, you'd hear them spend very little time talking about how good the policy is, and most of their time talking about what can happen if someone is not appropriately protected.

Think about it this way. You don't buy life insurance to own it. You buy life insurance because of the downside associated with *not* owning it.

Are you ready for another paradox about value? We've just said that the value of an intangible benefit is best understood in terms of the absence of that benefit. When researching life insurance options, for example, when a prospective buyer considers the impact of leaving their family without a steady income, or not having the resources to fund a college education, or the Internal Revenue Service laying claim to half of their estate, the value of a life insurance policy suddenly takes on new meaning. A life insurance salesperson can try to describe how wonderful their policies are until they are blue in the face, but it's the images created by the absence of being properly insured in the unfortunate time of need that ultimately sends a shiver up the customer's spine.

This same principle can be applied to most products. In the case of tech-nology, for example, having a highly available network is certainly desirable, but *not* having a reliable network can be disastrous. Here's another example. If you are considering the purchase of radial tires, a tread design that channels water out from underneath the tire in wet conditions is certainly a nice benefit, but it is nowhere near as valuable as its ability to prevent your car from hydro-planing, and skidding off the road into oncoming traffic.

Think about the product I sell—Question Based Selling. My product is very intangible. The only way to create opportunities in our business is to help prospective clients perceive high amounts of value in the programs we deliver. But, when I talk with the vice presidents of sales, they don't want to hear how wonderful my program is, they want to know how QBS will solve their problems. And, even though they often have different goals—from wanting salespeople to more effectively differentiate themselves, to alleviating competitive margin pressures, to ramping new salespeople up more quickly, or better qualifying opportunities—the idea of not accomplishing these objectives is what really creates a sense of urgency.

I suppose it's human nature to take the positive benefits of a product or service for granted. But the minute they go away, we consumers go berserk. Do you own a cellular phone? I bet you rarely think about all the wonderful benefits of having a cell phone, until it's time to make an important call and you can't get a strong enough signal.

So as a salesperson, you put yourself in a stronger position by positioning the value of your product or service in terms of the positive benefits it provides as well as the problems it solves or prevents.

The tendency to focus on the positive comes long before the customer actually makes a purchase decision. Early in the sales process, for example, when sellers are trying to get to higher levels within the account, a salesperson might say, *"Mr. Customer, I would like to get a few minutes with your CFO to show him how cost-effective our products are relative to increasing productivity and maximizing the return on your investment."* Sounds like a mini elevator pitch, doesn't it? Here's the reverse. *"Mr. Customer, would it make sense to spend a few minutes and bring your CFO up to speed, so he doesn't have a knee-jerk reaction and torpedo the idea?"*

In preparation for QBS training events, I always ask for a conference call to customize the material for the intended audience. But I don't ask for a manager's time so I can "understand their business and deliver better training." Although these are positive benefits, they don't necessarily create a sense of urgency. Therefore, I am more inclined to ask a vice president of sales for time on their calendar, "so we don't completely miss the boat at the upcoming training event." Both of these questions refer to benefits that would come from strategizing in advance. But how you ask does make a difference.

Regarding the broader issue of selling intangibles, it's true that even if the product you sell is tangible, the value of your proposed solution is not. It's also true that a salesperson will convey greater value to potential buyers by communicating intangible benefits in terms of the absence of their product or service, rather than simply depending on sophisticated corporate marketing jargon to say a lot of words, but not offer a lot of substance.

Education Is the Ultimate Goal

When we strategize about how best to communicate value in the sales process, what we are really talking about is education. And a large part of the opportunity to succeed in sales hinges on your ability to help prospective customers clearly understand the value being offered by your product or service. Education is a funny thing, however. While one might assume that the best way to educate someone on something is simply to explain it as eloquently as possible, as we are seeing, some things (like the perceived value of an intangible benefit) are difficult to explain.

Here's an example from my own business. In QBS, we spend a great deal of time talking about curiosity, and the role it plays in the strategic sales process. While other sales trainers completely ignore the importance of curiosity, I have built a very successful training practice on the fundamental concepts of sales effectiveness, one of which is the fact that curiosity is the genesis of every sale. As I have said many times, if a prospect or customer is not the least bit curious about who you are or the value you bring to the table, then you are not likely to succeed in the account. Everyone agrees with this.

However, in my early years of sales training, I found it surprisingly difficult to explain the concept of leveraging curiosity to sales audiences. I stood at the podium and told them, *"If you want to be successful in sales, then you must pique the prospect's interest."* Participants were polite, but I could tell the message wasn't getting through. The point finally hit home once I began explaining what happens in the absence of curiosity. "Let me put it this way," I say. *"If a prospective customer is not the least bit curious about who you are, or what you can do for them, then you have no chance."* Now, they all get it!

> **Secret #11** Customers often perceive greater value when they think about *not* having key features or benefits.

It's another one of life's crazy paradoxes. Sometimes the best way to communicate something is to explain what happens in the absence of it. This is an important lesson for salespeople, because as educators, you will find that customers often perceive greater value when they think about not having key features or benefits. Again, thinking about all the wonderful benefits one gets from owning life insurance isn't nearly as impactful as thinking about the absence of being appropriately covered in the event of an untimely death.

"...And That's What We Solve!"

Here's one more ironic twist. With regard to positioning, rather than trying to articulate all the wonderful benefits your product or service provides, the most impactful way to express the true value of your solutions may be as simple as articulating the problem and then saying, "We solve that!"

The logic here is as simple as the phrase. If you agree that customers are much more interested in solving their own problems than they are in hearing a salesperson's claims, then it stands to reason that your value proposition ought to center more around a discussion of their problems than your solutions.

The value clients derive from QBS is quite intangible, as I have said. Consequently, benefits like a wider sales funnel, reduced buyer resistance, and differentiation are difficult to communicate without sounding just like every other sales trainer sporting a bag full of slides. Therefore, I don't spend a lot of time trying to describe the "wonderful" benefits of QBS training. Instead, I spend most of my time talking with salespeople, managers, and executives about the challenges of the current selling climate. Then I challenge their thinking about the problems they are trying to solve. For example, I explain:

QBS is very different than traditional sales methods. That's because there's a problem with traditional sales approaches. In fact, this is exactly how I began the introduction in the book that you are now holding in your hands. Every sales training program I am aware of is founded on the premise that a salesperson must first uncover a need, in order to then provide value. My guess, Mr. VP of Sales, is that you agree with this. Me too! But, here's the problem. In today's business environment, just because a salesperson wants to ask a bunch of questions to uncover needs doesn't necessarily mean that prospective customers will "want to" share information with them. Likewise, just because you have a good story to tell, that doesn't guarantee you an audience within your target accounts.

The selling environment has changed. Customers have less time, more products and services are being offered, and sellers have become increasingly more aggressive. As a result, prospective buyers are more cautious and standoffish than ever before, making it more difficult for salespeople to penetrate new accounts. In fact, key people in important accounts are often working just as hard to get off the telephone as salespeople are to stay on it.

Furthermore, if your salespeople sound the same as everyone else in your market space, they forfeit their competitive edge—which, again, makes it difficult for sellers to penetrate accounts, fill the pipeline, qualify accounts, differentiate their solutions, and create a sense of urgency for moving forward.

These are very real challenges impacting sales organizations on a daily basis...and that's basically what QBS solves.

Personally, I have learned the hard way that spending most of the time with prospective clients talking about their potential problems is way better than trying to promote myself with accolades about the value of my product or service. Granted, this aforementioned passage is a condensed version of my value proposition for QBS. But it delivers the message. Times are tough in sales, and QBS has ways to solve that. That message resonates with sales management. In the same way, as prospective customers relate to the verbal pictures you paint about challenges they currently face, they will naturally look to you as someone who can help address those issues.

Personal	Company	Product
Integrity	Vision	Quality
Honesty	Stability	Consistency
Thought Leadership	Industry Leadership	Good Reviews
Competence	Congruence	Cost Effective
Confidence	Goal-Oriented	Good Fit
Capability	Geographic Coverage	Flexibility
Responsiveness	Proven	Support
Accountability	Track Record	Warranty
Follow-Through	Employee Morale	Customer Satisfaction
Comfort Level	Loyalty	Meets Standards
Humility	Customer-Focused	Innovative
Attitude	Customer Satisfaction	Nice Looking
Being Forthright	Longevity	Feels Comfortable
Knowledge	Helpfulness	Size
Experience	Controls	Color
Expertise	Operational Efficiency	Specifications
Understanding	Compliance	Safety

The graphic above illustrates the three areas of intangible value: Personal, Company, and Product. Note that the personal intangibles on this list come from the customer's perception of the sales rep. In a perfect world, you would have all of these qualities going for you, in which case, getting appointments and securing commitments would be easy. The same is true with your company and products. There may be even more intangible benefits than are shown on the list, but if you could somehow convey all of these, you would be well on your way toward making a sale.

First and foremost, customers want to know that you understand their problems, issues, and concerns. By understanding this, most of my conference calls with sales executives begin with me asking a simple question like, "How can I help?" Most clients will mention a few symptoms of their current environment, but what they really want is someone to help diagnose and solve the root cause of the problem. That's why I take the time to lay the groundwork by explaining that the selling environment has changed. Notice that I went on to explain that there is a problem with traditional sales methods, and that sounding just like everyone else is the quickest way to commoditize your value proposition. In a typical conference call, it's not unusual for me to spend fifteen or twenty minutes talking about the challenges sellers now face, and why continuing with an old-school approach is no longer a viable option.

The net effect is this: At the very moment in time when a prospective client begins to form the impression that, "Hey, this guy understands my problem… and he might even be able to help us solve it!"—that's when you start to establish some serious credibility as a valuable resource.

Here's the cool part. After articulating the customer's problems to the point where your value proposition essentially is, "These are the type of challenges we help customers solve," the next question customers ask is, "How do you do that?" Doesn't that sound like an invitation to provide more detail into the specific aspects of your product or service? It's also an excellent opportunity to suggest a face-to-face meeting, or other appropriate next steps. Either way, the net result of the conversation is very different than what would have happened had I gone down the traditional path of trying to articulate or describe all the "wonderful" benefits of Question Based Selling.

This strategy applies with virtually any intangible sale. Take financial services, for example. With the rollercoaster ride people experienced in the last ten years, there is a fair amount of skepticism toward stockbrokers and financial advisers. Now, when a financial adviser calls a prospective client, just telling them about his track record is no longer enough to gain their confidence. Instead, by articulating the challenges investors face and demonstrating that he understands what might be most important to this customer, the adviser has put himself in a position to transform a customer's skepticism into potential interest.

Here are a few examples of what this positioning might sound like in a couple of different industries:

Financial Adviser

"Mr. Customer, although we are in the business of providing financial products and services, just providing advice is not good enough for most clients anymore. People don't want to hear about the latest hot stock pick, and they don't want to be pressured into making unwise investments by commission-hungry brokers. Instead, clients want solid thinking and sound direction. They want an integrity-based financial partner who will help maximize their return on investment and minimize their risk. They also want someone who will invest the time to consider their individual financial status as well as their longer-term investment objectives. Mr. Customer, *that's basically what we do for the clients we serve.*"

Real Estate Agent

"Mr. Customer, I understand you're thinking about listing your home and that you are currently in the process of selecting an agent. The way I see it, the real value homeowners get from an agent comes after the listing agreement is signed. In today's real estate market, selling a home is not as simple as just taking a picture and registering your home with a multiple listing service. No, if you want to get quality offers on your property, it must be proactively marketed to other real estate agents and to the buying public. Leads have to be monitored and followed up on, and feedback should be used to adjust to market conditions and deal with any issues a prospective buyer may have. The bottom line is, if you want results, you need to choose an agent who will put forth the effort as if they were selling their own home...*which is exactly what we do!*"

Medical Sales

"Dr. Prospect, there are several medicines you can choose from to fight foot fungus. The problem is, most patients don't just want a temporary solution. They want permanent relief. So, the ultimate goal is to prescribe a treatment that eliminates the current symptoms of itching, chafing, burning, and peeling, with the added benefit of eradicating the underlying medical condition after a few weeks of continued usage. *And, that's basically what this new product does.*"

Notice that the salesperson in these examples doesn't spend a lot of time talking about product features. Interestingly, they don't spend a great deal of time talking about the problems they solve either. Instead, they are very specifically talking with customers about potential problems and challenges that might exist. You see, customers have challenges whether you offer a solution to them or not. I have come to believe that the first thing customers want to know is whether you understand their current dilemma or situation. If any of the challenges you raise resonate with the client, then your introductory "blurb" will undoubtedly expand into a more in-depth exchange of ideas regarding the customer's financial objectives, real estate concerns, or medical challenges.

> **Secret #12** The first thing customers want to know is whether you understand their current goals, dilemma, or situation.

There is another angle on this strategy of bonding with customers on their problems, issues, and concerns. One of the best salespeople I know is a real estate agent with RE/MAX in Atlanta named Jerry Saunders. Jerry has been my agent for twenty-five years. I can tell you that as a perennial skeptic, the last thing I want is some pushy real estate agent trying to "sell" me a house.

At the very first house Jerry took me to in 1987, he unlocked the front door, walked into the foyer, and said, "You don't want this house." That really threw me. "I don't?" I asked, a bit baffled. "Why not?"

Jerry pointed to some barely noticeable cracks in the sheetrock, and to some places where the molding was separating from the wall. A quick trip to the basement revealed the house had been built crookedly on the foundation. We left. Wow! Jerry wasn't trying to sell me just any house. He was actually trying to help me buy the right house. How do you think that affected his credibility as an agent?

By the time we made it to the third house, I had gained some confidence as an experienced "house looker." Sure enough, he unlocked the door and we walked in. "I don't want this house," I announced. When Jerry walked in behind me and saw what I saw, he said, "Yuck!" The carpeting was Pepto-Bismol pink, the walls were painted in a dreary peach color, and all the moldings had been painted brown. Yuck was right. But then he pointed out that whichever house I ended up purchasing, I would probably have to replace the carpeting and repaint. "So, Tom, what you really need to be looking for are things like floor plan, structural stability, location, and value relative to the market."

We looked at a dozen houses that day, and sure enough, I bought the one with the obnoxious pink carpet. Once we repainted and put in neutral colored carpeting, the place looked totally different. Thanks to Jerry, and the credibility he had gained with me, I was able to look for what was most important in making a house purchase as opposed to letting cosmetic first impressions fool me into making the wrong decision.

Now that I have worked with Jerry several times, I have noticed a trend.

When Jerry Saunders sees a potential problem, he points it out. He highlights benefits as well. But one of the reasons he has become so successful in real estate is because he has tremendous credibility with clients, much of which comes from his willingness to talk directly about actual problems, as opposed to trying to sell real estate by only focusing on the positives, the "silver lining," if you will, like so many other agents do.

The way I see it, customers will spend all kinds of time with someone they believe can help them address problems, issues, or concerns, but they have very little time to spend with someone who is just another sales caller. Of course, the only way for prospective customers to know whether you can help them is to get their problems out on the table. That doesn't happen by blasting potential buyers with the latest elevator pitch and having your value proposition get commoditized, however. Nor does it happen because you incessantly probe customers for needs. Let me say it again. You bond with customers by talking more about what's most important to them (their problems), rather than whatever might be most important to you (your solutions).

> **Secret #13** You bond with customers by talking more about what's most important to them (their problems), rather than whatever might be most important to you (your solutions).

The question you must answer is: Do you want to be seen as a valuable resource in the eyes of prospective customers, or as just another sales caller? I choose the former. The good news is how you position your value proposition will have a lot to do with how you are being perceived in the marketplace.

Summary

In today's business environment, customers simply aren't going to move forward with a purchase until they feel comfortable that it's the right decision. What makes customers feel more comfortable? Yes, your product or service has to provide the right fit, and yes, your company must also be viable in the marketplace. But at the end of the day, the customer's comfort level comes from how he or she feels about the salesperson and his or her extraordinary ability to represent the product or service.

So, let's agree that credibility is an important quality for a salesperson. So are knowledge, experience, integrity, and thought leadership. The question now is, how can you convey these qualities to potential customers, especially if they are outwardly skeptical toward vendors? I call it traction. We want to gain maximum traction with prospective clients who have needs that we can satisfy, and we want to convey our intangible benefits in order to start building value as quickly as possible.

What's the best way to convey intangible benefits to potential buyers? That's a very good question. Stay tuned for the answer!

Chapter 2

EXPANDING YOUR VALUE PROPOSITION

Buyers are motivated by what they need. If someone needs to protect against financial loss, for example, they buy insurance. If someone wants to keep pace with industry trends, they might upgrade their technology. Virtually every purchase is an attempt to solve a problem or accomplish a goal, thereby satisfying a need.

By helping prospective buyers identify potential needs, sellers can expand their opportunity to provide solutions—and more opportunities means increased sales. In this chapter, we'll examine how you can help prospects broaden their needs, which will ultimately create a greater sense of urgency to move forward.

Ring…ring… ring… Begrudgingly, I closed the newspaper, climbed out of my comfortable chair, and lunged for the telephone. Sure enough, it was another one of those pesky sales callers. You know, where the phone rings just after you've crashed into the La-Z-Boy, following a long day at the office.

On the other end of the call was a salesperson named Brent, who was selling septic tank improvement products. *Septic tank improvement products?* I remember thinking. *That's a new one on me.* But as a consummate student of the sale, I indulged him—at least for a few moments.

Brent was an energetic young salesman who successfully secured a few minutes of my time, and then dove headfirst into his sales pitch. He explained that he represented a company that distributes chemical enzyme systems. (What's a chemical enzyme system, you might ask? Apparently, it's a process that enables septic tanks to function more efficiently.) Brent rattled off a list of product features and their corresponding benefits. Then he added, "Our products are EPA approved and environmentally safe."

After his opening barrage, I asked, "How much do your septic tank improvement products cost?"

"Our products are extremely cost effective—less than three dollars per month," Brent responded confidently. He then tried to close the sale by offering a five-year supply of his product for the special low price of $179.

"There's only one problem," I replied. "I subscribe to the theory that if it ain't broke, don't fix it. And as far as I know, my septic system is working just fine, which makes your product too expensive at any price. But thank you anyway." *(Click.)* Then, before settling back into my chair, I forwarded my calls to prevent any further unwelcome interruptions.

Brent didn't sell me his product that day, but it wasn't because he lacked enthusiasm or because he had an inferior product. Frankly, he could have been the world's greatest salesperson offering the best septic tank improvement product and the answer would have been the same—*No thanks.* The reason is simple. I wasn't a qualified prospect because I didn't perceive a need.

> **Secret #14** Without needs, there are no solutions; and without solutions, it's virtually impossible to establish value.

Brent was convinced that homeowners would save money by using his product. But it doesn't really matter what the salesperson believes. The buyer is the one who actually makes the decision, and since my septic tank seemed fine, there was no reason to spend $179. Brent failed to uncover a need that would fuel the sales process; therefore, he missed an opportunity to either solve a problem or improve my existing condition.

This scenario makes an interesting case study because salespeople all over the world try some variation of this approach—offering solutions without first identifying the need. But, buyers don't have needs just because you offer solutions. It's the other way around. You can only offer solutions if the buyer has needs. Guess whose job it is to uncover needs? It's the salesperson's job.

Where Do Needs Originate?

Sellers cannot provide value until the prospect first recognizes the existence of a need. Needs are what initially motivates them to investigate potential solutions and needs are what motivates them to buy. Of course, the more needs you uncover, the more likely it is that prospective buyers will find value in the solutions being proposed. From there, it's the implications of those needs that ultimately drive purchase decisions.

Too often, sellers are taught that the best way to find qualified opportunities is to go out looking for pain. That's essentially what my friend Brent was doing. He was calling to see if I was currently experiencing a problem with my septic tank. Turns out, *I wasn't.* The assumption is, if prospects are currently experiencing a problem, then they must have needs. On the surface, looking for pain makes sense because pain causes prospects to seek relief. It also motivates them to want to prevent problems from occurring in the future.

Searching for problems is not a bad strategy. Pain can be a very powerful motivator indeed. In fact, frustration and discontentment have been the catalysts for some of the most lucrative opportunities of my sales career. But we must realize that pain is *not* the only source of prospect needs.

Needs Come from Both

Needs are also created by desire. Otherwise, why would anyone spend $80,000 to buy a new Mercedes Benz? It's not because they're feeling some sort of pain. More likely it's because they desire the luxury and elegance that only Mercedes Benz can offer. These desires *are* needs, but they are hardly problems in the traditional sense. If the customer's objective was simply to solve a problem, they could have purchased a Honda for less money and still had adequate transportation.

The same is true with artwork, fine jewelry, pleasure boats, furniture, oriental rugs, sporting goods, video equipment, musical instruments, and vacation property. People purchase these products to satisfy a need—a need that comes from desire, rather than pain.

In QBS, we define a need as a discrepancy between *what is* and *what could be.* In layman's terms, needs are formed when people who are dissatisfied with the status quo (*what is*) recognize that they would be better off if their situation was improved (by *what could be*). Prospects who are currently experiencing pain will seek relief, while those who wish to satisfy a desire will buy things to improve their existing condition—and the larger the discrepancy, the more your prospects will need a solution.

Secret #15 To alleviate *pain*, prospects will seek relief. To satisfy a *desire*, prospects will attempt to improve their existing condition.

This is where implications come in. The customer might currently have a problem, but what are the implications of that problem? If there are many, then you can foster many reasons for them to purchase your product or service. Of course, the more reasons a customer has to alleviate a pain or satisfy a desire, the greater the customer's sense of urgency will be to move forward.

These discrepancies can manifest themselves as either a lack of something required (to alleviate pain), or a lack of something preferred (to satisfy a desire). To illustrate, suppose your laptop computer crashed for the third consecutive day. If you depend on a PC to run your business, then you suddenly have a serious problem—a pain caused by a lack of something required. Having lost my own computer system before, I know that this situation will quickly manifest itself into a need by creating a discrepancy between *what is* (an unreliable laptop) and *what could be* (a system that works).

A discrepancy can also be created by desire—a need to improve the status quo. If an AT&T salesperson showed a corporate CFO how he could reduce his company's telecommunications costs by changing carriers, and the CFO became excited about saving money, then a discrepancy would be created between *what is* (his current long distance expenses) and *what could be* (significant reductions in cost). As a result, the CFO's contentment with his previous carrier would be replaced by a desire to improve the status quo.

In Question Based Selling, this is important because we must recognize that needs and the implications of those needs come from both pain and desire. If your goal is to uncover needs in order to provide solutions, you can expand your opportunity (to sell) by offering relief to those prospects who are currently experiencing pain, and a vision of value for those who wish to improve their existing condition.

Perception Isn't Everything

Going back to the story of the septic tank salesman, I want to point out an interesting irony about needs. Just because Brent didn't successfully uncover a need on the telephone doesn't mean a problem (or opportunity) didn't exist.

Because I was not aware of any septic tank problems, I did not perceive a need for the product Brent was offering. But after a few days, Brent's call prompted me to wonder if our septic system was indeed functioning properly. For all I knew, it could have been seeping raw sewage into the ground. What do I know about septic tank maintenance?

As I thought more about it, I remembered seeing septic tank service trucks around the neighborhood. These service trucks would indicate that our neighbors were either currently experiencing problems with their septic systems, or they were trying to prevent problems from occurring. I made a few calls and discovered that septic tanks do need regular maintenance, so I scheduled an appointment with a local company, AAA Septic Services, to come out and give us a "complimentary" evaluation.

The service rep asked, "When was your system last serviced?" My honesty revealed my ignorance, which he used as an opportunity to educate me further. He explained that like anything else chemical or mechanical, septic systems need to be serviced on a regular basis to function properly; otherwise, the homeowner could face any number of undesirable and costly consequences.

As I learned more about septic tank maintenance, it became obvious that we did have a need. It was a classic case of what you don't know *can* hurt you. Gladly, I authorized a work order for AAA to service our system. In addition, I agreed to purchase the very same maintenance product Brent had offered less than a week earlier to help avoid potential problems in the future.

When My Perspective Changed, So Did My Needs

When Brent called, I didn't think I needed septic system maintenance. But within seven days of his call I was signing a purchase requisition for the very same septic tank improvement product. The question is, what changed?

Oddly enough, my actual needs didn't change between Brent's call and AAA's recommendation. The status of my septic system was virtually the same as it had been a week earlier. What changed was my perspective. New information created a discrepancy between the current status of my septic system, and the recommendation I was getting. When I found out that septic systems do need regular maintenance, and that there are serious consequences if regular maintenance is not properly performed, I quickly recognized the existence of a need.

Furthermore, the need for septic tank maintenance was not actually driving the purchase. It was all the implications that the AAA service professional brought to light that really got my attention. For example, if I let the system fail completely, then my entire backyard would probably need to be dug up, including our new backyard patio that had been poured less than a year before. In addition to the excavation, I would also be looking at a repair cost somewhere in the neighborhood of ten times the cost of preventative maintenance, not to mention the time, hassle, and odor that would come with such a mess.

As you can see from this anecdote, the actual need had been there all along. My desire to avoid the undesirable implications of the problem existed as well. My friend Brent missed an opportunity to make a sale simply because he didn't understand the difference between active needs and latent needs.

Active Needs

People who are currently experiencing problems, frustration, pain, or an intense desire have immediate needs. In QBS, we call these *active needs*. If you were driving your car on a desolate stretch of interstate highway, for example, and your low fuel warning light suddenly started to flash, you would have an immediate need; in this case, for gasoline. Since you would be on the verge of running out of fuel, you would have an active need to resolve the problem. You would also start worrying about the implications of being stranded on a desolate highway without any fuel.

Similarly, if you were in a computer superstore and saw that the price of the laser printer that you'd been eyeing for the last several months had suddenly been reduced for a "today only" clearance sale, you might have an immediate need to take advantage of the opportunity. This is an example of an active need that comes from desire—also with several positive implications.

Active needs occur whenever a person is no longer satisfied with the status quo. Whether their dissatisfaction is caused by pain or desire, prospects with active needs are relatively easy to approach and sell to because they are already open to changing the status quo. In some cases, they may have already started actively looking for a solution.

> **Secret #16** *Active needs* occur when prospects recognize that they are no longer satisfied with the status quo.

Not surprisingly, people with active needs make wonderful prospects. In addition to having already recognized their needs, they appreciate a salesperson who is willing to work with them to find a solution. Consequently, the sales cycle tends to be much shorter, and decisions are made more quickly. In some ways, it's like feeding a hungry baby. All you have to do is dangle a few implications/benefits out in front of someone with an active need, and they get excited.

Wouldn't it be nice if every prospective buyer in your territory had active needs? But that's not reality. While it's enticing to think that people out there are desperately seeking our solutions, the reality is prospects with active needs represent only a small portion of your overall market opportunity.

Latent Needs

The larger and more significant portion of the market is comprised of prospects who do have needs for your product or service, but haven't yet recognized those needs. In QBS, we say that these prospects have *latent needs*.

Latent needs are needs that do exist but haven't yet surfaced as problems or desires. Prospects with latent needs fail to recognize that they are no longer satisfied with the status quo. As an example, suppose you and I were standing beside your car when suddenly we noticed that one of your tires was worn down to the cords. Instantly, you would have a need for new tires. The question is, did you have a need for new tires yesterday? Sure you did. The tread on your tire didn't wear itself down overnight. But until you actually recognized the existence of a problem, your need for new tires was latent. It existed, although you were not aware of it at the time. This is essentially what happened when Brent called me. I absolutely had a need for septic tank improvement products, but my need was a latent need.

Salespeople encounter prospects with latent needs all the time—especially prospects who say things like: "I don't need life insurance because I'm not planning to die any time soon." Or, "We don't have time to evaluate new technology, because we're too busy putting out fires." Here's my personal favorite: "We can't afford sales training right now, because sales have been slow."

Hello! The best time to buy life insurance is when you're not planning to die. Similarly, new technology might help eliminate some of those nagging system problems; and it makes all kinds of sense to invest in sales training if your sales numbers are weak, or your competition is getting tougher.

> **Secret #17** *Latent needs* exist when prospects fail to recognize that they are no longer satisfied with the status quo.

The primary reason latent needs exist is ignorance. I do not mean this in a derogatory way or use the term with malice. It's just that when prospects are not aware of a problem (or opportunity to improve their existing condition), they have no reason to change. Another source of latent needs is having a false sense of security. Going back to a previous analogy, if your car was just serviced and everything checked out fine, then it would be easy to assume that there's no need for additional maintenance.

The Lion's Share of Opportunity

The easiest way to create opportunities that otherwise wouldn't exist is to go out into the marketplace looking for prospects with active needs. But as we've said, active needs represent only a small fraction of the overall market opportunity, while latent needs make up the lion's share. For every prospect who is currently feeling pain, or who recognizes an opportunity to improve their existing condition, there are many more who might also benefit from your product or service. In fact, this relationship is highly skewed where prospects with active needs are more the exception than the rule. You can see this better if we extrapolate some numbers.

Everyone needs insurance, right? One might think so, but studies have shown that while 60 percent of middle-class Americans are underinsured, less than 2 percent are "in the market" to buy additional coverage. What does this mean for an insurance salesperson? It means that sixty out of every one hundred prospects need more insurance, but only two out of those people would be eager to have a discussion about buying additional coverage. These two people would have active needs, and the other fifty-eight would be said to have latent needs.

If you do the math, you will also find that prospecting for active needs is unproductive. Using the previous example, an insurance salesperson who only prospects for people with active needs would have to make fifty calls (on average) just to find one new opportunity. That's an extremely low return on their invested sales efforts. If that same salesperson went after the larger market segment, by targeting the other 60 percent who have latent needs, the number of opportunities that could be harvested from the same pool of prospects could increase dramatically. In other words, out of every fifty prospects, twenty-five or thirty might have a latent need for additional insurance, and thus, might be interested in hearing more about the insurance products being offered.

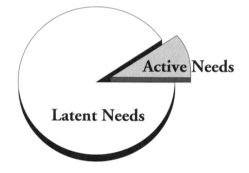

Total Market Opportunity

Most top performing salespeople will attest that the overwhelming majority of their sales success comes from their ability to transform a prospect's latent needs into active needs. This transformation is also how you escalate the prospect's sense of urgency to move forward with a favorable decision.

Increasing the Prospect's Sense of Urgency

Dangling potential solutions out in front of a prospect with latent needs is a low percentage play. No matter how good your solutions are, prospects with latent needs do not recognize the existence of a problem or opportunity, and as a result, are probably not going to buy. That's because they're complacent. They are already satisfied with the status quo, and the opportunity for improvement isn't enough to initiate or justify a change.

The opposite of complacency is urgency. Urgency tends to motivate people to take action when problems are either painful enough, or opportunities are enticing enough, to justify making a change. How can you increase a prospect's sense of urgency? Easy. All you have to do is transform their latent needs into active needs. And the greater the prospect's needs, the more incentive they have to alleviate the pain or satisfy the desire.

> **Secret #18** *How badly you're bleeding usually dictates how fast you drive to the hospital.* The greater the prospect's sense of urgency, the more likely they are to act on your solutions.

The following diagram illustrates the relationship between latent needs and active needs. Actually, it's a logical progression. After fifteen years of training salespeople, people ask me, "Tom, what are top performers really good at?" The answer is actually quite simple. They're good at turning latent needs into active needs, in order to increase the prospect's sense of urgency, which will ultimately increase their probability of success in making the sale.

As the prospect's perspective changes (like mine did in the septic tank scenario), the simple recognition of a latent need can transform it into an active need, and the prospect's sense of urgency for finding a solution will increase automatically. So will your probability of successfully completing a sale.

Escalating Needs Increase Probability

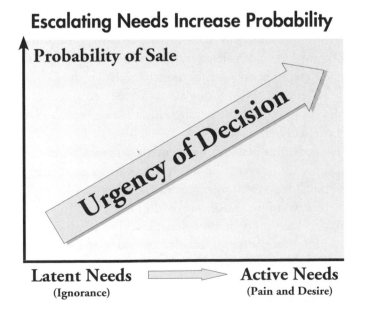

Turning a prospect's complacency into an active desire is the real game in professional selling. This is what allows sellers to go after the broader market opportunity—those prospects who have needs but haven't yet recognized the opportunity to improve their existing condition. It's what separates top sales performers from the rest of the masses.

While it is natural for prospects to find comfort in the status quo, sellers have to realize that potential buyers can't take advantage of opportunities they don't know about. This boils the sales function down into a process of mutual discovery, where sellers work together with prospective buyers to uncover problems and opportunities that otherwise wouldn't have been identified. Have you ever heard a prospect say, "I wish I had known about your production sooner"? Just like you and me, they can only act on the information they have at the time.

> **Secret #19** Uninformed prospects are much less likely to make a favorable buying decision.

The easiest way to increase a prospect's sense of urgency is to change their perspective. You can accomplish this by offering new information that will cause them to take notice. Better yet, you can ask questions that will help uncover needs, but more importantly, help them discover multiple implications that could potentially improve their existing condition. The following anecdote illustrates the point.

Changing the Prospect's Perspective

Pat Daley sells home security systems in Sacramento, California. Like many salespeople, Pat makes sales call after sales call, trying to uncover potential opportunities by asking people if they are currently "in the market" for a new home security system. His prospecting efforts have been diligent, but sales have been slow. Most of the people he talks to either have a security system already, or they feel secure enough without one.

Robert Dickens also sells home security systems in Sacramento. Even though he's calling on the same pool of prospects as Pat, Robert's business is booming. His pipeline is overflowing with new opportunities and his company is swamped with new orders. Business couldn't be better. In fact, his organization is straining to keep up with a rising demand for home security.

What's the difference between Robert's approach and Pat's, given that they are selling similar products within the same geographic area?

The difference is their target market. Pat is prospecting for people who already have an active need for a security system. Pat is looking for the two out of one hundred. Robert, on the other hand, works closely with his prospects to develop their need for home security. Robert has figured out that his greatest opportunity to make sales lies in his ability to create demand by helping potential buyers recognize latent needs. Furthermore, he understands that it's not home security that's actually driving the need for home security systems. Rather, it's the implications of not having a security system in place in the event of an unfortunate or undesirable situation. In his view, who wouldn't be interested in protecting their home and family?

To foster this demand for home security, Robert focuses on raising the prospect's awareness, and piquing their interest, which is the first step toward changing their perspective. His typical sales call sounds like this:

Robert: *"Hello, Mr. Prospect, my name is Robert Dickens, and I'm with SafeGuard Security Systems of Sacramento. Sir, are you aware that within a five-mile radius of your home, the number of break-ins, thefts, and violent crimes has nearly doubled in the last year?"*

Prospect: *"Really? I wasn't aware of that."*

Robert: *"Yes. It's unfortunate, but true. In fact, six incidents of criminal activity have been reported in your area within the last ninety days. That's why I'm calling. To protect people like you, SafeGuard Security has implemented a community-wide plan to eliminate these security breaches. Would you like to know how this plan works?"*

Prospect: *"Yes, I would."*

Robert: *"Through the end of next month, our company is offering residents in East Sacramento a complimentary security evaluation—and there's no obligation to buy anything. For those people who are interested in protecting their homes and families, we will dispatch one of our certified security experts to inspect your property and identify possible security risks. That way, you can minimize any temptations that might otherwise invite criminal activity."*

After getting the prospect's attention by raising their awareness, Robert schedules an appointment for himself or one of his company's security experts to come out and provide a complimentary evaluation.

What do you suppose a complimentary security evaluation consists of? Essentially, it's forty-five minutes of uninterrupted sales time. It's also an opportunity for Robert to transform the prospect's latent needs into an active desire by identifying the implications of any potential security problems.

As property owners learn more about how intruders target houses with insufficient lighting, inadequate door locks, or overgrown shrubbery, they predictably start to feel less secure. With each deficiency that Robert or one of his security experts points out, homeowners begin to visualize how burglars, rapists, or murderers could easily gain access into their home. Consequently, their sense of urgency for buying a security system increases significantly. According to Robert, once a homeowner takes the time to consider the risks, they invariably jump to the next question, which is: *How much does a security system cost, and how soon can you have it installed?* Bingo!

> **Secret #20** Urgency sells! It increases the prospect's desire to satisfy their needs, and it also increases your probability of success.

Robert is successful because he works together with his prospects to identify potential problems. That's not the case with Pat. Pat isn't doing much of anything to escalate the prospect's sense of urgency. Instead, he just goes after the small percentage of homeowners who already recognize their need for home security, but haven't yet purchased a home security system.

Robert is not only providing a valuable solution; he is rendering a valuable service. By giving his prospects an eye-opening dose of reality, he helps them to realize that they may not be as safe as they thought. This realization creates a discrepancy between "what is" (potential risks), and "what could be" (peace-of-mind protection). Keep in mind that Robert hasn't created the problem (crime), nor has he created the prospect's need for home security. He simply brings the issues to the forefront, so prospects can make informed decisions about enhancing their status quo.

Build a Repository of Issues & Implications

You'll hear me talk about needs development later in the book, and in that vein, you'll hear me say that uncovering needs is a flawed strategy. Would you rather be like Pat or Robert? Pat goes out looking for people who already recognize the full extent of their needs. Robert does the opposite, recognizing that if he raises important issues, and the implications of those issues, his probability of success increases dramatically.

I would make the case that a capable salesperson ought to already know what "might" be important to potential customers, before they even pick up the telephone or show up in person. In fact, the whole idea of uncovering needs in today's business environment is no longer relevant for two reasons. First, prospects with latent needs probably aren't going to share valuable information with a salesperson, because they don't even recognize the existence of a need. Second, and more importantly, as customers in general have grown increasingly more skeptical toward vendors, people are very reticent to share their needs (even if they are indeed recognized) with a salesperson they don't yet know or trust.

Thus, the play is no longer to try to uncover needs, but to facilitate a conversation where the salesperson raises potential issues and their implications. This facilitation is a proactive means of accomplishing two things. On one hand, your bringing up important issues could absolutely jog the customer's thinking and cause them to recognize key points that they might not have otherwise factored into their decisions. As well, raising important issues and implications is one of your greatest opportunities to gain credibility with potential buyers, as we will discuss in more depth when we get to the chapters on needs development.

The key is preparation. When I train sales teams on-site, they leave with a list of action items that are important in terms of implementing the QBS methodology.

The first action item on the list is always the same—to create a repository of decision issues and implications that could impact the customer. Notice I use the word "could," because we're not asking salespeople to be clairvoyant. You can't know what's important to a customer until you actually talk with them. But, you can absolutely make a list of potential issues and the implications of those issues, as a way to prepare yourself in advance for more productive conversations.

It's an easy assignment, really. Start by simply making a list of possible decision issues. What topics might be important to the customer? In the previous example of home security, the issue of safety might be obviously important to the decision making process. But, so might other issues like cost, installation,

Decision Issues

* *Performance*
* *Productivity*
* *Maintenance*
* *Educ. & Training*
* *Upgrades*
* *Data Mgt.*

integration with the Internet for remote monitoring, ongoing service, the company's track record, or how having a system might impact their home-owner's insurance.

If you sell technology, there are all kinds of issues that could affect cus-tomers ranging from performance, to productivity, maintenance, education/training, upgrades, and data management, all of which translate into potential cost savings. Note that these are just the decision issues. Behind each of these issues is a list of potential implications that can further the customer's thinking and increase their sense of urgency for making a decision. How many implica-tions factor into the decision? Let's do the math.

Do the Math

As part of this repository building exercise, I encourage salespeople to make a list of possible decision issues, and then for each of the issues on your list, make a sub-list of possible implications that could affect (or be impacted by) that particular issue. Just ask yourself, "Why might (issue) be important to the customer?"

If home security is indeed the issue, then it would be easy to make a list of why home security might be important. On that list might be things like protection against theft, fire, home invasions, personal safety, surveillance, valuables, damage to personal property, vandalism, financial loss, or peace of mind. That's ten.

If the issue at hand is productivity, then the list of implications might include things like: time to market, compensation, employee morale, customer satisfaction, training, installation, cost of goods sold, competitive positioning, profitability, and market share. There's another ten. You can do this for every issue on your list.

So, let me ask: What are the chances a customer will bring up all ten of these implications (for any given issue) to you? The answer is very slim. But, human nature is very predictable. So, if you were to ask the customer a question like: *Besides the obvious goal of maximizing productivity, what (specifically) are you most concerned about?* most will name one or two, and sometimes three. Now the question is, who is going to bring up the rest of the implications that might factor into their decision? If the customer's not going to bring them up, and you don't bring them up proactively, you leave the door wide open for a competitor to be seen as a more valuable resource. Raising issues and implications is what I mean when I talk about facilitating more productive conversations.

If we do the math on this, let's suppose there were fifteen issues that might factor into the customer's decision-making process. And, let's suppose you made a list of ten implications for each issue listed, you would suddenly have one hundred and fifty opportunities to provide value. That's a tenfold increase over just talking about the issue itself. This is very different than running around tossing out industry buzzwords in a standard elevator pitch. For the sake of argument, let's do a comparison between two salespeople: you before you made the repository list and you after. I would argue that the second you would outsell the first by an order of magnitude. How do I know this? Not only have I witnessed it with QBS students countless times, but if you look back to the earlier diagram that refers to the customer's sense of urgency, you will see that raising potential issues and implications that the customer wouldn't necessarily bring up on their own is the easiest way to turn latent needs into active needs. This, of course, increases the customer's sense of urgency, which increases your probability of success in making a sale.

What's the downside to this model? Two things—one is being over-prepared. Does it make sense to try to bring up each issue and every single implication in every meeting you have with potential customers? Of course not. So how many issues and implications should you raise? The answer is as many as it takes to create enough interest and urgency to fuel the sales process moving forward. Secondly, while this exercise is simple enough, making a list of ten implications per issue is not as easy as you might think. That's because these issues and implications are not top-of-mind. As a sales culture, we have trained salespeople that their job is to uncover needs. But what if the prospect doesn't know what they need? Worse, what if they aren't open to sharing with a salesperson they don't yet know or trust?

It's like physical exercise. The exercise will pay significant dividends, but only if you actually make the effort. This is where you challenge yourself to come up with a list of ten implications, so you will have an opportunity to challenge the customer's thinking when it's time to facilitate a needs development conversation.

Summary

Although the examples I cited deal with home security systems and technology, the same philosophy applies whether you're selling insurance, consulting, real estate, pharmaceuticals, financial services, industrial supplies, or heavy equipment. Transforming latent needs into active needs will escalate the prospect's sense of urgency for finding a solution, which, in turn, increases your probability of making a successful sale.

Identifying needs is fundamental to any successful formula in selling. No matter how exciting your solution may be, prospects who don't recognize their own needs won't recognize the value of your product or service. Speaking of value, what if it were possible to double your value proposition again in the eyes of potential buyers, so instead of one hundred and fifty opportunities to add value, you would have three hundred? That's what we'll do next when we talk about *Gold Medals* and *German Shepherds*.

Chapter 3

GOLD MEDALS AND GERMAN SHEPHERDS

To succeed in sales, sellers have to motivate potential buyers to "want to" take action. But we (as sellers) also have to recognize that people are motivated in different ways. While some people are motivated to run fast toward Gold Medals, many others will run even faster from German Shepherds.

In QBS, we will show you how to motivate both kinds of buyers. By making a few simple tweaks to the way you position your value proposition, you can double the number of benefits your product or service offers, and increase your probability of success in making the sale.

I go fishing up in Maine every summer," Dale Carnegie wrote in the mid 1930s. "Personally, I am very fond of strawberries and cream, but I find that for some strange reason, fish prefer worms. So when I go fishing, I don't think about what I want. I think about what they want. I don't bait the hook with strawberries and cream. I dangle a worm or a grasshopper in front of the fish and say, 'Wouldn't you like to have that?'"

This story prompts me to ask, why not use the same commonsense approach when fishing for customers?

Secret #21 If you want to motivate people, then it's more important to think about what they want, rather than what you want.

Most salespeople love to talk about the solutions they offer. They get excited about the value of their product or service and want to share this good news with qualified prospects. While some are more strategic in their delivery, others get excited and start spewing benefits like a volcano. In either case, their objectives are the same—sellers are trying to convey enough value with their solutions to justify a favorable purchase decision.

But, as Mr. Carnegie points out in his timeless and meaningful message, just because something is important to us (as salespeople) doesn't necessarily mean it's important to the customer. Sales presentations are breeding grounds for this type of disconnect. For example, have you ever had the experience where some portion of the audience is absolutely riveted to your presentation, while other people in the same audience are just sitting there with a glazed look, like a cat testing a new pair of eyes? Obviously, they are completely missing the point. In the real world of selling, this happens because people have different buying motivations.

Always Positive Is Not the Most Productive

Salespeople have tried numerous ways to address the fact that prospects are motivated differently. One of the most prevalent sales tricks is to try to motivate prospects with "happy gas." For decades, sellers have been told that attitude is everything, and the more enthusiastic you are, the more excited your prospects will become. You know the drill—flash a big smile and bubble over with energy in an attempt to get prospects excited about your product. Gag me! Especially in this new era of customer skepticism, this fluffy cloud approach to selling is just a facade that causes many salespeople to miss out on some otherwise lucrative opportunities.

Even salespeople who are not filled with happy gas still tend to emphasize the positive, pointing out all the wonderful benefits of their product or service, in an attempt to get prospects and customers excited. But as you are about to find out, always positive is not always the most productive approach in Question Based Selling.

True professionals are not "always positive." Instead, they radiate intangible qualities like competence, capability, and expertise by being serious and self-assured. This is very different from the eager salesperson who attempts to communicate value by having a permanent smile plastered on his or her face.

> **Secret #22** Competence, credibility, expertise, and value will outsell over-eagerness every time.

I'm not saying that you shouldn't be proud of your product or excited about a new opportunity. I'm merely suggesting that being super-positive and highly enthusiastic is not the best way to motivate *all* prospects. And as you'll see throughout Question Based Selling, being super-positive is not even the best way to motivate *most* prospects.

Problems with Behavioral Selling

Salespeople have also tried to address the fact that people are motivated differently by adjusting their own behavior. The last fifty years of behavioral research has generated numerous selling models that attempt to categorize prospective buyers into subgroups of prospects who have common personality characteristics and behavioral tendencies. Some of these subgroups include Drivers, Amiables, Analyticals, Expressives, Sensors, Thinkers, Intuitives, Judgers, and Feelers…just to name a few.

With a behavioral approach to selling, the thought is: if you can identify the type of person you are dealing with, and better understand how they are motivated, then you will be able to more effectively position the value of your product or service. I agree with the premise. The problem is, most behavioral selling models are very difficult to implement in the real world. I say this because after trying twice to implement this approach, I ran into the following four problems:

- When first engaging new prospects, it's impossible to know, in the initial moments of a conversation, whether you are dealing with a Driver, Amiable, Expressive, or Analytical. This puts the salesperson at a significant disadvantage, because prospects are going to form their impressions of you long before you will know how to position yourself.
- *You can't always judge a book by its cover.* Have you ever met someone who at first seemed like a "crusty old bird," but then once you got to know them, you found they were just an "old softy"? Other people are super sweet until you aren't looking, and then, wham! They stab you in the back. Needless to say, misjudging someone can be detrimental to your sales efforts.
- Very few salespeople (and I emphasize the word few) have the acting talent required to transform their personality to match their prospect's behavior without bumbling or sounding fake.
- Lastly, when you are dealing with multiple people in a strategic sale who all have different personality profiles, whose personality style should you try to match? Conventional wisdom would suggest that you target the biggest title in the room—assuming that he or she is the decision maker. But, I would hate to address the needs of the Driver, only to find out later that I failed to meet the needs of the Amiables, Expressives, or Feelers. I

can pretty much guarantee that the top decision maker in the room will ask their cohorts what they think after you finish your presentation and leave the room.

These problems lead me to conclude that behavioral selling models make for interesting theory; but trying to categorize people according to their personality type and then match your behavior to theirs is a highly ineffective way to try to manage a sale. The truth is, many salespeople end up outsmarting themselves by first misjudging their prospect and then mishandling the situation.

My experience has been that most salespeople perform at their best when they are just being themselves. They appear more comfortable and sound more confident, which allows them to focus on delivering value rather than trying to be something they're not.

> **Secret #23** Keep it simple. You will be more effective just being yourself, rather than trying to be something you're not.

This brings us right back to square one, where we concluded that potential buyers are indeed motivated differently. While I have always agreed with the premise that knowing how people are motivated allows sellers to more effectively position their value, I knew that there had to be a better way to manage these differences.

Solving the Personality Problem

People who are motivated differently can get excited about the same product for different reasons. This became apparent back when I started selling Superservers for NetFrame Systems. What's a Superserver? Simply put, it's a computer system that's powerful enough to support large corporate networks.

NetFrame put all its new field salespeople through a one-week orientation at corporate headquarters in the Silicon Valley. There we learned how to qualify new opportunities and how to position NetFrame's family of products. Upon completing the training, we were sent back to our respective territories to sell—*creating business opportunities that otherwise wouldn't exist.*

At first, I toed the company line—telling prospects how exciting our new technology was. I told them how NetFrame's unique multi-processing system architecture (MPSA) would improve their performance, productivity, and reliability. I also explained our systems were easy to manage and how that would end up saving the customer money.

As it turned out, some prospects did get excited about all the wonderful benefits NetFrame offered. But as time went by, I noticed that other prospects just weren't getting it. No matter how many "wonderful benefits" I threw out, they still weren't registering value, and I wasn't getting any closer to making a sale.

Finally, ignorance gave way to curiosity, and I started asking customers what they wanted. Guess what I discovered? While some prospects were very interested in all the positive benefits NetFrame offered, others were more interested in avoiding potential problems—they dreaded things like maintenance headaches, support issues, or overloading the network with excess traffic. Soon I discovered that prospects had very different reasons for buying our product. To motivate more prospects, it was clear that I needed to change the way I was positioning our value proposition.

The Metaphor That Stuck

In 1996, the Summer Olympic Games were held in my home city of Atlanta. As I watched athletes from all over the world perform in their respective events, I remember wondering what motivated them to compete at the highest levels. On the surface, it seemed logical to assume that these world-class athletes were driven by all the positive rewards that would go to the champion—fame, admiration, and of course, the gold medal. After training for most of their lives, who wouldn't want to experience "the thrill of victory"?

But as I watched the games unfold, it became obvious that while some athletes were motivated by *positive rewards*, many others were trying to avoid "the agony of defeat." Rather than think about all the accolades that would come from success, some athletes were motivated to run even faster, and jump even higher, because they were trying to avoid an undesirable outcome.

Carl Lewis, arguably one of the greatest track and field athletes of all time, and nine-time Olympic gold medalist, was an excellent example of this. After his last event in Atlanta, when he won the gold medal on his final attempt in the long jump, the sportscaster asked, *"Mr. Lewis, what were you thinking about just before you jumped?"* As it turned out, Carl Lewis wasn't thinking about medals, money, or having his picture on a box of Wheaties. Instead, he said his primary motivation was that his family was in the stadium and he didn't want to disappoint them by losing his final Olympic event.

Isn't that how many customers feel? Rather than hoping to benefit from all the wonderful things your product or service offers, they're trying to avoid potential problems, uncertainty, or even failure. In Question Based Selling, it's pretty clear that people are motivated differently—and while some are motivated by positive rewards, many others are motivated even more by negative aversion.

> **Secret #24** While some people run fast toward *Gold Medals*, many others run even faster from *German Shepherds*.

The fear of failure is a powerful influence. Imagine what would happen if a pack of German Shepherd dogs were actually chasing the Olympic athletes down the track toward the finish line. That would certainly motivate me to run faster. How about you? So what motivates your customers: *Gold Medals* or *German Shepherds*? In reality, some prospects you meet will be driven by positive benefits (*Gold Medals*), while others will be motivated by their need to avoid potential problems or feelings of uncertainty (*German Shepherds*).

The fact that people are motivated differently shouldn't surprise you. We see evidence of this every day. For example, why do people exercise? Isn't it true that some people exercise because physical activity is invigorating and it makes them feel energized all day (*Gold Medals*), while other people exercise because they're trying to lose weight or they want to reduce their risk of heart failure (*German Shepherds*)?

* More Reliable
* Cost Effective
* Less Overhead
* Easier to Use
* Easy to Manage
* Upgradable
* Proven Solution
* Performance

Why do people take vacations? Again, some people want to spend time with their families and see the world, while other people take vacations because if they don't, they'll go nuts. Can you see the difference?

I applied this principle to selling Superservers at NetFrame and quickly discovered that while some prospects were interested in positive benefits like better performance, productivity increases, and state-of-the-art technology, other prospects were more interested in protecting themselves against negative issues like downtime, maintenance problems, and corrupted data. Once I realized that my product could be positioned to address *Gold Medals* and *German Shepherds* (both), my sales took off, and it was truly amazing to see prospects who used to just sit there with a glazed look suddenly come alive.

The question is, what type of prospects do you want to sell to, those who are motivated by positive rewards or those who are motivated more by negative aversion? If you're like me, you'll want to sell to both.

Doubling Your Benefits Doubles Your Value

If you want to sell to people who are motivated by both *Gold Medals* and *German Shepherds*, then it's important to position benefits in ways that both will understand. How do you do this? Let me explain.

Positioning benefits is how sellers convey value. Ultimately, we want to establish enough value to justify the cost of our solution. Extrapolate this further, and we can logically conclude that the more benefits you bring to the table, the more value you can present to prospects and customers—thus increasing your probability of success for making a sale.

So let's make a list of benefits. When I deliver QBS programs to live audiences, I often ask participants to make a list of the compelling benefits their product or service offers. Then I go to the flip chart, and together we aggregate these benefits into a larger list that summarizes their company's value proposition. What we end up with is a flip chart filled with benefits—much like the diagram on the opposite page. As I did in the previous chapter, I encourage you to detail a list of the specific benefits that your product offers your customers.

The tendency is to position benefits positively, as *Gold Medals*. That seems to make sense, given that the dictionary defines a benefit as *something that promotes or enhances one's well-being*. Consequently, sellers all over the world run around telling prospects how terrific their products are because they provide wonderful benefits like reliability, cost effectiveness, lower overhead, ease of use, and the list goes on. These benefits are indeed wonderful, but mostly for those people who are motivated by *Gold Medals*. Other prospects, those motivated more by *German Shepherds*, might fail to register these positive benefits, in which case sellers would only connect with a portion of their intended audience.

We definitely want to motivate prospects who get excited about positive rewards. But we also want to reach those people who are trying to avoid potential problems, uncertainty, or even failure. You can accomplish this by positioning each of the benefits you offer both ways—as a *Gold Medal* and a *German Shepherd*.

Take one of the benefits from our diagram—cost effectiveness, for example. In addition to emphasizing the positive aspects of your product's cost effectiveness in terms of *Gold Medals*, it's just as important to let prospects know that your solution will also protect them against potential *German Shepherd* consequences like hidden expenses, high maintenance costs, or a low return on investment.

The same logic applies to other benefits like reliability and performance. To increase the value of your offering, you'll want to position these benefits both ways too. Let me illustrate.

Seller: *"Ms. Prospect, our reliability features will increase your productivity (Gold Medal) and also reduce all*

> *those pesky interruptions that would otherwise hand-cuff your business (German Shepherd)."*

—**or**—

> *"Performance is also an advantage—for two reasons. Because our systems use advanced technology, you can access more information (Gold Medal) without any risk of overloading the system with excess network traffic (German Shepherd)."*

Are you getting the picture? You can take any benefit from any company, for any product being offered, and position it both ways—as a Gold Medal and also as a German Shepherd.

Positioning benefits both as *Gold Medals* and *German Shepherds* accomplishes two very strategic objectives in the QBS sale. First, it's a risk reduction strategy. Instead of having some portion of your audience glaze over because they're simply not getting it, you will connect with more prospects by positioning value in a way that motivates them. Also, positioning benefits both ways means you no longer have to guess whether you are dealing with a Driver, Amiable, Expressive, or some other personality type. You will know in advance that prospects are motivated either by positive rewards or by negative aversion. This allows you to score points with those prospects who are motivated by *Gold Medals*, and also with those prospects who are motivated by *German Shepherds*.

Secret #25 By positioning both *Gold Medals* and *German Shepherds*, you will get more bang out of each benefit.

The flipchart diagram on the previous page listed eight specific benefits. The problem is that many of your competitors will claim that they too provide the same list of benefits. But you'll have the advantage if they focus only on the positives (as most sellers do), because they will address only eight value points. A QBS salesperson, on the other hand, who positions each of these benefits in terms of both *Gold Medals* and *German Shepherds*, instantly expands their value proposition to include sixteen value points, rather than just eight. Notice that your product hasn't changed, nor have the customer's needs. The only thing that changes is the customer's perception of your value—it doubles.

Here's the best part. Very few people are motivated only by *Gold Medals*, or only by *German Shepherds*. While some might lean one way or the other, the vast majority of prospects and customers are motivated by a combination of the two. Now let's do the math. Your ability to position twice as many benefits gives you an opportunity to present twice as much value; it also gives your prospects and customers twice as many reasons to move forward with a favorable purchase decision. This technique will ultimately help you justify your solutions and close more sales. As an added bonus, positioning both *Gold Medals* and *German Shepherds* will differentiate you from any competitors who are still being taught to focus only on the positive.

I Didn't Invent Human Behavior

The realization that prospects are motivated by positive reward and by negative aversion will forever change the face of professional sales. Those sellers who are willing to adapt and change the way they position benefits will reap significant rewards, while those who focus only on the positive will find themselves fighting against a severe competitive disadvantage.

Question Based Selling shouldn't receive all the credit, however. We didn't invent human behavior. Potential buyers have been responding to *Gold Medal* and *German Shepherd* influences for a long time. Just look at the advertising industry. Marketing executives figured out long ago that in order to generate greater returns on their advertising investments, they needed to target multiple segments of the consumer population. Do you remember the TV commercials for Fram Oil Filters—where the greasy mechanic looks directly into the camera and says, "You can pay me now (to install a new filter) or pay me later (to replace the entire engine)"? Fram recognized that while some people buy oil filters to make their engines run more smoothly (*Gold Medal*), many other people buy oil filters to avoid potential engine damage (*German Shepherd*).

Don't be alarmed! Targeting multiple market segments has become a common advertising practice for everyday products. Here's another example. Why do people buy Johnson's baby shampoo? Some people buy it because it's gentle on the hair (*Gold Medal*), while many other people buy Johnson's baby shampoo because it won't sting their baby's eyes (*German Shepherd*). Remember the slogan? "No more tears."

I can keep going. Why do people buy Miller Lite beer? Some people buy it because it "tastes great" (*Gold Medal*). Other people buy Miller Lite beer because it's "less filling" (*German Shepherd*).

The following chart highlights a number of everyday products and how they are being positioned to appeal to both kinds of buyers.

Product	Gold Medals	German Shepherds
Volvo automobiles	Efficient and stylish	Safe to protect family
Tandem computers	Maximum performance	Eliminates downtime
Microsoft	Technology leadership	Fewer integration issues
Johnson's Baby Shampoo	Gentle on the hair	No more tears
Miller Lite beer	Tastes great	Less filling
Fram oil filters	Smoother running engine	Prevents costly repairs
Life insurance	Retirement savings	Financial protection
Diet food products	High in taste	Low in fat
Organic detergents	Natural cleaning agents	Protect the environment
Weight-loss programs	Look and feel better	Lose those ugly pounds

Positioning Gold Medals and German Shepherds

Don't mistake this technique for negative selling. Positioning *German Shepherd* benefits is not intended to threaten, intimidate, or scare prospective customers. We are simply acknowledging that different types of people are motivated differently, which gives you an opportunity to position your benefits in a way that will more effectively meet the prospect's business and emotional needs.

Are you getting it? Some people confuse German Shepherd positioning with negative selling. They've been taught that benefits are supposed to be positive, but now we are talking about the potential downside of various products and services. Don't be confused.

Gold Medal benefits are easy to reconcile, because they sound positive. And, those sellers who have always been taught that benefits are good things, they'll be content. But let me ask: is protecting customers against potential downsides or risk a good thing too? The answer is a resounding yes. Doesn't your product or service do both? You provide positive benefits (*Gold Medals*) and you also protect customers against potential negatives (*German Shepherds*), which is definitely a good thing. In terms of positioning your product's value proposition, it's a two-for-one situation.

Corporate Marketers Take Note

In every company that I have ever sold for, the corporate marketing department played an integral role in the success of the sales organization. But I have noticed that the vast majority of product literature and corporate marketing programs are full of *Gold Medal* benefits, but they hardly mention *German Shepherd* risks. Like salespeople, corporate marketers have also been taught to put their best foot forward when positioning benefits, in an effort to communicate all the wonderful aspects their product or service offers.

Ironically, the way marketing departments position *Gold Medal* benefits is often in direct conflict with the sales organization. Sales managers want sales-people to go out into their respective territories looking for *German Shepherds*—problems or issues that are causing pain. But this causes an emotional discon-nect whenever a salesperson uncovers a prospect who is motivated by *German Shepherds*, and then turns around and starts positioning their company's value in terms of *Gold Medals*. That's essentially what happens every time you deliver a canned corporate pitch or hand someone a product brochure.

This problem can be solved if salespeople probe for both *Gold Medals* and *German Shepherds*, and corporate marketers make it a point to position solu-tions in a way that speaks to both motivations.

Just take the repository of business issues and implications that you created in chapter 2 and realize that any benefit, for any product, in any industry can be positioned as a *Gold Medal* and a *German Shepherd*. Your 150 implications suddenly double, where you now have three hundred opportunities to add value—while your competitors are running around with a fake smile and mes-sages that are filled with "happy gas."

Champions Also Need to Position Both Ways

What if you're selling to someone who is motivated exclusively by one or the other? For example, suppose you've been working with a major account for the last several months, and your internal champion (Matthew) is motivated by positive rewards. Matthew is an energetic optimist who loves state-of-the-art technology and high-performance solutions, and he is definitely motivated by *Gold Medals*. Knowing this about Matthew, should you position your solution to Matthew in terms of *Gold Medals*, *German Shepherds*, or both?

Traditional thinking would suggest that you should communicate with Matthew in terms that are most likely to motivate him. In that case, you would focus on *Gold Medals*. In QBS, we recommend just the opposite. Even if Matthew is absolutely driven by *Gold Medals*, that doesn't mean the rest of the committee, or the person who will ultimately sign the check, will be motivated the same way. Most strategic decisions involve more than one person, and someone other than your champion may have very different buying motiva-tions. Therefore, it makes sense to talk about both *Gold Medals* and *German Shepherds* so your internal champion can buy into the total value of your prod-uct and then position it both ways to other people in the organization.

In fact, don't be afraid to ask: "Matthew, would you like a couple of ideas about how other customers have positioned our solutions to secure the necessary approvals, or do you want me to back off and let you handle it?" Most internal champions will say: "Sure, I'll take a couple of ideas." The next thing out of my mouth is a question: "Are you familiar with the concept of Gold Medals and German Shepherds?" Their response is predictable. They will chuckle and say, "No, what's that?" Perfect!

That's your opportunity to teach them how to more effectively sell your product or service internally, to their colleagues or to upper management. Basically, they are inviting you to give them a lesson in positioning, which you should be more than happy to do, knowing that most customers have had very little formal sales training, especially if your success depends on their ability to sell internally.

Even Sales Managers Can Apply This Principle

Does your company have sales awards? A performance trip? Bonuses for reaching or overachieving sales quota? Most companies do. By offering incentives for good performance, management can encourage the sales organization to perform at the highest levels. But incentives like these only tap into some portion of how salespeople are actually motivated.

Like customers, plenty of salespeople are motivated by positive rewards—no question about it. But salespeople are also motivated by negative aversion. While many sellers are motivated to go the extra mile to receive a trip or an attractive bonus, others work just as hard because they have an intense desire not to fail. That's how it was for me. I appreciated all the bonuses, accolades, and awards that came with success, but I was motivated more by the fear of having an empty sales forecast, facing a disgruntled sales manager, or missing the annual performance trip.

Being motivated by *German Shepherds* is not some demented form of paranoia or pessimism; nor does it equate to having a negative attitude. Rather, the fear of failure is a very powerful and constructive motivational influence that, when channeled properly, can improve both your performance and your results.

> **Secret #26** Some of the world's most successful people get to the top because of their intense desire not to be on the bottom.

There's a lesson here for husbands, wives, parents, teachers, even sales managers. Accolades and rewards can motivate people to perform in desirable ways. But so can the need to avoid problems, uncertainty, or even failure. The message is this: if you want ordinary people to perform in extraordinary ways, then it's important to motivate them with *Gold Medals* and *German Shepherds* (both).

Summary

Knowing that prospects and customers are motivated by *Gold Medals* and *German Shepherds* causes salespeople to approach the sales process differently. Being able to connect with a larger audience puts a bounce in their step and bolsters their confidence. That's because Question Based Selling does what Dale Carnegie suggested so many years ago—we challenge salespeople to focus on what the customer wants, rather than what *we* want.

In addition to positioning the value of your product or service in terms of *Gold Medals* and *German Shepherds*, another way to increase your value proposition is by creating a sense of momentum that comes from other customer experiences, which we will talk about next in chapter 4.

THE HERD THEORY

In today's selling environment, traditional reference selling is highly overrated. Saying this may shock some people, since virtually every sales training program created in the last thirty years talks about the importance of leveraging references to establish credibility and convey value.

References are important, but so is differentiation; and it's no longer an effective strategy to use references just like everyone else. In QBS, we want to challenge the status quo in order to set ourselves apart from everyone else. This differentiation is achieved by leveraging the rest of the herd—which, ironically enough, includes "everyone else."

The use of references can help your selling efforts in two ways. First, a positive reference can increase your credibility by showing prospective buyers that the solution you are proposing has already been proven effective. Essentially, it's a way to show prospective buyers that other clients have already blazed the trail to success. By reducing the prospect's risk, you make it easier for them to move forward with a favorable purchase decision.

The second way references can be useful in the sales process is to stimulate buyer interest. When prospective buyers see that your product or service has already helped other customers solve a problem or improve their existing condition, chances are that they will want to know more about your solution. In this way, references can be used to pique a prospective buyer's interest.

Secret #27 Potential buyers are instinctively trying to reduce their risk of making a bad decision.

Potential buyers are always at risk in the decision-making process. If they make a good decision, they can be a hero. If they make a bad decision, however, they will quickly become the goat. It follows then, that buyers want to make the right decision. But, perhaps even more importantly, they will want to avoid making the wrong one.

Walk a mile in someone else's shoes, and you will find that most prospects have a fear of the unknown. They wrestle with questions like, what if the product fails to perform as advertised? How can we be sure this solution will address our needs? Are we getting the best deal? Prospects would love to be able to peer into a crystal ball and see what the future holds before they make decisions, but crystal ball technology is only available in fairy tales. That's why buyers have to rely on the next best thing—references.

The Problem with Traditional Reference Selling

The fact that other people or companies have already purchased, implemented, or deployed your solution is a proof statement that helps to reduce the buyer's risk. Proof of previous successes makes them feel more comfortable about your solution, and it increases their confidence about moving forward with a decision to purchase.

There are some problems with traditional reference selling, starting with the fact that positive references are a dime a dozen. Just about anyone can produce a list of happy customers. If five vendors are all vying for the same piece of business, chances are good that the prospect will receive very similar lists of "happy" customer references from all five competitors. As a result, prospects tend to dismiss the value of these prearranged references—after all, why would a salesperson who wanted to win the business give out a bad reference?

In addition, individual references are easily discounted as irrelevant or non-pertinent. Nothing irks a prospective buyer more than the suggestion that just because someone else made a decision to move forward, they should too. Suggesting that someone should buy just because some other soul did is an aggressive posture that tends to make prospects feel pushed, which is likely to cause them to respond by pushing back. Essentially, the validity of individual references gets discounted when customers think, *Just because your solution worked in their environment, doesn't mean it's right for us.*

These challenges tend to put salespeople in a precarious position. Buyers still want to limit their risk prior to making a significant purchase decision, but individual customer references aren't always enough to differentiate the uniqueness of your solution, especially if those references are being met with some resistance.

Why the Herd Theory Works

Question Based Selling has changed the paradigm for reference selling. Rather than pointing to individual references as a way to prove that your solution is indeed viable, the Herd Theory surrounds prospects with a general sense of momentum—to establish credibility and convey a greater sense of value. Momentum ultimately reduces the buyer's risk. It's a little like handing them a crystal ball.

For example, if you could demonstrate that everyone else was already interested in, and excited about, your product or service, wouldn't that communicate a greater sense of value and lower the prospect's risk? That's precisely how the Herd Theory works. Showing prospects that "everyone else" is already moving in a certain direction is a very effective way to motivate potential buyers to move in that same direction.

Here's a little metaphor that illustrates the Herd Theory in action.

A Quick Lesson on Herd Behavior

Have you ever seen a herd of cows and noticed that they all tend to move together in the same direction? Have you ever wondered why this phenomenon occurs? Let's challenge our thinking by taking a closer look.

Imagine yourself driving down a country road, surrounded by rolling fields of farmland, as far as the eye can see. Suddenly, something catches your attention—it's a herd of cows up ahead, in a nearby field. Curiosity causes you to pull off the road to investigate further. And there you sit, in the middle of nowhere, watching the Herd Theory in action.

For unexplained reasons, you step out of your car, scramble over the fence, and catch up to the cows as the herd slowly meanders across the field. Curious as to why they are all moving in the same direction, you maneuver yourself toward the center of the herd to ask a very simple question.

Fortunately for this metaphor, the cow in the center speaks fluent English. So you tap the beast on the shoulder and ask: *"Pardon me, but…why are you walking in this particular direction?"*

When I tell this story in person, whether it's in Minneapolis or Madrid, I always ask the audience, *"How do you think the cow in the center of the herd will respond?"* So, let me ask you. How would you respond if you were surrounded by the rest of the herd?

I bet you answered with the same response I hear from salespeople all over the world. Invariably, they say, *"I'm moving in this direction because everybody else is."*

Whether we're talking about a herd of cows, a school of fish, or a flock of birds, the behavior is the same. Individuals in the group are significantly influenced by the direction of their surrounding herds. It's just not feasible to assume that a hundred cows could individually make simultaneous decisions to all face the same way and walk in the same direction.

People, too, are influenced by the direction of their surrounding herds. Just look at commercial advertising. All you have to do is switch on the television, and you will see ads for all kinds of products that attempt to motivate target audiences by showing them how "everyone else" is benefiting by moving in a certain direction. Coca-Cola, for example, doesn't try to convince consumers that they should drink Coke products. Rather, they try to convince you that everyone else is drinking Coke. Think about it this way—other than by creating this type of momentum, how else would large tobacco companies persuade young people to try cigarettes?

Leveraging "Everyone Else"

The bottom line here is simply this. Buyers are influenced more by the direction of their surrounding herd than by specific recommendations from individual references. Again, most prospects are reluctant to take the plunge just because someone else did. But they are definitely influenced when "everyone else" seems to be moving in a certain direction. Perhaps that's because there's safety in numbers and prospects would like to benefit from everyone else's experiences. They would also like to learn from everyone else's mistakes. But one thing is for sure—nobody wants to reinvent the wheel.

> **Secret #28** How the rest of the "herd" feels is more important than any one person's opinion or recommendation.

Surrounding prospects with the perception that "everyone else" is already moving in a certain direction is a very powerful QBS technique. As we get deeper into the book, we will show you how to leverage this strategy to penetrate more new accounts, build greater value in your sales presentations, and overcome objections. The Herd Theory also gives sellers a way to provide the emotional reassurance that helps prospects feel comfortable enough to pull the trigger on a buying decision.

This approach is very different from traditional reference selling, however. With the traditional approach, sellers use individual references to suggest: *Since other customers are already using our solution, you should use it too.* This is a push strategy—one that attempts to encourage, nudge, and ultimately push prospects toward the salesperson's desired result.

The Herd Theory is a pull strategy. Rather than pushing prospects by suggesting that they should buy just because other customers have, the Herd Theory lets prospects know that everyone else is already moving in a certain direction, in order to ask: *Would you like to know why?* Essentially, we leverage the momentum of the surrounding herd to build credibility. The implication is if "everyone else" is already moving in a certain direction, then something about it must be good. As an example, how do you know whether a truck stop restaurant on the interstate has good food? Just count the number of trucks in the parking lot at mealtime. More trucks means better food. (Make that a herd of trucks.)

But, the Herd Theory also has a wonderful way of making prospects curious—so they will want to know more. If your product or service appears to have momentum in the marketplace, then why wouldn't prospective customers want to know more about how it works or why people are selecting it?

How It All Started: A True Story

Although the Herd Theory has evolved into a key component of the QBS methodology, this approach was conceived more out of desperation than design. Its origin dates back to the year 1990, when I had just accepted a position with KnowledgeWare, Inc., the leading provider of Computer-Aided Software Engineering (CASE) software tools.

At the time, KnowledgeWare was growing by leaps and bounds. They had just experienced a very successful initial public offering, and were in the process of rapidly expanding their customer base. As is often the case, they wanted to double the size of the sales force in order to penetrate more accounts. Consequently, I was brought in to sell in the Southeast.

This was an exciting opportunity; and, although my territory hadn't yet been assigned, I was chomping at the bit to get started. Product training was the first step, so I tried to learn as much as I could about CASE tools.

Two weeks into the job, the vice president of sales called me into his office and told me that there was a "slight" problem. Apparently, the company had hired too many salespeople. After a recruiting frenzy prior to the start of their fiscal year, it was discovered that KnowledgeWare had staffed a total of seven salespeople in the Southeast region, but they only had six available territories. And because I was the last person hired, I was suddenly the odd man out. This was not what I expected to hear after only two weeks on the job.

"What does this mean for me?" I asked. The vice president said he didn't know yet, but he committed to figure it out and get back to me as soon as possible.

Numbly, I went back to my product training. Ten days later, I found myself back in the VP's office. Apparently, there was an opening in the Midwest. With five available territories in the central region, there were currently only four salespeople. "How would you like to sell CASE tools in the Midwest?" he asked. It didn't take a rocket scientist to figure out this was my only option, so I accepted.

The actual territory assignment was still up in the air. During the previous sales year, the top performer in the Midwest was responsible for two states, Kansas and Missouri. To grow the business, KnowledgeWare's management had decided to cut his territory to make room for another sales rep—me. But since he had been the top producer in the region, he was allowed to divide the territory as he saw fit—and as you would expect from any hungry salesperson, he definitely took the better half.

"Tom, I've decided to keep Missouri," he announced. That made sense since he lived in St. Louis. "But I'm also going to keep Kansas," he added, "and you get Kansas City."

Kansas City? *That's not a territory*, I remember thinking. *Kansas City is just a dot on the map.* Having never been there, I couldn't help wondering how a cow town in the heart of the Midwest could ever be a desirable place to sell Computer-Aided Software Engineering tools. *Should I go out and buy a western hat and some boots? Maybe I should learn to chew tobacco.* These and other wild thoughts ran through my head after being handed this "brass pig" for a territory. Not knowing what the future held, I was off to Kansas City.

The Standard Approach Wasn't Working

KnowledgeWare kicked off its new sales year on July 1. I had been on board just over a month. We received our annual quotas, and it was time to head out into the territory to start selling.

Armed with limited CASE tool knowledge, an extremely short list of prospects, and a telephone, I started calling prospects in Kansas City. Using the standard approach, my initial sales calls sounded something like this:

Seller: *"Mr. Prospect, my name is Tom Freese, and I'm with KnowledgeWare, Inc., the leading provider of*

*development software, based in Atlanta. We develop
and sell Computer-Aided Software Engineering tools,
and I wanted to get together with you to discuss how
our products can address your programming needs."*

Essentially, I was calling new prospects to see if they would be interested in investigating, evaluating, or hearing more about our product. Not surprisingly, I didn't get many hits. Most of the people I called were likely receiving a steady stream of sales calls that sounded very similar to mine. While prospects in Kansas City were always polite, I was having serious trouble getting my foot into any doors. It wasn't the rejection that was bothering me, however. It was the fact that each "No, thank you" significantly reduced the size of my already petite territory.

My Desperation Move

Things were not going well. During my first thirty days in Kansas City, I worked hard to penetrate new prospect accounts, but with very limited success. I needed to try something different. So, in a desperate attempt to cultivate new business, I decided to host a KnowledgeWare product seminar.

KnowledgeWare's corporate marketing department featured a traveling "road show"—a group of presentation specialists who would blow into a city, provide an exciting "dog and pony" presentation, and then blow out. My strategy was: if I could just fill the room with seminar participants, this event would give me an opportunity to generate interest, uncover needs, and motivate prospective customers to further investigate our solutions. I put a stake in the ground by scheduling a road show presentation in Kansas City for late August. While the week before Labor Day isn't necessarily the best time for a seminar, it was the only open timeslot in the foreseeable future.

Fortunately, I was able to leverage KnowledgeWare's business partner relationship to secure the large auditorium at IBM's regional headquarters in downtown Kansas City. It was a terrific facility with all the trappings that would enable us to host a world-class event for up to one hundred people. This venue also gave us some much-needed credibility and a built-in endorsement from the world's largest computer manufacturer at the time—IBM.

All we needed was attendees, which was my responsibility. With less than a month remaining until the seminar, it was do or die. But if I was having trouble getting new prospects to meet with me, how in the world would I get them interested in attending a product seminar?

Mailing Invitations and Doing Follow-Up

I decided to send out a mass mailing that would canvass every potential customer in the Kansas City area. But rather than send a blanket invitation to each company, I targeted individuals. I hoped this would give my invitations a personal touch. It would also give me a reason to follow up with them.

Shortly after the invitations were mailed, I started calling. Like an idiot, I used the same approach as before, hoping that prospects would be interested in coming to the seminar to hear about all the wonderful benefits our product offered. Unfortunately, most prospects just assumed that I was yet another salesperson begging them to attend another sales seminar.

As you might have already guessed, the first few prospects I contacted responded with the same level of disinterest as before. I quickly realized that responses like "It sounds good, but…" or "We'll think about it" were not accomplishing the objective. With limited success, I tried to confirm attendees, but once again, it was obviously time for something different. That evening, at a restaurant called The Golden Ox, on the west side of Kansas City, the Herd Theory was conceived. Little did I know how much impact this technique would have on my long-term sales success.

The Rest of the Story

When the idea for the Herd Theory hit me, I was picking at my dinner, worrying that, with only two weeks remaining before the seminar, very few attendees had been confirmed. My systems engineer and I were both nervous and not very hungry. In our favor was a solid company with a quality product, as KnowledgeWare had already become the industry leader in other parts of the country. We also knew that the road show event had been very well received in other cities, and we were convinced this format would produce a positive result if we could just get people to attend the presentation—butts in seats!

I started wondering, what if KnowledgeWare was the de facto standard for application development in Kansas City? What if everyone else was already using KnowledgeWare's products? Would that make someone who hadn't yet been exposed to KnowledgeWare's CASE tools interested in finding out more about the technology? In other words, if the rest of the herd was already moving in KnowledgeWare's direction, wouldn't other prospects in Kansas City want to know why? That was it! People would surely be interested in attending this event if they knew that "everyone else" was interested in attending, too.

The next day, I started calling prospects, but with a different purpose. I wanted to build a sense of anticipation and excitement around the event. So, rather than begging them to attend, I let prospects know that I expected participation from everyone else, and my purpose in following up was simply to make sure they didn't get left out. The actual dialogue went something like this:

Follow-up Call (Script)

Seller: *"Hello Mr. Prospect, my name is Tom Freese, and I'm the regional manager for KnowledgeWare in Kansas City. I wanted to contact you about the CASE application development seminar we are hosting at IBM's Regional Headquarters on August 26. Do you remember receiving the invitation we sent you? (Pause for a response)*

"Frankly, we are expecting a record turnout—over one hundred people, including development managers from Sprint, Hallmark Cards, Pepsi Co., Yellow Freight, Kansas Power & Light, the Federal Reserve Bank, Northwest Mutual Life, American Family Life, St. Luke's Hospital, Anheuser-Busch, MasterCard, American Express, Worldspan, and United Airlines, just to name a few.

"I wanted to follow up because we haven't yet received an RSVP from your company, and I wanted to make sure you didn't get left out."

Granted, this was a highly positioned approach, but it was also 100 percent accurate. I wanted prospects to know that IBM was endorsing this event. I also wanted to let them know that I expected "everyone else" to participate. I accomplished this by rattling off an impressive list of marquee company names that we were "expected" to attend. Most importantly, I wanted to make sure that they *didn't get left out.*

"Left Out of What?"

Leveraging the rest of the herd has a customer service flavor, more than the traditional sales role. Rather than begging prospects to attend, I was simply calling to make sure that they didn't miss out on a very important opportunity. That's the beauty of this technique; if you say to someone *I just wanted to make sure you don't get left out*, the next four words they will say are: *Left out of what?* When prospects become curious about what it is that they might miss, they almost always ask for more information.

> **Secret #29** When you're trying to make sure someone doesn't get "left out," their next four words will be: *Left out of what?*

Nobody wants to miss out on a potential opportunity, particularly if "everyone else" already seems to be moving in that direction. Keep in mind that while most prospects are naturally cautious, they are also naturally curious—and their desire not to be left out will likely generate a request for additional information. How did I respond when prospects asked for more information? That was easy. Their request was my invitation to pique their interest further by giving them information about the problem we solved and getting them excited about the upcoming event.

Securing Their Commitment to Attend

After piquing the prospect's interest, there's no time like the present to close. In this case, that meant getting them to agree to attend our presentation in Kansas City. Once we let them know we were expecting a record turnout, it was easy to ask for a commitment by saying: *Do you have your calendar handy?* Everyone has their calendar handy. Now the only question was, were they available on the date of the seminar? If so, I simply asked if they would like me to reserve a seat for them. Mission accomplished!

If the prospect was not available to attend the presentation on August 26 but was interested in finding out why "everyone else" was interested in KnowledgeWare's CASE tools, I suggested one of the following alternatives:

- *Would you like to send someone else?* Perhaps there was someone else on their staff or in their organization who could attend the presentation in their absence. That would benefit them and certainly help get our foot in the door.
- *Perhaps we could schedule a make-up event?* For those people who had scheduling conflicts, I would probe to see if there was any interest in coordinating a second event.
- *What about an on-site presentation?* Some people don't like public seminars. For them, I suggested that we come on-site for a more detailed discussion about KnowledgeWare and how our CASE tool products could enhance their specific development environment.

I even used the Herd Theory to let prospects know what other companies who had scheduling conflicts were doing. I also made it a point to expand each opportunity by asking prospects if there was anyone else in their company who would benefit from attending this event. I offered to contact these referrals, but I always asked the prospect to forward a note letting them know we had talked. If you ask nicely, most people are happy to accommodate this request. Then the person who they referred you to won't mistake your call as just another salesperson cold-calling into the account.

The Results Speak for Themselves

By the time August 26 arrived, we had confirmed attendees from most of Kansas City's largest corporations. Development managers, programmers, and software engineers from Sprint, Hallmark Cards, Pepsi Co., Yellow Freight, Kansas Power & Light, the Federal Reserve Bank, Northwestern Mutual Life, American Express, MasterCard, and Anheuser-Busch were all coming, largely because "everyone else" was going to be there.

Sure enough, when they arrived, everyone was there. We had a record turnout of 119 attendees! IBM's auditorium was packed to the rafters with customers, and our event in little ol' Kansas City set an attendance record for KnowledgeWare road show seminars that went uncontested for the rest of the sales year.

Many prospects even took the time to thank me for calling and making sure they didn't get "left out." The momentum we had communicated became a self-fulfilling prophecy—people were excited about the presentation because everyone else seemed excited. Even the IBMers who attended were astonished, as they too would benefit from this event. It was a win-win for everyone involved.

When it came time to kick off the actual presentation, I took the stage and introduced the program. I thanked everyone in the audience for their time and reviewed the objectives of the event. Then, before the seminar began, I took one more opportunity to leverage the herd by saying, "Before we actually get started today, I would like to turn your attention to the back of the room." Everyone turned around in their chairs. There stood thirty-seven IBM sales reps, lined up against the back wall. I continued, "I would like to thank IBM for their support of this event, and to give you (the audience) an idea of just how exciting KnowledgeWare's product is, when was the last time you saw this many blue suits, white shirts, and red ties assembled in one place?" Everyone clapped!

The truth is, in the days prior to the seminar I invested the time to call every IBM sales rep in the Kansas City office (over fifty people) to make sure they knew we were hosting one of the year's largest seminar events. I also made sure that they knew "everyone else" was going to be there. Not surprisingly, the local IBMers didn't want to be left out either.

> **Secret #30** Most prospects are very interested in, and highly influenced by, what "everyone else" is doing.

After this seminar, there was no longer a shortage of opportunity in Kansas City. We knew all along that we were selling a valuable solution, and we also knew that people would buy if we could just get them to evaluate our product. By the end of the year, my brass pig of a territory finished No. 1 in sales, and KnowledgeWare did, in fact, become the de facto standard for CASE tool software in Kansas City. We also closed more new-name accounts than any other commercial sales territory in the country—all because we leveraged the momentum of the surrounding herd.

Momentum Comes in Different Shapes and Sizes

When people think of references, they think of "happy" customers. This makes sense, since salespeople would want customers who are satisfied with their products and services to positively influence other potential buyers. Happy customers are not the only source of momentum in your strategic sales, however.

The Herd Theory can be just as effective with non-customer references. That's essentially what we did in Kansas City. We let prospects know that "everyone else" was interested in hearing more about our CASE tool solutions. Even before we had customers, we were able to leverage other prospects to create a sense of momentum that helped us establish credibility and generate interest. As a result, everyone wanted to know why the rest of the herd was also interested in what KnowledgeWare had to offer.

> **Secret #31** If the rest of the herd seems to be moving in a certain direction, other prospects and customers will want to know why.

Non-customer references give sellers an excellent opportunity to be creative. Herd momentum comes in all shapes and sizes, and you can customize the surrounding herd to meet the needs of your specific sales situation. For example, if you are talking to a bank, you might leverage your success at other financial institutions like Citibank, First Union, Transamerica, Chase Manhattan, Bank of America, Bank of Boston, American Express, and VISA. If you call on regional hospitals, you might tell them about your success at St. Jude's Children's Hospital in Memphis, Mt. Sinai in Miami, Emory University Hospital in Atlanta, Sloan-Kettering in New York, and Humana Healthcare in Nashville.

You can build momentum using the media too. *Ms. Prospect, would you like to know why the* Wall Street Journal, Forbes Magazine, Newsweek, USA Today, *and* Entrepreneur Magazine *have all featured articles about the success of our newly announced product?* If your product is relevant to their business, they will surely want to hear more.

You can also leverage your partners, particularly if your company has strategic industry relationships or if your product is sold through reseller channels or distribution. Letting prospects know that you are currently partnered with companies like IBM, Microsoft, Accenture, Ernst & Young, Deloitte, PricewaterhouseCoopers, Forrester Research, and Gartner can be very powerful for establishing credibility and piquing the prospect's interest.

If you represent a brand-new company or you sell a product that has just been released, you may not yet have the luxury of existing customers. The Herd Theory can still work by drawing a parallel between yourself and other success stories that create a sense of momentum. Call it guilt (or success) by association. As an example, it wasn't long ago that Microsoft was just a fledgling start-up company. Now, they are one of the most successful businesses ever. Perhaps you can build a parallel by letting prospects know that your company will do for the Internet or cable TV business what Microsoft has done for PC software. If you sell pharmaceuticals, perhaps you can create momentum by letting prospects know that your product is expected to be as popular as Tylenol. The key is linking yourself with success stories that prospects can easily relate to.

You Can Even Leverage Your Competition

Most salespeople would agree that using a prospect's direct competitor as an individual reference can be a little dicey. For example, it would be hard to say to Chase Bank, "You should buy our product because Citibank is one of our best customers." You are more likely to get an immediate mismatched response like, "We don't want to be like Citibank."

If you change the underlying message, however, you can absolutely leverage the momentum of competitive companies. For example, if you're selling a product whose marquee customers include telecommunications giants like AT&T, Sprint, Verizon, and T-Mobile, and you are trying to penetrate other new accounts in the same industry, you can very effectively leverage the Herd Theory. You can accomplish this by rattling off an impressive list of telecommunications companies that are already moving in your direction, and then ask, "Would you like to know why all these companies are already using our product?" Who wouldn't want to know why other companies are moving in a certain direction—especially when they are in the same industry?

Popcorn Credibility

We have all heard the unmistakable sound of popcorn popping. It's that rapid-fire popping sound that tells us that the popcorn is bursting with activity. You know, *Pop, pa, pa, Pop, Pop…Pop, pa, pa, Pop, Pop!*

After a few minutes, when most of the kernels have popped, the popping sound slows down in a way that's also unmistakable. It's how you can tell that the popcorn is finished—when the popping sound slows to an intermittent *pop…pop…pop…pop…pop…pop* sound.

Applying the Herd Theory is more than just naming a list of references. You must also be able to name those references with a certain amount of credibility—popcorn credibility. It should sound like popcorn popping, as you demonstrate a higher level of competence and credibility by confidently rattling off an impressive list of customers, prospects, media references, or partners.

In the context of a sales call, it might sound like this:

Salesperson:	*"Mr. Prospect, you mentioned that you wanted to increase revenue and decrease expenses. That's exactly why companies like Delta Air Lines, Citibank, Lockheed Martin, HP, Goldman Sachs, Lanier Worldwide, Motorola, West Corporation, Constellation Energy, and Transamerica have all chosen our product. Would you like to know what they're doing to accomplish the same objective?"*

Lots of salespeople can name two or three customers, but then their popcorn stops popping. From there, it's a struggle to name more—in which case, they actually lose ground because they can't demonstrate credibility.

> **Secret #32** When surrounding prospects with herd momentum, you gain credibility as long as your "popcorn" keeps popping.

Now that you understand the concept, here's an exercise you can use to increase your own popcorn credibility when dealing with prospects and customers in the strategic sales process.

Exercise: Increase Your Popcorn Credibility

In our live QBS training programs, we show audiences how to increase their popcorn credibility using a simple exercise. I usually start by asking everyone in the audience to get a partner. For our purposes here, you can practice this exercise by yourself.

Once everyone has a partner, I ask each participant to make a pre-exercise commitment. On a piece of notepaper, write down how many herd references you think you can name in rapid succession. This will give you a baseline for assessing your results. *Hint:* Top salespeople can usually rattle off between twenty-five and thirty herd references.

For the actual exercise, I ask partners to stand facing each other. While one partner holds up their hands and counts on their fingers, the other person rattles off as many herd references as they can name—with popcorn credibility. It's best to begin with customer references. This enables participants to focus on the technique. Later, I encourage you to try this same exercise using prospect references, partner references, and media references.

When everyone is ready, I give the signal, and participants begin naming references until their popcorn stops popping. Long pauses indicate that you are no longer gaining credibility, so the counting stops. The number of herd references that were counted is how many you can name with popcorn credibility. Now, compare your score to the number of reference names you wrote down prior to the exercise.

How does your pre-exercise commitment compare to your actual results? The typical salesperson who participates in this exercise can name between eight and fifteen reference names in rapid succession. That's good for the first time through. Do not despair if your results were lower than expected. I've seen plenty of experienced salespeople stumble after naming only three or four references. The key is increasing your skills so you can quickly create a robust list of herd references with top-of-mind awareness to establish greater credibility in the sales process.

Practice Makes Perfect

The best way to increase your popcorn credibility is to improve your recall. Sellers who can confidently rattle off an impressive list of herd references can surround their prospects with a powerful sense of momentum. To do so, you must be able to easily recall herd references out of memory. This is not a function of IQ, however; it's a function of practice.

Sellers can easily increase their popcorn credibility if they are willing to practice ten minutes a day for a full week. For this relatively small investment, you will be shocked at how large the benefit is. For best results, take out a piece of paper and physically create several different herd lists, categorizing reference names by industry, size, or how long they have been customers. By taking the time to write them down, these references will be more accessible in your top-of-mind memory for easy recall later.

Then each day, practice naming the references you've listed. Practice naming them by category and make it a point to learn a few specific data points about each member of your herd. As you get more sophisticated, practice rattling off your reference names by geographic location or in alphabetical order. The more specific you can be, the more credibility you will convey. In just a few days, your confidence will soar, and you will be well equipped to leverage a sense of momentum that will make your prospects and customers feel more comfortable, and motivate them to move forward in the sales process.

Do You Have a Pencil?

Sooner or later, most prospects will ask for references. They will want to contact a handful of other customers in an attempt to uncover any potential "gotchas" before making their final decision.

The problem is, while most sellers are quick to respond with a canned list of satisfied customer references, prospects usually get a similarly generic response from every vendor—a list of five or six account names, laid out on nice paper, with glowing remarks about each. Vendors hope this gesture will make prospects feel more comfortable, but it often doesn't.

If you really want to differentiate yourself, here's something you can try. The next time a prospect asks you for references, say, "Sure. Do you have a pencil?" (Note: Don't ask for a pen. It sounds too rhetorical. Instead, ask if they have a pencil and you're more likely to get a favorable response.) They'll reach for the nearest writing instrument and say, "I have a pen. Will that work?" You say, "Sure, that will be fine. Write this down."

Once they're ready to write, you start naming references from memory. Be sure to give your prospects a chance to write all the information down. Include the name of the company and the primary contact in the account. For maximum impact, I like to rattle off their telephone number (and extension) as well. You might even give them a quick synopsis about the issues these references faced, and how their issues were resolved by implementing the proposed solution.

You can literally watch a prospect's face light up as you name five, ten, even fifteen references off the top of your head. This is the ultimate implementation of popcorn credibility and the Herd Theory. It is also a terrific way to demonstrate that you know your business better than any other salesperson they have ever encountered. You want them to come away thinking that some of your competitors don't even know their families as well as you know your customers. Your credibility will skyrocket; and chances are, they won't even call your references. Why bother? Your demonstration of competence will make prospects feel more comfortable than a hundred canned references ever could.

> **Secret #33** A salesperson's ability to demonstrate account-specific knowledge translates into greater credibility.

Memorizing account-specific detail isn't difficult. Most salespeople talk to their best references so often that they know a great deal about these accounts already. But if you have trouble remembering details, make a cheat-sheet. Put a list of pertinent facts in your daily planner, so you can glance at it while prospects are writing down the references you name. Salespeople get just as many points for being prepared as they do for having a good memory.

Applying the Herd Theory throughout the Sales Process

The Herd Theory is a powerful technique for establishing credibility and for generating interest at the beginning of the sales process. Prospects will surely be curious when "everyone else" seems to be moving in a certain direction—and if they're curious, they will certainly want more information. The Herd Theory can also be useful later in the sales process to provide the emotional reassurance prospects need to pull the trigger on a purchase.

Buyers are nervous, particularly when they're faced with an important decision. That's why herd references are so valuable. The same momentum that you used to pique the prospect's interest can also be used to overcome objections and show customers why your product provides the best solution.

Feel, Felt, Found: A Distant Cousin

When an objection is raised, many salespeople gravitate to an older technique that's commonly known as *Feel, Felt, Found*. This is how I was originally taught to handle objections and reassure prospects that they were indeed making the right decision.

Here's how this technique (Feel, Felt, Found) works. When a prospect raises an objection, the salesperson acknowledges the concern by saying: *I understand how you feel.* The salesperson is then supposed to cite at least one example of how many other customers have *felt* the same way, but here's what they *found* that helped resolve their concern. The actual dialogue might sound like this.

Prospect: *"I'm concerned that your price seems too high."*

Salesperson: *"I understand how you feel. Other customers have felt the same way. Take Bank of America, for example, who had similar concerns about price until they found that the value of our product far outweighed its cost."*

The intentions of this Feel, Felt, Found strategy are admirable, but the problems are twofold. First, this approach tends to invite mismatching. As we said before, pointing to individual success stories makes it easy for prospects to say: *But we're not Bank of America.* The other problem with Feel, Felt, Found is that you can only use it once per sale. Otherwise, using this technique over and over to address multiple objections can make you sound like a broken record.

> **Secret #34** Surrounding prospects with a credible herd reduces your risk because you become the messenger, not the message.

The Herd Theory accomplishes the same objective as Feel, Felt, Found, but without the risks. Most objections aren't unique and many of the prospects you engage will have similar questions and concerns. But rather than trying to use individual successes to make people feel comfortable, the Herd Theory uses momentum as the primary intangible to make easier to overcome.

In fact, you can use the same herd that you rattled off earlier in the sale to give your prospects a clearer sense of direction. To accomplish this, let them know that companies like Sprint, Hallmark Cards, Pepsi Co., Kansas Power & Light, the Federal Reserve Bank, Yellow Freight, Northwestern Mutual Life, and Anheuser-Busch have all had similar concerns. Then ask: *Would you like to know what they did to ensure their success?*

Of course they will say *yes.* Now you're providing a valuable service. Rather than trying to talk prospects into buying, you're letting them know that many of your existing customers had similar questions before they finalized their decisions. This gives you an opportunity to share what these customers (i.e., the rest of the herd) did to ensure their success. This positions you as the messenger and not the message, which significantly reduces the likelihood of a mismatch.

Summary

By creating a sense of momentum in the sale, you will have a strategic advantage. Since the beginning of time, it has always been easier for people to follow the crowd than to strike out on their own. That's why leveraging the Herd Theory is such a powerful strategy in QBS. If you can challenge the prospect's thinking by reassuring them that they are indeed moving in the right direction, you will increase your probability of making a sale, and you will also reduce the buyer's risk. It's the perfect win-win scenario.

Identifying needs and positioning value is fundamental to any successful formula in selling. No matter how exciting your solution may be, prospects who don't recognize the existence of a need won't appreciate the value of your product or service. How can salespeople help prospective buyers recognize more needs? Stay tuned, as that's what we'll cover in Part II (chapters 6 through 10).

Chapter 5

MISMATCHING: THE AVOIDABLE RISK

In high school physics, students learn that for every action, there is an equal and opposite reaction. That's exactly what happens in the strategic sale. The harder you push, the harder your prospects and customers tend to push back. In Question Based Selling, this creates a counterproductive response behavior we call mismatching.

In this chapter, you will learn what causes mismatching to occur, how it makes prospects even more cautious or standoffish, and most importantly, how to minimize the effects of mismatching for greater sales results.

Have you ever had one of those conversations where the person you are talking with seems to contradict or clarify everything you say? You make a point, and they immediately take the opposite position. Or, you interject a comment, and they feel a need to share something even better or more impressive. Needless to say, these are very frustrating behaviors that usually put a damper on further discussion.

In everyday conversation, this occurs more often than you'd think. For example, make an innocent comment like, "I hear it's supposed to be nice this weekend," and you might be surprised how often people will take the opposite position. In some cases, they will say, "Really? I thought it was supposed to rain," or be "too hot," or "too windy," or "too humid." Perhaps they'll contend that the weekend is "too far away," or "too close," or maybe they'll just lament about the upcoming weekend because they have to "clean the garage." In each of these responses, the person is mismatching your original supposition that the weekend is supposed to be "nice."

Mismatching is a form of disagreement. It's an instinctive and emotional behavior that causes people to respond or push back in a contrarian manner, usually by taking the opposite viewpoint on what's being said.

The human body has certain natural reflexes. Blinking is a good example. If I were to flick my fingertips toward your eyes, you would blink. My action would cause an instinctive response. You wouldn't have time to evaluate the situation, and you would not make a conscious decision to contract your eyelid muscles. Reflexes would just take over, and you would instinctively blink.

While blinking is a physical reflex, mismatching is an emotional reflex, but it works much the same way. It's an emotional knee-jerk reaction that causes people to respond in a contrarian manner.

To see mismatching for yourself, try this simple experiment. Walk into a customer's office (or your manager's office) and cheerfully ask, "Did I catch you at a good time?" Watch carefully to see how they respond. More often than not, they will respond cautiously, saying something like, "That depends on what you need." Next, try the opposite. Walk ten steps down the hall into someone else's office and ask, "Did I catch you at a bad time?" Once again, observe their response. In many cases, they will instantly invite you in, saying, "No, no. It's okay. What can I do for you?"

People will mismatch just about anything. One afternoon while I was raking leaves in my side yard, I was lamenting to my neighbor that yard work is cruel and unusual punishment. He replied by saying, "What do you mean? Working in the yard is relaxing and enjoyable." Later on that same day, I thought it would be interesting to try the opposite—so I commented to my other neighbor that yard work is "relaxing and enjoyable." Sure enough, he took the opposite position, telling me why having to work in the yard was depressing. Was it pure coincidence that each neighbor took the opposing viewpoint? I don't think so.

> **Secret #35** Mismatching is the instinctive tendency of individuals to resist, push back, or respond in a contrarian manner.

Do people mismatch every time? Of course not. Mismatching is not a programmed response; it's a behavioral tendency. But mismatching does occur, especially for those of us in sales. Even when it's just an innocent comment, you might be surprised at how often prospects, customers, coworkers, and business partners will take the opposite position.

Agreement Brings People Together

In sales, buyers and sellers are coming together as partners in a mutual exchange of value. The key word here is *mutual*. When a sales transaction occurs, it should be good for the buyer and good for the seller, both.

This doesn't happen by accident. To have a mutual exchange of value, sellers must first get prospective buyers to agree that they have a need. Once a need is identified, then sellers must get prospects to agree that their product or service provides enough value to justify its cost. We show you how to uncover needs and present value later, but for now, let's focus on the psychology of the sales interaction.

Success in selling is largely a matter of bringing people together. We want prospective customers to feel comfortable, and we want them to openly share their needs, thoughts, feelings, and concerns. Essentially, we want to be invited to participate in a more in-depth conversation—because the more you know about the prospect's needs, the more opportunities you will have to provide valuable solutions.

> **Secret #36** Agreement is the emotional bond that brings people together to form mutually beneficial business relationships.

Contrast this with the feeling many prospects have when first meeting a new salesperson. Until they get a sense that the salesperson can truly add value, they usually are cautious and reluctant, unwilling to share their needs, thoughts, feelings, and concerns. They have not yet established a trust with the salesperson and, therefore, before you have a mutual relationship, prospects are more likely to push you away than invite you in.

Mismatching Is a Form of Resistance

For all the reasons agreement is your ally in the strategic sales process, disagreement is your enemy. Instead of bringing people together, disagreement drives them apart. In conversation, disagreement leads to an increased sense of resistance. When people disagree, they tend to distance themselves emotionally to avoid further confrontation or debate. They are also more cautious and reluctant to share ideas and opinions. Now let me ask, would you rather be openly invited into a more in-depth conversation or cautiously pushed away?

Mismatching is a form of resistance that communicates disagreement. As you saw earlier, someone who mismatches is essentially disagreeing with you. They're pushing back against something you said, or something you've done. Instead of agreeing that the coming weekend will be "nice," as in our example, mismatchers will disagree by saying it's going to be too hot, too windy, or too humid.

> **Secret #37** Mismatching conveys disagreement, which increases your risk and lowers your probability of success.

Because mismatching communicates disagreement, it has a destructive influence on sales conversations. Instead of fostering a sense of mutuality, mismatching causes discord, where people who mismatch are either trying to control the conversation or satisfy their own need to add value.

This is important because your ability to minimize the negative effects of mismatching can significantly reduce your risk, which in turn increases your probability of success. But to minimize the negative effects of mismatching, you must first understand what causes this behavioral tendency to occur.

Where Mismatching Originates

Because mismatching is a behavioral reflex, virtually everyone does it, albeit to varying degrees. In fact, when I explain mismatching to sales audiences, I can literally watch the expressions on people's faces change as they recognize their own behavior in some of the examples. Remember, mismatching is a very common and instinctive behavioral mechanism.

The question is, why do people mismatch? So far, we've talked about mismatching in terms of disagreement. This makes the act of mismatching sound like an intentionally malicious offense. Oddly enough, it's usually not. Mismatching is usually more of a defense mechanism than an intuitive response.

> **Secret #38** Mismatching is more of an instinctive defense mechanism than an intuitive response.

Mismatching is rarely driven by someone's desire to disagree; in fact, the opposite is true. It's usually driven by the need to feel valuable. Let's face it— most of us want to be smart. We want to be respected and we want to feel that we are contributing something valuable in the conversation. Behavioral scientists would characterize this as our need to self-actualize.

As such, people have an instinctive desire to feel valuable. We also have some basic needs for social acceptance. But trying to add value in a conversation can unfortunately lead to mismatched responses. For example, if someone were to say, "The ceilings in this house are very tall," and someone else responded by saying, "I agree," how much value have they added to the conversation? The answer is none. By simply agreeing, they are not offering any new ideas or additional information.

Therein lies the challenge. People who want to feel valuable look for opportunities to interject new information into the conversation. They want to add something of value, something the other person may not have noticed or considered. In our very first example, the mismatcher interjected information in an attempt to share why the upcoming weekend might be something other than "nice."

> **Secret #39** A mismatched response satisfies the needs of the mismatcher more than it disagrees with the content of the discussion.

People are natural mismatchers—but not out of disrespect toward others. Rather, it's because we are naturally insecure. And that's the key point: while agreement is certainly an emotional bond that brings people together, it often fails to satisfy our internal and instinctive need to add value.

Mismatching Comes in Four Different Flavors

I hope you're getting the picture that mismatching doesn't reflect poor behavior. In fact, some of the most well-intentioned people are the most fervent mismatchers. But in the sales process, while we want prospects and customers to contribute to the conversation, we don't want their need to add value to foster a sense of disagreement or create discord. This would only make your conversations less productive.

The good news is that mismatching is an avoidable risk. By understanding why mismatching occurs and learning how to recognize a mismatch when it happens, you can minimize its negative impact on your sales conversations.

In Question Based Selling, we have identified the four most common mismatch responses. Each of these behavioral tendencies is outlined below.

The Contradiction

Telling someone that they are wrong is one of the fastest ways to shut down a conversation. But that's essentially what happens whenever someone contradicts what another person says.

Contradiction is the most common mismatch—and it means just what it says. A contradiction is a reflexive response that directly rebuts a comment or statement. Our earlier anecdote about whether it was going to be a nice weekend is a perfect example of a contradiction. Here's another example:

Salesperson:	*"I've prepared an agenda for today's meeting. I would like to begin by talking about performance, cost effectiveness, and growth. Then we can talk about maintenance options."*
Prospect:	*"It's premature to worry about maintenance."*

The prospect's knee-jerk reaction to the salesperson's prepared agenda is a classic mismatch. Rather than thoughtfully responding to what the salesperson has suggested, the prospect in this example immediately contradicts by saying the first thing that pops into his head. It's likely that maintenance issues will come up in the meeting, but for now, the prospect takes the contrarian position in an attempt to have some control over what's on the agenda.

In another example, if you were to say, "The ceilings in this house are very tall," someone could easily contradict you by saying, "Actually, the ceilings in this house are quite typical for homes in this part of the city." Even when someone is trying to be helpful, a contradictory response still impedes the conversation's natural flow and discourages additional discussion.

Unnecessary Clarification

My sales engineer joined me for a very important meeting with one of our most lucrative prospect accounts in the Southeast. The vice president of operations opened the meeting by sharing a problem that his company was having with unscheduled downtime.

Prospect:	*"Our old system has consistently been out of service for approximately one hour per day to replicate files. This is unacceptable. We would like to find a way to reduce our system's downtime to no more than fifteen minutes. Can you help us?"*

Of course, this was music to my ears. Reduced system downtime was one of the strengths of our solution, and this vice president had just built a perfect case for why he needed our product.

But then my engineer jumped into the conversation, and in an attempt to add value, he responded by saying:

Engineer:	*"Actually, we reviewed your system logs and your downtime for replication is only fifty-five minutes per day."*

Everyone looked bewildered. If the prospect's tolerance for downtime is fifteen minutes, what difference does it make if the current system outage takes an hour or fifty-five minutes? Either way, the prospect still has the same problem—too much downtime. This is a good example of an unnecessary clarification, where the mismatch shuts down the conversation just as fast as a contradiction would.

Ironically, my engineer was just trying to participate. He was trying to add value by enhancing the accuracy of the discussion. Needless to say, pointing out a senior executive's inaccuracy is both counterproductive and unnecessary. We must remember that while we have an instinctive need to feel valuable, prospects and customers want to feel valuable too.

> **Secret #40** Prospects and customers have an instinctive need to be perceived as valuable too.

Rather than listen to the essence of what's being communicated, chronic mismatchers have a need to clarify or restate everything that's being said. While a certain amount of detail is valuable, there's a point where clarifying unnecessarily becomes detrimental to your selling efforts.

One-Upmanship

One-upmanship is another type of mismatching. You see this with kids playing in the schoolyard, trying to outdo each other. One person makes a statement (or tells a story), and someone else jumps in trying to make an even bigger impact by saying, "The same thing happened to me, only worse."

One-upmanship is a mismatch because of what it communicates. Instead of acknowledging the value of another person's contribution, the mismatch actually reduces their significance by communicating *I'm better than you.*

Unfortunately, this behavior often finds its way from the schoolyard into many business situations. For example, prospects sometimes mismatch an overly polished salesperson because the prospect wants to be perceived as equally charismatic. As a result, these prospects tend to say things like: *If you think your proposal is aggressive, you should see the discount your competitor is offering!*

Sellers can also one-up their prospects. After a prospective customer has finished describing their needs, countless salespeople have made the mistake of jumping in and saying something like: *You think you have needs? You should see what another one of my customers is facing. They have so many problems with their systems that...* Can you see why one-upping someone else creates a mismatched response?

In selling (and in life), a productive conversation shouldn't be a contest, and suggesting *I'm better than you* only increases your risk of failure.

The Dreaded "I Know"

Last, but not least, is the dreaded "I know" response. This type of mismatch occurs when the need to acquire additional information is superseded by one's own feelings of inadequacy or low self-esteem.

Have you ever noticed that some people aren't open to hearing your advice? College kids, for example, seem to know everything. Try offering some constructive advice to one and you'll see what I mean. It's amazing how worldly an eighteen- or nineteen-year-old can be. In most cases, however, this response is just a defensive reaction. Again, people want to feel valuable. My daughter, at just five years old, after only three weeks of school, said to me, *"Dad, I don't need any more advice, because I'm in kindergarten now."* While it takes most parents twenty years to raise a child, we finished in five. Wow!

It's not that people are averse to improving themselves. It's just that most people have a reflexive need to protect against feeling inadequate.

This knee-jerk "I know" response tends to close off a conversation and degrade the importance of another person at the same time—a double whammy. There are numerous variations of this mismatch, such as *I already knew that* or *So I've heard*. With this type of response, the mismatcher ends up sending the following message: *I'm not stupid...so please keep it to yourself next time.* As you might guess, these kinds of statements tend to shut down a conversation, which is problematic for sellers who are trying to engage new prospects. Here's a quick scenario to illustrate how the "I know" response can work against a seller.

Suppose a prospect shares what she believes to be an interesting point with her salesperson, Jennifer. Like most of us, contributing to the conversation makes prospects feel smart and valuable; and by listening intently, Jennifer has a wonderful opportunity to strengthen her relationship with this client.

All she has to do is listen and nod, but Jennifer has an intense desire to be perceived as knowledgeable. She's had to fight to get ahead in the business world, and she wants to be respected as an expert in her field. When presented with new ideas or information, Jennifer's reflexive tendency is to mismatch by telling prospects that she already knows.

Prospect:	*"I've heard the county commission is considering a tax reduction for commercial property in North Fulton."*
Jennifer:	*"I know. I heard that last week."*

The "I know" mismatch creates an interesting problem for Jennifer and others like her. Because Jennifer's self-concept is largely based on being in the know, her need to mismatch is purely a defensive reaction. Essentially, she's more interested in protecting her own image (of being in the know) than being attentive to the conversation and to her customer.

Jennifer isn't trying to create a problem. She's just trying to make sure others see her as a credible professional. But this does creates a problem when her need for credibility downgrades the importance of another person's input.

> **Secret #41** Mismatching shows a fundamental lack of interest, which stifles conversation and chips away at the self-worth of other people.

Jennifer surely doesn't mean to degrade the importance of what her prospects are saying. To her, saying "I know" means the same as, "I agree." To the customer, however, "I know" usually sounds more like, "I'm already aware of that piece of information, so could you please shut up." Jennifer's intent may have been pure, but her mismatched response sends a very different message—and there's a big difference between *I agree* and *Shut up*, don't you think?

What Mismatching Means for Salespeople

Prospects and customers have feelings, too. They don't want to be contradicted, corrected, or one-upped, and they especially don't want salespeople to make them feel inadequate. Therefore, if you are mismatching your prospects or customers, you are undermining your own success.

> **Secret #42** If you are a habitual mismatcher, then you are shooting yourself in the foot and you must STOP immediately!

Habitual mismatching is relatively easy to change. A manager, mentor, coach, or sales trainer should be able to work with you to identify the specific behavior and make the necessary adjustments. Correcting this behavior will significantly improve the quality and depth of your sales conversations.

Dealing with potential buyers who habitually mismatch is not so easy, however. You can't just tell them to stop. In fact, you will find that prospects and customers tend to mismatch salespeople automatically. Don't be offended. People are naturally cautious and skeptical of anyone who is trying to get into their pockets. I know how I feel when an overzealous salesperson walks up and asks *How can I help you today?* Be honest. Aren't we all a little wary of being pushed into buying a product or service we don't really need? This caution breeds resistance—and the more cautious people are, the more likely they are to mismatch.

The old school of selling attempts to address this by coaching salespeople to be more and more aggressive. The strategy is: when prospects are cautious or reluctant, you must push even harder to overcome their objections. In today's selling environment, however, aggression usually backfires. We learned about this in high school physics. For every action, there's an equal and opposite reaction. In sales, that means the harder you push, the harder your prospects and customers will push back.

Telling Is Not Selling

What does the concept of mismatching have to do with Question Based Selling? The realization that prospects and customers are going to push back is a rude awakening, particularly for those sellers who go around telling prospects why their solutions are superior. If we assume that most people have a natural tendency to mismatch, then telling customers why your product is great will often cause them to mismatch, telling you why it's not. It's a consistent pattern. Telling prospective buyers how superior your proposal is may cause them to point out (or think about) areas where your offering is weak, or where your competition has an advantage. Moreover, if you tell prospects that you would like to wrap up the deal within a certain time frame, they're likely to start telling you why that's not going to happen.

Telling is not selling. This is an old saying in sales, but it's also true. Most people love to buy, but very few want to be told, and even fewer want to be "sold." Buyers today don't want to be pushed, persuaded, or otherwise convinced. It's only natural; after all, who wants to feel that they're being manipulated into buying something they don't need?

Nonetheless, corporations spend millions of dollars each year telling their salespeople what to say. As a result, salespeople are being sent out into their respective territories to deliver some version of the following elevator pitch.

Salesperson: *"Mr. Prospect, you should buy this product from me, because we offer you the best value, and you would benefit the most if I am the one who sells it to you."*

Very few salespeople would use these exact words, but this is precisely what customers hear when they're feeling sold to. I equate it to jamming one of those giant foam fingers you see at college football games into a customer's face, saying, "I'm going to sell you this product whether you like it or not." Of course people mismatch. Wouldn't you push back too?

Perhaps you're starting to see the challenge. To succeed in sales, you must uncover needs and then educate prospects and customers on the value of your product or service. This is how you will help them recognize an opportunity to improve their existing condition. But, using force to accomplish these objectives only increases your risk and decreases your probability of success. There has to be a better way.

Five QBS Strategies That Reduce Your Risk

Just because mismatching is an instinctive response doesn't mean we have to passively stand by and let this behavior negatively affect our sales results. Similarly, just because a prospect mismatches doesn't mean we should write them off as not being a potential opportunity. Two of the largest sales in my career were made to chronic mismatchers.

But since mismatching is not a typical objection, it should not be handled like one. When people contradict, clarify unnecessarily, or respond defensively, they are usually trying to add value to the conversation in an attempt to satisfy their own needs.

Unfortunately, when a prospect mismatches something a salesperson says or does, many sellers jump immediately into objection-handling mode—having been trained to squelch objections as they arise. They assume that if they can overcome the objection, it will go away. This formula doesn't work with a mismatched response, however, because you wouldn't want to squelch your prospect's need to add value, or their desire to contribute to the conversation.

When mismatches are treated as objections, salespeople end up finding themselves in the awkward position of trying to overcome a prospect's behavioral quirks—namely their intrinsic need to add value. Whoops!

> **Secret #43** Mismatching is *not* an objection; therefore, it should *not* be handled like one.

The QBS strategies and techniques outlined in this book are intended to minimize the undesirable effects of mismatching on the sales process. For salespeople, this is a risk-reduction strategy. Instead of being pushed away, you will find yourself working together with more prospects and customers to create and nurture mutually beneficial business relationships.

Here are five strategies that will minimize your risk of mismatching.

Ask More Questions and Make Fewer Statements

Minimizing the mismatching instinct starts with prevention. If we can identify and prevent those things that cause people to mismatch the things we say or do, then we can avoid the negative reaction.

In conversation, statements are easily mismatched. Declarations are even worse. That's because most definitive statements take a position that can easily be disagreed with. For example, the statement "It's supposed to be nice this weekend" is a declaration that's easily mismatched when someone takes the opposite position, saying that it's going to be "too hot," "too windy," "too rainy," or something else that disagrees with the original supposition.

The same thing is likely to happen if a salesperson tells a prospect: *Your boss needs to be at the presentation next week.* Prospects can easily mismatch this statement by saying, *There's no need for anyone else to be involved at this point.*

It's virtually impossible to make a statement that cannot be contradicted, clarified, one-upped, or interpreted defensively. In fact, the more definitive your statements are, the more susceptible they are to being mismatched. Cautious prospects are particularly wary of statements made by salespeople since they don't want to be pushed, persuaded, or otherwise convinced to buy a product or service they don't really need.

Secret #44 If your current approach to sales is statement-based, then your comments will actually invite mismatched responses.

While statements are easily mismatched, questions are not. Questions help diffuse the emotional triggers that fuel the need to mismatch. That's because it's impossible to disagree with a question. If we go back to our now familiar example and change the statement to a question, we can avoid a mismatched response altogether by asking: *What's the weather supposed to be like this weekend?* How can anyone disagree with that question? In reality, questions actually help to satisfy the other person's need to add value by inviting them to contribute to the conversation.

Asking questions, rather than making statements, also helps to minimize risk by giving sellers greater latitude in their conversations. I remember one instance where my company partnered with GE Capital on a multimillion-dollar computer sale to the Georgia Lottery. David Reddaway of GE Capital and I took the senior vice president of the Georgia Lottery to an upscale seafood restaurant for dinner, where we had a nice mix of business and personal conversation. Because our guest was African American, I wanted to ask his opinion on a recent news story regarding racism in America. Most people would say that controversial topics like politics, religion, and sex should be avoided at all costs, particularly in a business setting. But in this case, I was truly interested in his opinion; so I asked.

I thought David was going to spit up his fish. His eyes got big, and I could feel his anxiety from across the table. He was shocked that I would bring up such a politically sensitive issue over dinner. In reality, it wasn't risky at all. Since I had taken no position on the subject myself (only asked a question), this prospect couldn't mismatch with an opposing viewpoint. Frankly, he was flattered that I was interested in his opinion. By the end of the evening, we had had a terrific meal and an insightful conversation; and we also closed the deal.

To minimize (or avoid) the risk of mismatching, it's important that sellers learn how to ask more questions and make fewer statements. This is one of the fundamental premises of Question Based Selling.

Credibility Reduces the Prospect's Need to Resist

If you agreed with our earlier conclusion that prospects are naturally cautious of salespeople, then you will probably also agree that the more credibility you establish with prospects and customers, the less standoffish they will be.

Establishing credibility should be one of your primary objectives in the sales process. In addition to communicating a greater sense of value, credibility also reduces your risk. Credibility reduces the prospect's need to mismatch because they start feeling comfortable with you, rather than cautious of you. It also opens the door to more productive conversation. People who believe that you are indeed credible are more willing to openly share. Instead of pushing you away, prospects and customers will invite more in-depth conversation. Chapter 8 will show you how you can use QBS to develop strategic questions that can significantly enhance your credibility much earlier in the sale.

Curiosity Neutralizes the Mismatching Reflex

The opposite of resistance is intrigue. To intrigue someone is to arouse their interest, or make them curious—according to Webster. When someone is intrigued, they want to know more. In QBS, we raise the issue of curiosity, because we want prospects and customers to invite us into more in-depth discussions about their needs and the value of our product or service. This is how you can create more opportunities to provide solutions.

Making prospects and customers curious is the most effective way to engage them in a productive sales conversation. That's why curiosity is such a big part of the QBS methodology. People who are curious will want to hear more about your product or service, while those who are not curious won't. We cover this at length in chapter 7. For now, I just want to make the point that curiosity neutralizes the mismatching reflex. People cannot be curious and mismatch at the same time.

> **Secret #45** It's impossible for someone who's curious to be inviting you in and pushing you away at the same time.

You can watch the dynamics of a conversation change when someone becomes curious. Curiosity causes them to physically lean into the conversation and give you their undivided attention. And when they ask a question to satisfy their curiosity, they are actually requesting your help—and it's impossible to ask for help and push you away at the same time.

Reversing the Positive

Another way to reduce the negative impact of mismatching is to turn it around so that the responses you receive are actually in your favor. We'll discuss this in more depth in chapter 10 when QBS shows you how to neutralize the disposition of your questions—to solicit more open, honest, and accurate responses. But here's a preview of this technique to pique your curiosity.

Throughout the course of a day, I ask a lot of questions like: *Did I catch you at a bad time? Am I interrupting? Is next week too soon for a presentation? Will the pricing in this proposal make your boss nervous?*

Each of these questions has a negative tone (or disposition), so when someone takes the opposite position they are actually mismatching in my favor. This technique is called reversing the positive.

Reversing the positive is not a manipulation strategy, however. Sellers should not approach potential buyers saying: *You don't want to buy any of this junk, do you?* in the hopes that they will mismatch, saying: *Yes, I do...I do!* But you can absolutely inject some humility into your questions by leveraging the negative so people will want to engage, rather than push you away.

Momentum Helps Reduce the Mismatching Instinct

Shortly after opening the southeastern regional sales office for NetFrame Systems, I landed a meeting with the vice president of information systems at Georgia Pacific. NetFrame was a relatively small company at the time, and this was a huge opportunity for me, and for NetFrame.

The meeting was held in the executive suite on GP's mahogany row. People were seated around a huge conference table with giant leather chairs in a room with lots of windows and a fabulous view of downtown Atlanta.

At the time, NetFrame only had one other big-name account in the Southeast—Delta Air Lines. I was hoping to leverage our success at Delta so the good people at Georgia Pacific would see how much better off they could be by purchasing our product. So, in the meeting, I told them how Delta had saved money by purchasing our solution as opposed to upgrading their existing equipment. I also showed them how Delta was able to reduce their system downtime and increase their productivity.

I went on and on talking about Delta until the vice president raised his finger and said, "Hold on just a minute while I check something." He wheeled his chair over to the window and began to look around. Everyone wondered what he was doing. When he finished scanning the area, he turned back to me and said, "Just as I thought, we don't fly airplanes here at Georgia Pacific."

That day, I learned a very important lesson about reference selling, and about mismatching. Individual references are easily mismatched. Remember when your parents used to say that you shouldn't jump off a cliff just because your friend Johnny did? It's the same with prospective buyers. Most won't make a buying decision just because the guy down the street decided to take the plunge. They need more evidence, which is why QBS approaches the topic of reference selling very differently. Instead of trying to motivate potential customers with individual references, we talked about leveraging the momentum of the rest of the herd in chapter 4. If everyone else already seems to be moving in a certain direction, prospects will feel much less of a need to resist or push back.

Summary

So far, we've discussed mismatching in terms of a verbal response. But it's important to note that mismatching also poses a silent risk. Some prospects will disagree, but they will remain silent—because they would rather disagree quietly than contend with the ego of a defensive salesperson.

Whether it's verbalized or silent, a mismatched response that takes the opposite position can affect your sales efforts negatively. But understanding this reflexive behavior gives you a strategic advantage over other sellers who are pushing to get into new accounts, pushing to move opportunities forward, and pushing to close deals by the end of the month, quarter, or year.

As we get deeper into the QBS methodology, you will see that forcefulness is not the best way to lead qualified prospects toward a mutual solution. Instead, QBS focuses on bringing people together, to increase your probability of success, and to reduce one of the most prevalent risks in the sale—the risk of mismatching.

Part Two

Leveraging the Most Powerful Tool in Sales

Everybody says you have to ask questions. Sales managers, sales trainers, and consultants all advocate the importance of asking good questions in the sales process. Initially, you must ask for an appointment. Then you must ask questions to uncover needs. And, as you near the end of the sale, you must ask for the order.

Good questions are important. Even the Bible says, "Ask and ye shall receive." In addition to helping sellers gather information, however, questions can also be used as strategic tools—to help establish your credibility, uncover the prospect's needs, and develop mutually beneficial business relationships. Used properly, strategic questions can become the single most powerful tool in your sales arsenal. But, asking too many questions can make prospects feel uncomfortable, and the wrong question at the wrong time can kill a conversation.

In Part Two of *Secrets of Question Based Selling*, I'm not going to tell you to ask questions—you already know that. Instead, we're going to examine the strategy of what to ask, and how to ask it. As a result, you will discover that every question you deliver has certain attributes—a Scope, a Focus, and a Disposition. And, how you manage these three strategic attributes will ultimately determine how productively your prospects and customers respond.

Of course, before you start blasting prospects or anyone with questions, you must first earn the right to ask. In other words, prospective buyers must want to engage. What makes a prospect "want to" engage? That's what you're about to find out.

Chapter 6

CONVERSATIONAL LAYERING

Prospects won't buy from every salesperson who comes calling. They can't even afford to spend time with everyone who calls. This makes it tough on salespeople who are trying to break into new accounts. To uncover needs and present solutions, salespeople must first earn the right to engage.

Of course, relationships are the key to selling effectively. You've heard it many times before: people buy from people. But this raises an important question. If relationships are the key to selling effectively, what's the key to building effective relationships? The answer is Conversational Layering.

Some people enjoy mountain biking. Other people like tennis, fishing, or horseback riding. Me, I like golf. Several months ago, I had an interesting experience during a golf outing one Saturday morning. Since I was a single, I was paired with three other players to complete a foursome. I shared a golf cart with a lively fellow named Bud.

Bud and I were strangers to each other, so we chitchatted for a few holes before broaching the subject of business. "Bud, what do you do for a living?" I asked. Bud said that he worked for a small technology company in Atlanta. Then he went on to tell me a little about his business. I would have guessed that Bud was a professional of some kind who was in his early fifties.

"What do you do?" he reciprocated.

I said, "After seventeen years in the trenches of sales and management, I developed a strategic methodology called Question Based Selling. Now I travel all over the world teaching salespeople and sales organizations how to be more effective."

For some reason, what I said struck a nerve with my new friend Bud. His face lit up and he turned to me in the golf cart and said, "I'll have you know that you're sitting next to the greatest salesperson on the East Coast!" While this seemed like a bold statement, I could tell that he wasn't kidding. Now, I was curious.

"Really?" I replied. I wasn't trying to challenge his assertion, and I certainly wasn't being judgmental. I was, however, very interested in knowing what made him the "greatest salesperson on the East Coast." So I said, "I'm not trying to challenge you, but what makes you the greatest?"

"Relationships," Bud said confidently. "Relationships are the key! Tom, you have to understand," he added, "that people buy from people, and customers have to feel comfortable enough to share their true thoughts and concerns."

On that, I agreed. Relationships are important. But I still wanted to know what made him the greatest salesperson, so I persisted.

"Bud," I said, "the reason I'm asking is because next week I'll be speaking to several hundred salespeople in a hotel ballroom in Washington D.C., and I'd like to tell them that I met the greatest salesperson on the East Coast. I would also like to share with them that you believe relationships are the key to selling effectively. Then I'd like to share some of your secrets. So my question to you, Bud, is: 'What are the four or five things that you do that give you a competitive advantage in developing business relationships?'"

A blank expression suddenly came over Bud's face. After making such a bold declaration, he pondered my question about having relationships for a moment and then said, "I guess you just have them."

His response was par for the course (no pun intended). I mean, it's incredible how many books and sales trainers espouse the importance of relationships in the sales process, but then don't tell you "how" to be more effective in creating or maintaining them. I found this very frustrating as a salesperson. So, when I hear people like Bud say *I guess you just have them (relationships),* I can see why so many salespeople focus on having relationships without ever thinking about what causes those relationships to occur. Fortunately, this is about to change with the introduction of Question Based Selling's Conversational Layering Model.

The Conversational Layering Model

Relationships *are* important in the strategic sale because people *do* buy from people. But that doesn't mean sellers should just head out into their respective territories to "have" relationships with prospective customers. Instead, we must ask ourselves: if relationships are the key to selling effectively, then what's the key to building effective relationships?

The answer is Conversational Layering. Whether you're trying to crack into a brand-new prospect account or expand an existing opportunity, the sale ultimately breaks down into a series of events and activities that are intended to engage qualified prospects in productive sales conversations, and then lead them forward in the sales process toward a mutual exchange of value. The key word here is process.

As I said earlier, the QBS methodology is based on cause and effect. In that vein, sellers must first "earn the right" to have a relationship with prospective customers. As sellers, we can't just pick up the telephone and start barraging potential buyers with questions about their needs. Likewise, we can't just start telling them about our solutions either. Instead, we must first earn the right to engage them in a productive and mutually beneficial conversation about their needs and the value we provide.

By applying this same logic to the entire sales process, I created a layered model that defines each of the prerequisite steps that must occur on the way to a successful sale (see diagram below).

Conversational Layering

This is the Conversational Layering Model. In this model, relationships are definitely a key component of the sales process, but as you can see from the graphic, relationships are not the actual catalyst of the sale. Imagine how you would feel if a salesperson called and said, *"Hi, this is Kerry Thomas of ABC Company, and I would like to have a relationship with you."* Most people wouldn't respond very favorably to this approach. That's because the salesperson hasn't yet *earned the right* to engage you in a business relationship.

The Conversational Layering Model is a recipe for success. Using the word "recipe" almost makes the sales profession sound overly simplified. Some people like the word "strategy" or "formula," as this is certainly a formula for achieving success. Perhaps I should ask: do you want the act of selling to be relatively easy or overly complex? When I pose this question to live audiences, the overwhelming response is: *Let's make it easy.* Be careful what you wish for.

You see, a recipe has two component parts. First, you have to have a list of ingredients. If you like to bake, for example, you will need to identify the ingredients that will ultimately be required to complete the project. Things like flour, water, eggs, sugar, baking powder, and perhaps even a touch of rum might be included in your list of ingredients. Secondly, you would need a procedure for implementation. For example, if you took a cake out of the oven after 35 minutes at 375 degrees and then added the flour, instead of a delicious cake, you would get more of a dusty omelet.

The Conversational Layering Model is your recipe for success in sales, with a list of ingredients and a procedure for implementation, as depicted by the progression of the arrows.

Jumping Ahead Increases Your Risk

I always thought that a career in the military would have been great if it were somehow possible to enlist as a colonel. Think about it—instant rank, a company car, a plush office, and lots of medals. Unfortunately, it doesn't work that way. To achieve the rank of colonel, one must first earn the right, which means climbing a ladder that starts at the very bottom—in boot camp.

Similarly, it would have been great to be a concert pianist, especially if it was possible to jump ahead to the professional ranks without having to study or practice. As an instant success, I'd play beautiful music before packed audiences in Carnegie Hall. But I took piano lessons for a couple of weeks, and quickly discovered that piano players don't just jump ahead to Carnegie Hall.

The same argument could be made about selling. We could take the position that salespeople can't jump ahead in the sales process—but in reality, they can. Most sellers don't have anyone looking over their shoulder, so there's nothing to stop them. As a result, many sellers do exactly that. They try to jump ahead (to uncover needs and present solutions) without first gaining credibility or securing the prospect's interest.

I say if you're going to jump ahead in the sales process, then why not jump all the way to the end? Here's an idea. Pick up the telephone and call one of your most lucrative prospects, saying, *"Hi, Mr. Prospect, I've got Thursday afternoon open on my schedule, so why don't I bring by a stack of purchase orders and sign you guys up? That way, we can save you the hassle of having to work through a diligent evaluation."* Of course, this is silly—you can't ask for a commitment without first presenting a solution.

Jumping ahead in the sales process is a high-risk proposition, and one that significantly reduces your probability of success. But that's exactly what salespeople do when they ask for a commitment without first accomplishing each of the prerequisite steps in the Conversational Layering Model. The same thing happens when you try to jump ahead into a relationship without first earning the right to challenge the customer's thinking.

Secret #46 Jumping ahead in the sales process increases your risk of failure and reduces your probability of success.

The belief that relationships are the key to selling effectively causes many sellers to jump ahead and focus their energy on building relationships, hoping to create new prospect opportunities to sell. The problem is, jumping ahead in the sales process is not a very effective means of creating relationships. So we're back to the same question: if relationships are the key to selling effectively, then what's the key to building an effective relationship? The answer will change your perspective about sales. It will change the way you think about your prospects and customers. Most importantly, it will also change the way they think about you.

Crossing the Sales Chasm

The very first sales training class I ever attended was one of the well-known Xerox sales courses. I remember one of the premises of this course was: if you want prospects and customers to openly share their thoughts, feelings, and concerns, you have to ask *open-ended* questions. As a young buck who didn't know much about professional selling, I thought getting people to open up by asking open-ended questions sounded reasonable, so that's what I tried. Great in theory, perhaps, but it was a different story when I approached real prospects with my newfound questioning strategy.

It's one of the great ironies of selling. Salespeople are taught to "open" their conversations with open-ended questions, but prospects and customers are usually reluctant to open up and share their thoughts, feelings, and concerns with someone they don't yet know or trust, especially a salesperson. Think about how you would respond if a cold call interrupted your dinner, and the salesperson said, *"Hello, Mr. Prospect, my name is Joe Smith, and I'm with Mutual Equity Brokers. What are your financial goals and objectives for the next five years?"* While some people might actually answer this question, most will not. Instead, they're more likely to think, *You don't have the right to ask me that*, and hang up.

Secret #47 Unless a relationship already exists, most prospects are reluctant to openly share with a salesperson they don't yet know or trust.

I often ask audiences in QBS programs to raise their hands if they have ever received a sales call like the one I just described. Sure enough, most everyone's hand goes up. "Now, I want you to keep your hand raised if you afford the typical sales callers more than fifteen seconds of your time." Virtually everyone puts his or her hand down. Imagine that—even salespeople don't like to be on the receiving end of a cold call—and most don't even stay on the phone long enough to find out what's being offered.

It's safe to assume that prospects in your target market probably feel the same way. Like us, they have better things to do with their time than entertain sales callers, and they don't want to have a relationship with every peddler who comes calling. As a result, prospects tend to be cautious, standoffish, and hesitant, especially when it comes to answering a bunch of open-ended sales questions.

This presents an interesting problem for the strategic salesperson. In order to have an opportunity to provide value, the strategic salesperson must first identify a need. We talked about this in chapter 2. But just because we want to probe for needs doesn't mean prospects are ready to openly share their thoughts, feelings, or concerns with a salesperson they don't yet know or trust. This creates a *chasm* between their needs and your value—until something happens that causes prospects to suddenly "want to" engage.

The Sales Chasm

Their Needs   What Makes Prospects Want to Engage?   *Your Value*

Most prospects are reluctant to share with a salesperson they don't yet know or trust. Even qualified prospects with a sense of urgency and an active need are cautious of salespeople who jump ahead and start asking questions that are overly invasive. Consequently, sellers are caught in a catch-22—where prospects are reluctant to participate in a meaningful conversation without an existing relationship, but sellers can't initiate a relationship until the prospect is willing to participate in a meaningful conversation.

It's a Paradigm Shift

One of the most significant differentiators between Question Based Selling and other methods is our belief that salespeople shouldn't be trying to *get* prospects to make a buying decision. We shouldn't try to *get* prospects to answer questions, and we shouldn't even try to *get* them to listen to our sales pitch. Instead, QBS focuses on getting prospects to *want* to buy, to *want* to answer questions, and to *want* to listen. It's more than semantics. It's a paradigm shift.

What is it that makes prospects and customers "want to" engage? If you refer back to the Conversational Layering Model, you will notice that it is a series of prerequisite steps that must be completed to move an opportunity forward in the sales process. For example, in order to ask for a commitment, sellers must first present solutions. Presenting a solution is the prerequisite for securing a commitment. That makes sense—after all, why would anyone move forward with a purchase without a thorough understanding of the proposed solution?

But just as you can't ask for the order without presenting a solution, you can't just show up and present your solutions without first uncovering a need and qualifying the opportunity. Again, prospective buyers would only *want* to attend a sales presentation if the solution being offered was able to address a specific need.

> **Secret #48** To secure a commitment, you must first present a solution; but to present solutions, you must first uncover a need.

By working backward in the Conversational Layering Model, we can very quickly identify each of the prerequisite steps that must be accomplished in order to move an opportunity forward. Think of it as a logical progression.

Needs development is one of the most important components of the sales process. It's a prerequisite for presenting a solution. But as we already mentioned, you can't just blast prospects with a bunch of sales questions in an attempt to uncover needs. You must first earn the right to ask, which means building a mutually beneficial business relationship.

The Key to Building Effective Relationships

Relationships are definitely important in the QBS sales process, but I still can't agree with my golfing partner's philosophy that salespeople should just "have" them. For sellers to successfully establish relationships, prospects must want to engage further. What makes them *want* to? Once again, working backward in the Conversational Layering Model, it's clear that the key to building effective relationships in the strategic sale is credibility. Credibility is the prerequisite for every relationship.

Can you see the difference? Rather than jumping ahead and just trying to befriend customers or force a relationship, QBS focuses on getting prospects to want to engage by leveraging credibility. We believe that without credibility, you can't possibly have a truly productive business relationship. Why would you or anyone else enter into a relationship with someone whom you didn't consider credible? Fortunately, the converse is also true. The more credibility you can establish as a competent professional, the more your prospects and customers will *want* to engage.

> **Secret #49** Credibility is the basis for every relationship; the more you have, the more your prospects will *want* to engage.

Unfortunately, salespeople have a bad habit of trying to communicate credibility by claiming their own greatness, usually in the form of an *elevator pitch*. This isn't an effective strategy anymore because competitors are all out there telling prospects that they're great, too. In chapter 8, QBS will show you how to establish credibility by being question-based, but not by asking the typical open-ended questions that I cautioned you about earlier. Rather, you will learn how to significantly enhance your credibility by asking a series of *diagnostic questions*.

It's not time yet, however, to explore diagnostic questions because we must first earn the right to ask. While credibility is the prerequisite for relationships, it's still not the beginning of the sales process. In other words, sellers can't just pick up the phone and rattle off a bunch of diagnostic questions. Instead, they must first secure a *forum* for selling.

The QBS Sales Forum

In order to have an opportunity to earn credibility, build relationships, uncover needs, present solutions, and ultimately secure a commitment to buy, we must have an environment that's conducive to selling. That means we must have two things: the prospect's time and their attention.

In Question Based Selling, we call this combination of time and attention a *sales forum*. This is where the sales process actually begins. To successfully engage new prospects (or existing customers) in a productive conversation, we must have a reasonable slice of their time and attention. While this may seem like a fundamental concept, I make the point because we sometimes forget that we are not the only ones calling on lucrative prospect accounts. Just ask your customers how many sales calls they have to fend off on a daily, weekly, or monthly basis.

Prospects also have to manage the hustle and bustle of their daily routines—which oftentimes isn't so routine. In fact, it's amazing how many people are vying for the decision maker's time and attention. If the boss calls a critical meeting, or if an important project needs to be completed by the end of the week, prospects suddenly have less time, and it becomes that much more difficult for salespeople to get their attention.

As if that's not enough, sellers also have to compete with all the non-business concerns that can occupy a prospect's mind. If the kids are home sick, the car is in the shop, or the prospect has a community service meeting later that evening, these scenarios tend to eat away at the prospect's availability as well, eroding their time and attention.

Now ask yourself this question: Given that prospective customers have more responsibility than ever before, and they are being pressed to accomplish greater results in less time, why should they give *you* a precious slice of their time or their attention? This is the challenge that salespeople face on a daily basis, with new accounts and also with existing accounts.

> **Secret #50** Sellers have to compete with everyone (and everything) for a slice of the prospect's time and attention.

Some salespeople try to secure their prospect's time and attention by being persistent. They leave a continuous onslaught of voice-mail messages in the hopes that prospects will eventually call them back. The problem is that if you're not the only salesperson calling on the account, then your "professional-sounding" messages are likely to sound just like everyone else's—in which case, you'll fall victim to a phenomenon we call *Charlie Brown's Teacher Syndrome.*

Charlie Brown's Teacher Syndrome

Do you remember Charlie Brown—the ever-popular Peanuts character most of us grew up with? Although it has been a while since the original comic strip was created, it's amazing how many people still remember Linus, Lucy, Schroeder, Snoopy, and the gang. But do you remember Charlie Brown's teacher? Trust me when I say that most of your prospects do.

When I present Question Based Selling to live seminar audiences, I like to ask the following question: *How many people in the audience use the telephone to make sales calls?* Virtually everyone raises his/her hand. *I want you to raise your hand again if you find yourself leaving lots of voice mails when making these calls?* Once again, most everyone raises a hand. Then, I ask the tough question. *How many prospects actually return your calls after you leave a message?* For most salespeople, the answer is *not very many.*

Do you know why your prospects aren't calling you back? I could guess, but if you would like to know for sure, then I suggest you try a little experiment. It's one of the exercises we do in the live QBS sales training program, and it's designed to show salespeople why their prospects aren't calling them back. Even though reading a book is different than attending a live QBS presentation, I encourage you to work through this exercise with us here.

To start, it's important to capture the type of messages you are currently leaving on your prospect's voice mail. To accomplish this, let's create a role-play scenario. Picture yourself dialing the phone and calling a new prospect (who in this case, is me). After a few rings, the call rolls into my voice mail, where you hear a standard greeting that says something like: "Hello, you have reached the voice mail of Tom Freese. I am not able to take your call at this time, but if you leave your name and number, I will call you back." What would you say? Whatever it is, write it down on a small piece of paper.

At this point in the exercise (in the live program) we've captured a room full of professional-sounding voice-mail messages. We use these messages to play out the scenario from the prospect's point of view. But, as you're about to discover, the messages we leave on a prospect's voice mail are often very different from what the prospect actually hears when he plays them back.

To show the audience what I mean, I briefly disappear backstage and then re-emerge playing the role of the prospect they just called. For effect, I lumber up to a mock desk and say, "I can't believe I've been in meetings since 7:00 a.m. Now, it's after 1:00 p.m. I'm hungry—but the cafeteria is closed, and I've got a staff meeting in a half hour. On top of that, the monthly report is due tomorrow, I have to meet with the company auditors, the kids are home sick, the car is in the shop, and the boss is in a bad mood. Oh well, I guess I'll check my voice mail."

Next, I pretend to dial the phone and do my best impression of the electronic voice that tells how many messages are waiting in the queue:

Voice-Mail Recording: *"Extension 3254...you have sixteen new messages."*

Now, if I'm an important person at a key prospect account, how many of these voice-mail messages might have been left by salespeople? Probably a bunch. And to put it in perspective, yesterday I would have received a bunch of sales calls, and I can probably look forward to the same bunch tomorrow. While many prospects would like to ignore their voice mail, they can't—because an important customer might be calling, or the boss, or a family member from home may have called and left a message.

To simulate the prospect listening to his voice-mail messages, I call on various audience members to read the messages they have written down, presumably the ones they left on my hypothetical voice-mail system earlier in the exercise. With me still playing the role of the prospect, the rest of the simulation goes something like this:

—BEEP— (I choose someone in the audience to read their message.)

Seller: *"Hello, Mr. Prospect, my name is Justin Wilson, and I'm with XYZ Manufacturing, a company that prides itself on providing the highest quality products in the industry. I'm calling because I want to see if there is an opportunity to get together to discuss your manufacturing requirements and the capabilities of our product. At your convenience, would you please call me back at (209) 555-9900?"*

—BEEP— (I choose someone else to read their message.)

Seller: *"Hi, Mr. Prospect. This is Gail Truman of ABC Company. I was hoping to get a few minutes of your time to see if there's a potential fit between your company's needs and the solutions we provide. When you get a chance, would you please call me back? My office number is (315) 555-8782."*

BEEP. Someone else reads their voice-mail message. BEEP. Another message. BEEP. I keep going until we accomplish the objective of the exercise, which is to discover that it doesn't take long before all these professional-sounding voice mails all start to sound surprisingly similar, if not the same. With the exception of the caller's name and the company they represent, these messages are virtually interchangeable.

This is a tough lesson to learn. But, while sellers are often proud of the voice-mail messages they leave, prospects are quick to tune out whenever the next salesperson's message sounds just like the last one. In QBS, we have a name for this. I call it *Charlie Brown's Teacher Syndrome.* Do you remember how Charlie Brown's teacher sounded? You never see the teacher in the actual cartoon, but we do hear a muffled vocal that sounds like a muted trumpet. No real words, just noises—something like: *"wah…wah…wah…wah…wah."*

If your voice-mail message sounds just like everyone else's, then your prospect is more likely to hear a recorded message that sounds a lot like Charlie Brown's teacher. By the time the prospect gets to the fifth or sixth voice-mail message (out of sixteen), they are more likely to hear:

—BEEP—

Seller: *"Hello Mr. Prospect, my name is Justin Wilson, and I'm with XYZ Manufacturing, a company that prides itself on…wah…wah…wah. I'd like to…wah… wah…wah…so we could have the opportunity to discuss…wah…wah…wah."*

Voice-mail messages from Charlie Brown's teacher are quickly deleted. Even if you take the time to craft what you think is a spectacular message, what you say may be very different than what the prospect actually hears. To them, you are just one of many callers, so when your prospects hear *"wah…wah… wah,"* it's easy for them to immediately gravitate to the position of *No thanks, we already have enough…wah…wah…wah.* As a result, the salesperson fails to secure the prospect's time and attention.

Garnering the prospect's time and attention is fundamental to your success in selling. In essence, if you want to have a real chance to take a swing at the ball, then you must first give yourself an opportunity to stand up to the plate.

Overcoming Prospect Reluctance

Charlie Brown's Teacher Syndrome isn't restricted to voice mail. This phenomenon can also occur when prospects pick up the phone in real time or if you are meeting them face-to-face. Within seconds, prospective buyers start forming their first impressions, and if your approach sounds just like everyone else's (i.e., *wah…wah…wah*), they will quickly tune out.

Sellers have tried to overcome this phenomenon in a number of different ways. Some salespeople try sneaking up on their prospects. Commando selling, I call it. That's where the salesperson devises a strategy that will hopefully get them into and done with a deal before the prospect even realizes what happened. I'm not a big fan of commando selling tactics, but not surprisingly, there are plenty of books out there on the subject.

In Question Based Selling, we want prospects and customers to want to engage. Rather than tricking them, we want them to want to afford us their time and attention so we can have a mutually beneficial discussion about their needs and the value of our products. What makes a prospective buyer want to give a salesperson their time and attention? The answer is in the upper left-hand corner of the Conversational Layering Model, and it's just one word—curiosity.

The Spark That Makes Prospects "Want to" Engage

Have you ever noticed that top performing salespeople are consistently penetrating new accounts while average performers seem to struggle for every appointment? It's not because top performers are better conversationalists. It's also not because they're better closers. It's because they know how to secure a prospect's time and attention—by piquing their curiosity.

If you take another look at the Conversational Layering Model (see diagram on page 99), you will see that curiosity is the key that unlocks the rest of the sales process. Curiosity creates the spark of interest that causes prospects to want to know more about you and the solutions you offer.

It's a relatively simple formula. Curious prospects will choose to engage. But if a prospective buyer is not the least bit curious about who you are or the solutions being offered, you won't succeed in getting their time or their attention.

> **Secret #51** Curiosity is the key that unlocks the rest of the sales process.

Rather than try to force a relationship with prospects that are naturally cautious of salespeople, a question-based salesperson initiates the sales process by piquing the prospect's curiosity to secure their time and attention. It's what gives you an opportunity to establish credibility, build relationships, uncover needs, present solutions, and ultimately secure the prospect's commitment to buy.

Did you catch that nuance? Question Based Selling is *not* just about asking good questions; it's also about creating questions in the customer's mind in a way that challenges their thinking about you and your solutions. Ah ha! Finally, we can cut through all the gobbledygook training that talks about the goals of the sale, and instead, focus on exactly how to accomplish those goals.

Conversational Layering is almost too straightforward to be considered strategic. But consider this. When a prospect is curious, and they also believe that you are a competent and credible resource, engaging them in a mutually beneficial business relationship becomes significantly easier. It's one of the great secrets of Question Based Selling.

Summary

There's an old saying that you can't teach an old dog new tricks. If we translate this into sales terms, it means some salespeople would rather press on with their most familiar approach than try something different. Change *is* difficult, and I'm not offended when people resist new ideas. Not everyone can be a top performer. But for those who strive to achieve the next level of success in sales, Question Based Selling offers a proven and repeatable sales model that will enable you to engage more prospects in more productive sales conversation.

That said, some salespeople cringe at the thought of appending additional steps onto the front end of the sales process. They figure it's tough enough to build relationships without having to think about making people curious and establishing credibility, too. To them, having to *earn the right* to challenge the customer's thinking seems like extra work. Let me assure you, it's not.

Extra work is all those sales calls that end in rejection. Extra work is also all the voice-mail messages that fail to generate a return call. QBS's Conversational Layering Model is designed to save you all this "extra work." Even better, it's another risk reduction strategy—less mismatching. Prospects who become more curious instantly become less cautious. Instead of holding you at arm's length, they will instinctively want to know more. And the best part is, a curious prospect will not only return your calls, they will call you back first.

> **Secret #52** Salespeople who understand how to make prospects curious will never have to worry about being successful.

What (specifically) can you do to make prospects and customers more curious? That will be our focus in chapter 7. Our objective here was more strategic. We wanted to point out the difference between jumping ahead to force a relationship, to starting to think about what makes prospects *want* to engage. Hopefully, I've piqued your curiosity enough to read on.

LEVERAGING CURIOSITY IN THE STRATEGIC SALE

One of the questions I end up asking salespeople all over the world is very simple: "What are you doing to leverage curiosity in the sales process?" Interestingly enough, the most common response I hear back is, "Huh?"

Curiosity is indeed the genesis of each and every sale, yet it continues to be the least talked-about subject in sales training. Essentially, it's the spark that makes people want to find out more about the products and services you offer. In this chapter, you will learn how to leverage curiosity as a strategic tool to secure a greater share of your prospect's time and attention, which should translate into significantly increased sales results.

The newly hired salesperson, trying desperately to rationalize his lack of production during the first month on the job, explains to his boss, "Sir, I can lead the 'horses' to water, but I can't make 'em drink."

"Make 'em drink?" the sales manager sputters. "Making customers drink is not your job. *Your job is to make them thirsty!*"

The sales manager in this anecdote makes an interesting point. It's not a salesperson's job to make people buy. Rather, the salesperson's function is to uncover new opportunities, and then pique the prospect's interest enough so they will want to know more about the products and services being offered.

> **Secret #53** The more curious your prospects become, the more opportunities you will have to add value and provide solutions.

Throughout Question Based Selling, we want prospective customers to become curious. We want them to ask questions, and we want them to be "thirsty" for more information about the value we provide. But this requires a fundamental change in strategy for many salespeople. Rather than just launching into a litany of features and benefits in an attempt to pique your prospect's interest, QBS would recommend that you first pique the prospect's interest in order to create more opportunities to identify potential needs and present solutions.

If you want to engage new prospects in productive sales conversations, you essentially have two choices. You can be aggressive and try to force your will upon them, or you can make prospects curious enough to want more information about the value you provide—so *they* will invite *you* in. Not surprisingly, most of us would rather be invited in by willing prospects than try to rely on brute force.

The Conversational Layering Model (from chapter 6) introduced the notion that curiosity is the key that unlocks the rest of the sales process. If a prospective buyer is not the least bit interested in who you are, or what you can do for them, then you are *not* likely to get their time or attention. Fortunately, the opposite is also true. As prospective buyers become more curious about the value you might be able to offer, it becomes much easier to create new opportunities to sell. This is actually good news for salespeople because it simplifies the sales process. It also puts you in control of your own destiny. In other words, if you can make prospects curious, then you will have many opportunities to establish credibility, build relationships, uncover needs, present solutions, and secure the commitments necessary to move forward with a sale.

Now, the question is, what is it exactly that makes people curious?

The Easiest Way to Make Someone Curious

There are lots of ways to make people curious. You can make them curious by saying something that piques their interest. You can also leverage curiosity with provocative voice-mail messages or by sending intriguing emails. We will analyze each of these as the chapter unfolds, but for starters, let's begin by talking about the absolutely easiest way to pique someone's curiosity.

Piquing someone's curiosity doesn't have to be difficult. In fact, the easiest way to pique someone's curiosity is to simply say, *Guess what?* Virtually everyone you say this to will instantly stop what they're doing and respond by saying, *What?* That was easy. For the moment, at least, you have this person's complete and undivided attention.

You can produce a similar result by saying, *Can I ask you a question?* That's another easy *yes*. Test it out for yourself. Simply walk up to the next person you see and say, *Excuse me, but can I ask you a question?* This question usually stops people in their tracks because they instinctively begin to wonder what you are about to ask.

Both of these questions are designed to create what we call a *mini-invitation*, which is a prerequisite to customer engagement. We said earlier that you must first have a prospect's time and attention in order to position the value of your product or service. In the Conversational Layering Model, we characterized this as having a *forum* for selling. But sometimes (especially in sales) you have to walk before you can run.

At the very beginning of the sales process, sellers haven't yet earned the right to challenge the customer's thinking. You certainly are not going to ask for or secure several hours of the prospect's time prior to building some credibility with them. It's more likely that you are just trying to get through the initial moments of the call. So, by asking for smaller commitments—what we call mini-invitations—you make it easier for prospects to engage, at least initially. From there, what you do to pique the prospect's interest further will ultimately determine whether the sales process moves forward or stalls.

> **Secret #54** Making prospects curious only takes a minute, but it gives you an opportunity to establish relationships that can last a lifetime.

This is important because success in the larger sale is usually the result of an accumulation of smaller successes along the way. And, if you are able to consistently secure the prospect's attention, you will create many more opportunities to expand your sales conversations.

To illustrate, my needs development strategy is very consistent from sales conversation to sales conversation. For example, I don't start probing for needs without first asking, *"Can I ask a couple specifics about your current _____ environment?"* Likewise, I rarely offer a suggestion without first asking, *"Would you like to hear some feedback?"* We use this technique throughout QBS to garner the prospect's time and attention—by creating a mini-invitation—which is far more effective than trying to bully your way into a conversation.

I'd like to add that leveraging curiosity in the strategic sales process is not some sort of manipulation strategy. On the contrary, asking a question to make sure it's "okay" to proceed is not only good manners, it demonstrates that you are sensitive to the individual situation and you are also very respectful of another person's needs. Let me ask you, do customers appreciate it when a salesperson is respectful of their time and space? Of course they do. I don't apologize for being respectful.

Voice Mail: Friend or Foe?

For many sellers, voice mail has become the enemy. It's the gatekeeper that stands in the way of a salesperson talking directly with the prospect they are trying to reach. As I said earlier, well-intended salespeople are leaving thousands of voice-mail messages every day, but only a small fraction of these calls are ever returned.

Prospects, on the other hand, think voice mail is terrific. Automated messaging systems give them the flexibility to be out of the office or away from their desks, yet they can still receive important messages. Voice mail also enables key decision makers to screen incoming calls, so they can focus on their business rather than be interrupted by constant solicitations. Email serves as a similar screening process for customers.

Some sales trainers teach salespeople to hang up when they get a prospect's voice mail and not leave a message. Instead, they would rather you keep calling and calling until the person you're trying to reach actually picks up the phone. The busier the prospect, or the more averse they are to receiving sales calls, the less productive this strategy is, however.

Other trainers suggest that you should leave increasingly forceful voice-mail messages so prospects will feel a sense of obligation to call you back. The problem is, these messages often fall victim to *Charlie Brown's Teacher Syndrome* (chapter 6), because salespeople end up leaving the same old well-worn messages over and over.

In Question Based Selling, we want to differentiate ourselves from the typical sales caller, but not just for the sake of being different. We want to differentiate ourselves for the sake of being more effective. This means leveraging curiosity on voice-mail messages to get more callbacks and, ultimately, to engage more prospects in productive sales conversations.

> **Secret #55** Rather than positioning value to pique the prospect's interest, Question Based Selling piques the prospect's interest in order to position value.

I completely understand what it feels like to receive very few return calls when leaving voice mail. But once I learned how to make people curious, voice mail became a terrific asset and a good friend. In fact, one of the secrets to my success in selling was that I had a very high engagement rate—later on in my sales career, 80 to 85 percent of the voice-mail messages I left generated a return call. Let me say that again: four out of five people that I called were calling me back. Why did they return my call? It's because when I left a voice-mail message, I didn't think about features, benefits, solutions, needs, or relationships. I thought about only one thing—what could I say that would cause this person to become curious enough to call me back?

Leveraging curiosity does require some thought and a pinch of creativity, as there is no magical script that will guarantee your success on every attempt. But there are many ways that you can pique someone's interest (when leaving voice mail) in order to engage potential customers in a mutually productive sales conversation. Let me give you a few ideas to get you started.

Subsetting from a Larger List

I was proud of posting 200 percent of my sales quota for multiple successive years during the latter part of my sales career, but I was equally proud of ramping up in a very short period of time. To accomplish a quick ramp-up, one of the things I would do if I came to work for your company is make myself a list of new announcements. I would create a Word document with my initials, simply called "TF—New Announcements," that would help provide content that could give my voice-mail messages more purpose. Filling out the document itself would be relatively easy. Note that this document was for my use only, as I would not send or forward it to customers or prospects.

I would simply visit the company's internal intranet and literally cut and paste anything that had happened over the last three to four months that might be relevant to a potential customer. I might even type some keywords into Google to see if there were any industry-wide announcements that might be relevant. Don't be too picky when you're accumulating data. I would cut and paste almost anything that might possibly bring something of interest to my prospect base. Once I had compiled a robust list of possible new announcements, I would whittle the list down to thirteen of the most impactful things on my document. Why thirteen, you might ask? You can use a different number if you like, but for me, thirteen is a number that seems like a lot and is still small and manageable enough to not overwhelm or intimidate prospective buyers. This technique would allow me to then leave a message that sounded like the following:

Salesperson: *"Hi, John, this is Tom Freese with ABC Company. I'm on the team that works with commercial accounts in the tri-state area. We've had thirteen new* *announcements over the last three and a half months, two of which might directly impact your business, and one of them is time sensitive…so, I wanted to try to catch you in the office this afternoon. If you get a chance today, could you please call me back at (770) 840-7640? I should be here today until around 5:15 p.m. Thank you in advance.*

The technique is what we call subsetting. Once you have compiled a robust list of the various new announcements over the last three or four months, you can very easily pick out two or three that would affect virtually anyone's business. Now, my message has both purpose and relevance, to the point where if the customer wonders what new announcements would affect his business, especially those things that are indeed time sensitive, they will surely call me back.

Note that these new announcements don't all have to be product related. For example, if the EPA came out with new compliance regulations that could affect your customer, that might work just as well.

Raising a Flag

You can use a similar technique by raising a flag in place of time sensitivity. Note that you don't need to raise a "red" flag. That means danger or warning, and sounds too close to Chicken Little claiming that "the sky is falling." Here's what an appropriate message might sound like:

Salesperson: *"Hi, Jim, this is Tom Freese with ABC Company. I'm on the team that works with commercial accounts in the tri-state area. We've had thirteen new announcements over the last three and a half months, two of which raised a flag with respect to your business…so, I wanted to try to catch you in the office this morning. If you get a chance today, could you please call me back at (770) 840-7640? I should be here today until around 11:45 a.m. I appreciate your help.*

Just to point out a couple of important nuances, let's look at the first and last sentences. In my two introductory sentences I simply want to introduce myself and my role within the company. But, notice that rather than focusing on my own title, I focus on my role—in this case, being on the team that works with commercial accounts in the tri-state area.

If you think about it from your prospective customer's point of view, would you rather be supported by a team or by a rogue individual? Most people would say they'd rather be supported by a team. When I train live audiences, I simply ask, how many people are on a team of some kind? Virtually everyone's hand goes up. So we are all on a team.

At the end of my message I say, "If you get a chance today, could you please call me back?" This sends a very clear request for action. When do I want them to call me back? The answer is "today," as I said in the message. But, instead of demanding that they call me back on my terms, I preceded that comment with very respectful and customer centric verbiage, by saying, "If you get a chance today…" These are very productive words. I'm not demanding; I am respectfully requesting.

I also tend to (but not always) time stamp my messages as well, by saying, "I should be here this afternoon until 5:15 p.m. or 11:45 a.m. today." When people listen to their messages on voice mail, they write down, Call Steve, Call George, Call Tom Freese (before 11:45)…" Which one sticks out? The one that's time sensitive, of course. Bingo!

Now I just have to fill in the middle (the meat) of my voice-mail messages with something relevant and I'm off to the races.

A Question That Only You Can Answer

Salespeople aren't always calling new prospects. Sometimes we're calling people where there is already an existing relationship—for example, you might have an existing relationship with customers, business partners, or other contacts in your industry. Calling someone familiar can be much easier than making a cold call, but you still have to compete with everything else that's vying for that person's time and attention. So rather than leave the same old generic-sounding message, you might leave a voice-mail message that says:

Salesperson: *"Hi, Susan, this is (your name and affiliation). I was hoping to catch you for a minute because I have a question—that only you can answer. If you could please call me back, I should be here in my office this afternoon until around 4:30 p.m. My number is (770) 840-7640.*

Will Susan return the call? If your voice-mail message makes her curious, she will. This technique is particularly effective because it's personal without being pushy. It also conveys a certain sense of urgency. After all, any question that "only you" can answer must be important. It's also very easy to implement. Before you dial the phone, just think of a question that only your prospect can answer. Examples include: *Susan, how do you feel about* _____*? or What is your opinion on* _____*?* These are questions that only Susan can answer (by definition) because you are soliciting her thoughts, feelings, and/or opinions. By the way, most people you are already familiar with love to give their opinions, and they will likely be flattered that you asked.

Something Made Me Think of You

Using a similar approach, you can make existing contacts curious by leaving a voice-mail message that says, "Hi, Richard. I decided to pick up the telephone and call because something happened yesterday just before lunch that made me think of you. If you get a minute, could you please call me back at (770) 840-8640? I should be in the office until around 11:15 this morning. I appreciate your help."

If you were Richard, would you return the call? Most people would, especially if they receive the message before 11:15 a.m. They would want to know what had happened that made you think of them. Note: when they do return your call, be ready with a story or anecdote that will lead the conversation into your business reason for calling.

> **Secret #56** The more curious prospects become, the sooner they'll call you back.

What's a County Tax Record?

Dave Brown is a commercial real estate agent in Atlanta. After hearing about Question Based Selling through a mutual friend, Dave offered to buy me a steak dinner if I would give him a few pointers. I'm a sucker for a good steak, so I accepted his invitation.

Over dinner, Dave went to great lengths to explain that selling commercial real estate was somehow different from other types of sales. "How is it different?" I asked. Then he started to describe an all-too-familiar scenario, where he was making call after call, and leaving message after message, but very few prospects ever called back. So far, selling commercial real estate didn't sound much different than selling anything else.

He went on to explain that the objective in commercial real estate was to match landowners who wanted to sell their property with builders who needed land to develop. The challenge was, most property owners who *did* want to sell had already enlisted another agency, while those who didn't want to sell would rather not be bothered. Keep in mind that Dave was just one of many commercial real estate agents in the Atlanta market at the time lobbing cold calls in to landowners who, for all practical purposes, were usually not very excited to receive yet another sales call. Consequently, it was difficult to find new prospect opportunities.

After dinner we drove to Dave's office, where I asked him to show me how he made sales calls. He plopped down behind a large wooden desk and pulled out a list of prospects. Then he dialed the telephone, waited for the answering machine to beep, and left the following message.

Salesperson: *"Mr. Prospect, my name is Dave Brown, and I'm with ABC Realty, the leading commercial real estate brokerage firm in Atlanta. Our firm specializes in getting landowners the highest value for their property. I would like to have an opportunity to talk with you about the possibility of listing your property. Please call me at (404) 972-4545."*

I asked Dave if he remembered the Charlie Brown cartoons. He did, and we both chuckled when he realized his opening blurb sounded like Charlie Brown's teacher. Everyone trying to sell commercial real estate in Atlanta was calling the same pool of prospects, and they were essentially leaving some version of the same professional-sounding voice mail. So, by the time the prospect actually listened to Dave's message, it sounded more like: *"Hi, Mr. Prospect, this is Dave Brown with ABC Realty, the leading…wah…wah…wah firm in Atlanta. We specialize in…wah…wah…wah, and I wanted to get together with you to… wah…wah…wah."*

The root of Dave's problem was easy to identify. Since the voice mails he was leaving sounded just like everyone else's, prospects weren't giving his message any more attention than the other real estate calls they were dismissing on a regular basis. Therefore, the problem was simple: if Dave didn't even get a chance to stand up at the plate, he would never have an opportunity to take a swing at the ball. Dave knew it was time for something different. He just didn't know what.

I pulled out a diagram of the Conversational Layering Model and explained that curiosity is the key that unlocks the rest of the sales process. Furthermore, I pointed out that if a prospective customer is not the least bit curious about who you are or what you can do for them, they will quickly disregard your voice-mail message. Now Dave was curious. All we had to do was figure out what would make prospective landowners curious.

Having never sold real estate, I didn't profess to have all the answers. But we nosed around his office for a few minutes, thinking that maybe we could come up with a few ideas.

"What kind of books are these over here on your shelves?" I asked.

"Those are real estate law books," Dave said.

"What about inside your glass cabinet?" I probed.

"Those are multiple-listing guides," he answered.

Dead-end on both counts. "What about these?" I asked, pointing to a pile of computer printouts on Dave's credenza. It was a stack of county tax records. What's a county tax record, I wondered? Apparently, in the state of Georgia, real estate agents can print a county tax record for any parcel of property—complete with a description of the property, tax information, and the original purchase price. "Now, that's interesting," I said. "Can you print one for the next person on your prospect list?"

While I drafted a calling script, Dave headed off into the adjoining office to print a copy of Mr. Jones's county tax record. When he returned, I handed him a copy of a script that I had just created. "If you get Mr. Jones's answering machine, this is the message I want you to leave." In addition, I said, "When you make the call, I want you to be holding Mr. Jones's tax record in your hand." I didn't care if he held it over his head or behind his back, as long as it was in his hand. Then, Dave dialed the telephone, listened for the beep, and left the following message:

Salesperson: *"Hi, Mr. Jones, my name is Dave Brown, and I'm with ABC Realty. I'm holding a copy of the county tax record for your property at (such and such address) in my hand…and I have a question. If you would, could you please call me back at (404) 972-4545? I should be in the office first thing tomorrow morning."*

Do you think Mr. Jones will return the call? You betcha he will! Wouldn't you? What's more important is why he'd call back. Dave's message was designed to do one thing—to make the property owner curious. As we said, curious prospects will choose to engage. It's important to note that while this particular messaging technique is highly positioned, it's also 100 percent accurate. When Dave makes these calls, he *is* holding a copy of the prospect's county tax record in his hand, and he *does* have a question.

I like to use this anecdote as a teaching tool during live QBS training seminars because it encourages salespeople to think outside the box. At a minimum, it's very different than leaving the same old "professional-sounding" voice-mail message. Let me ask, would you return the call?

The next question is, what should you say when Mr. Jones calls you back? Were you wondering this too? It's simple. You tell him why you called. Let's play out the scenario and you will see what I mean.

Mr. Jones:	*"This is Ed Jones returning your call. You left a message on my answering machine last night—something about my county tax record?"*
Salesperson:	*"Yes, Mr. Jones, let me pull your file. As I said on the message, my name is Dave Brown, and I'm with ABC Realty here in Atlanta. The reason I called is because we are currently working with three builders who are looking for 100-plus acre tracts of land. I don't have any idea if you would ever be interested in listing or selling your property, but I noticed on your county tax record that you currently own 248 acres at the corner of Buford Highway and Route 141, so I thought I would pick up the telephone and see if it makes sense for us to have a conversation."*

Not everyone who returns Dave's call will be ready to sell their property. Some people may never be ready. But again, if you want to have any chance to swing at the ball, you must first give yourself an opportunity to stand up to the plate. This means getting real "live" prospects on the telephone, and then causing them to *want* to engage in a productive conversation about their needs and the potential value you provide.

You might be shocked to know that most of the prospects who return Dave's call actually thank him for calling. That's because rather than trying to force his way in, Dave takes an understated approach that also provides a valuable service. Owning land is an important investment, and, as such, investors *do* want to know about potential opportunities when they arise. Even if they are not ready to sell at this time, this technique still initiates a conversation where Dave can begin to build a relationship that could yield potential opportunities in the future.

When was the last time you were thanked for making a prospect call?

Create Associative References

When targeting new prospects, it's always a good idea to look for possible inroads into the account. Perhaps you have a previous contact or existing relationship in some other part of the business that you can leverage to get to a key decision maker. Having an "in" is definitely to your advantage. However, when there are no inroads into a new account, most sellers tend to gravitate to some version of a standard cold-calling script.

QBS takes a different approach. Salespeople can't always count on having an existing relationship or reference to pave their way into a new account, but they can always create and leverage an associative reference.

What's an associative reference? An associative reference is a contact you manufacture within your targeted prospect accounts that legitimizes the reason to call key decision makers and initiate a productive dialogue. Essentially, an associative reference communicates a sense of familiarity that allows you to pique the interest of decision makers in order to cause them to *want to* engage further.

Here's an example. Suppose you wanted to penetrate a division of Ford Motor Company, but you had no inroads into the account. Sure, you could just pick up the telephone and start lobbing cold calls in to Greg Simms, the general manager of the division and ranking decision maker. But I wouldn't, because it's likely that Greg Simms is already being deluged by sales calls from other vendors who *all* want a share of his time and attention.

Most strategic salespeople have been taught to target the end user, rather than go through the purchasing department. That makes sense because typically, the end user has the need and the budget, while purchasing just facilitates the transaction. Nonetheless, it may be a good idea to start with purchasing (or some other department), because they often make great associative references.

Hence, I might lob a call into the purchasing department at Ford. After a few rings, a gruff-sounding person usually answers the phone, her name is usually Doris, and she's usually in a bad mood. Perhaps you've had the occasion to talk with her. Here's how that conversation usually goes:

Purchasing:	*(ring…ring) "Purchasing, this is Doris!"*
Salesperson:	*"Hi, Doris, my name is Tom Freese, and I'm with XYZ Corporation. I'm working on a manufacturing problem, and I was hoping you could help me. Did I catch you at a bad time?"*
Purchasing:	*"No, no…this is fine. What can I do for you?"*

Doris may provide me with a wealth of information—in which case, I would ask about upcoming projects, who makes decisions, and other relevant stuff. I would also ask about the purchasing process for the products I represented. Generally, I would try to have as productive a conversation as Doris would allow. Then, after I hung up with Doris, I would call Greg Simms and leave the following voice-mail message:

Salesperson: *"Hi, Greg, this is Tom Freese with XYZ Corporation. I just got off the phone with Doris in purchasing—and I have a question. If you get a chance today, could you please call me back at (770) 840-7640? I should be here in my office today until around 3:45 p.m."*

Do you think Greg Simms will return that call? If he's curious about what's up with Doris in purchasing, he absolutely will. Once again, this approach is highly positioned, but it's also 100 percent accurate. I *did* just get off the telephone with Doris, and I *do* have a question. So, what should I say when Greg Simms calls back and wants to know why I was talking with Doris in purchasing? Again, the strategy is simple—you tell him why you called.

Salesperson: *"Mr. Simms, thanks for returning my call. As I said on your voice-mail system, I'm the district sales manager with XYZ Corporation in the Detroit area. Recently, I heard that Ford was getting ready to fund a large distribution project in the Northeast. I wasn't sure who to contact, so I called the purchasing department and spoke to a nice woman named Doris. Since she didn't know many details regarding this project, I wanted to reach out to you—to see if it would make sense for us to have a conversation about the solutions we might bring to the table. Are you the person I should be talking with about this?"*

Doris in purchasing has become an associative reference for me. She isn't the end user, and she typically wouldn't make the actual decision. She might not even be able to help identify the right person. But whenever you leave a message saying you "just got off the phone with Doris in purchasing," the recipient of your voice mail will call back because they will be curious about what's up with the person being referenced. Furthermore, it's much easier to engage someone when it appears that you have presumably already made it past a gatekeeper in the account.

Associative references don't have to come from the purchasing department. For example, this technique can be implemented just as effectively by contacting the decision maker's counterpart within the same company. Talking to Greg Simms, for example, creates an opportunity for me to call John Hutchison, the general manager of another division within Ford. Using the same approach, I might leave a voice-mail message saying, *"Hi, John, this is Tom Freese, and I'm with XYZ Corporation. I just got off the telephone with Greg Simms over at the Birmingham plant, and two questions came up in our conversation that I think fall under your bailiwick. If you get a chance, can you please call me back today at (770) 840-7640?"*

Leveraging curiosity provides a wonderful opportunity for salespeople to be creative, but it's critical that sellers don't ever cross the line. You do not have to breach your integrity to make people curious, and if you are creative and consistent, you won't have to.

> **Secret #57** A highly positioned, curiosity-inducing voice-mail strategy will only be effective if it is also 100 percent accurate.

Although I have cited a few examples of how sellers can use voice mail to leverage curiosity to increase their callback rate, there are thousands of ways to make prospective buyers curious. Whether you sell to doctors, accountants, lawyers, corporations, or individuals, if they are curious about who you are or what you can do for them, they will choose to engage. If they are not the least bit curious, then you will not have an opportunity to sell. It's that simple.

Sending Intriguing Email Messages

Do you take email for granted? Many salespeople do. They fall into the trap of thinking that email is an enabling technology, one that gives them easy access to prospects and customers. In their minds, all they have to do is send an email message and they will automatically get through to busy prospects. The problem is, email provides easy access for everyone else too, including your competitors. As a result, prospects and customers are being deluged with electronic messages, and it's no longer unusual for decision makers and key influencers to receive fifty, eighty, or more than a hundred email messages per day. Prospects then have to sift through all the fluff to get to the really important information.

When I send an email message, I don't consider it "fluff." To me, it's a valuable document containing important information. As a result, I want the recipients of my email messages to read and consider the content of them, preferably sooner than later. That's why I focus on leveraging curiosity with email. Much like with voice mail, leveraging curiosity causes people to give your email messages a higher priority, and as a result, you get an increased share of their time and attention.

When you send email messages to prospects, customers, or coworkers, they usually review them by downloading messages onto a personal computer, or scanning them on a smartphone. As you know, messages are displayed in a list showing the date and time of the message, who the message is from, and its subject. The date and sender fields are automatically assigned, but the "subject" field provides another wonderful opportunity for sellers to pique the prospect's curiosity.

When a prospective customer reviews their email messages, you can assume that they are going to prioritize messages by sender and by subject. Messages that appear to be more important or urgent are undoubtedly going to be opened and read first. But so are the messages that make these folks curious.

Unfortunately, salespeople have a bad habit of using the subject field to satisfy the recipient's curiosity, by telling them what the message is about. There's some irony in this practice. If you reveal the purpose of your message in the subject field, then why do they need to read it?

Much like the headline of a newspaper, a question-based salesperson wants to leverage curiosity in the subject field in order to increase the amount of mindshare we get from prospects and customers. Therefore, our objective is simple—we want prospects, customers, and coworkers to notice the subject, become curious, and consequently open the email to read what it says. As an example, here's a subject heading that I have used many times in email messages to pique the recipient's curiosity:

To: mrprospect@largecorporation.com
From: tfreese@QBSresearch.com
Date: May 23, 2002
Subject: What would happen if…?

Most people who receive an email that says "What would happen if…?" will instantly double-click on the subject to find out what the message is about. As an added bonus, if your message heading makes them really curious, it's likely that yours will be one of the first messages they open.

Again, be creative. There's an infinite supply of subject phrases that you can use to make your email messages more provocative. Here are some other phrases that will accomplish the same objective.

Subject Phrases: *Two Questions...*
                        On second thought...
                        Wanted to ask a favor...
                        Would like your opinion about...
                        Per George Thompson...

Each of these subject phrases is intentionally intriguing by design. In my mind, the subject field's only purpose is to pique the recipient's curiosity so they will *want* to open the message and read it. And as with voice mail, the more curious they become, the more they will want to read your email. Note that the easiest way to come up with valuable subject fields for your email messages is to skip over the subject and compose your actual email message. Then, go back and look at what you wrote. Within the context of your messages, there will be all kinds of phrases you can use (followed by a "...") that will make people want to know more.

What's the purpose of the "..."? It means there's more to come. How do they find out what else is in your email? Simply open it up and read it.

Secret #58 With email, the subject should make prospects curious so they will make your message a high priority.

Leveraging curiosity is not a manipulation strategy. With QBS, we are not trying to get prospects to buy things they don't want, nor are we trying to force ourselves upon new prospects. We're simply trying to initiate a conversation and see if it makes sense to engage further. What makes prospects and customers *want* to engage further? That's what we will examine next.

Five QBS Strategies That Make Prospects Curious

Curiosity is a very powerful human emotion. It's also the catalyst for each and every sale, and it fuels the rest of the sales process. But we still haven't answered the question: What makes people curious? Actually, there are five things—curiosity inducers, I call them—sellers can use to make prospects *want to* engage. These include provocative questions, partial information, glimpses of value, newness or exclusivity, and momentum.

Provocative Questions…and Statements

Provocative questions (and statements) tend to make people curious. They make people wonder why you asked (or said) what you did. Earlier, we made the point that the easiest way to grab someone's time and attention is to simply say, *Guess what?* This is an example of a provocative question, one that causes most people to wonder, *What?* The same thing happens when you say, *Can I ask you a question?* Whomever you ask will surely say *yes*, but they will also start to wonder what you are about to ask. It's human nature.

I intentionally use provocative prose to name chapters, subsections of the book, and the book itself. I want readers to wonder what's new about Question Based Selling. I also want them to think about what it means to "Challenge the Customer's Thinking by First Challenging Your Own"—from the text on the cover. Again and again, I intentionally use provocative questions and statements to pique the reader's interest, particularly those who are striving to double their sales results. Does it work? You tell me. Did you read the preface titled "The Best Sales Experience I Hope You Never Have" or the epilogue titled "For Sales Managers Only"?

In addition to piquing the prospect's interest early in the sale, there are numerous opportunities to use provocative questions and statements later in the sales process to lead potential buyers toward a favorable decision. You will see examples of this technique throughout Question Based Selling.

Partial Information

Some sellers spend lots of time trying to satisfy their prospect's curiosity, but they invest little time trying to create it. I suppose they just assume that their value lies somewhere within the information they provide to customers, so they go around spewing a fountain of features and benefits about all the wonderful value their company and products offer.

If, however, you agree that curiosity is indeed the key that unlocks the rest of the sales process, and that depth of conversation is the salesperson's friend, then satisfying a prospect's curiosity along the way actually cuts short the customer's incentive to engage in more depth. Think about this: if the prospects you call on already had all the information they would need, then they wouldn't have any reason to meet with you. Likewise, if the prospect's curiosity isn't piqued after you initially meet, then there's no reason to schedule a next step—like a formal presentation. They would already have all the information they needed. And if a prospect gets everything in your presentation, then there's no reason for follow-up afterward.

> **Secret #59** Average sellers try to satisfy their prospect's curiosity. Top performers try to make prospects even more curious.

If you want prospects and customers to "want" more information, then rather than trying to tell them everything upfront, you have to leave some meat on the bone. That means sharing enough information to convey value and pique their curiosity further, but not so much that you remove their incentive to move on to the next step of the sales process.

As an example of using partial information to make a prospect curious, suppose a salesperson approaches a prospect and says:

Seller:	*"Ms. Prospect, my engineer ran a series of tests on your internal systems over the last several days and he thinks you are about to have a serious customer service problem."*
Prospect:	*"What kind of problem?"*

Wouldn't you be curious if someone told you that you are about to have a serious customer service problem? Of course you would; in which case, you'd want to hear more. Once you have the prospect's attention, you can appropriately manage the conversation by asking additional questions.

Seller:	*"In researching your network configuration, we found that one of your file servers may be corrupting data. The good news is, we think we have a solution. Can you get the committee together so we can discuss the problem and present possible alternatives?"*

Partial information can also be a very effective strategy later in the sales process. Curiosity is what motivates prospects to attend presentations, and curiosity is also what gets decision makers to sit down at the negotiating table—to work out the details of a purchase. For example, if you wanted to wrap up a deal, you might say:

Seller:	*"Mr. Prospect, several weeks ago we submitted a proposal for your upcoming project. If our management was willing to offer a special incentive to close this deal by the end of the year, would you want to sit down and work through the details?"*

The prospect may say, *"Sorry, we're not ready to purchase anything."* Then again, they might say, *"Sure, let's take a look at the offer."* Frankly, most prospects will say *yes*, because they'll want to know more about the "special incentive." Keep in mind that you're not asking for a commitment here. You are simply asking if your prospect would like to sit down and discuss something that might be beneficial for both parties. This type of approach makes for a very soft sell, which most prospects appreciate.

Some salespeople push back against this concept of using partial information. They worry that withholding information could breach their integrity or somehow come across as unprofessional. If you have similar concerns, then let me ask you this question. How long does your initial interaction with a typical prospect usually last? Five, ten, maybe fifteen minutes? Prospects are busy people, and it's virtually impossible for a salesperson to articulate the full value of their offering within such a limited window of time. Most salespeople simply can't cover all the features, benefits, cost comparisons, configuration details, upgrade options, support options, and warranty information in a few minutes. Consequently, we salespeople are always dealing in the world of partial information, like it or not. Now the question is, do you say things that satisfy your prospect's curiosity so they say, "Leave me alone," or do you say things that leave potential buyers wanting more?

One note of caution about using partial information to pique your prospect's curiosity: the play here is not to be vague. Prospects tend to interpret messages that are overly vague as either devious or unimportant. That's why we've suggested that you should leverage partial information, as opposed to not enough information.

Glimpses of Value

Another way to pique a prospect's curiosity is to use glimpses of value. This strategy is powerful because dangling valuable benefits in front of potential buyers usually entices them to want more information about how those benefits would impact them. Of course, when they ask for more information, you've accomplished the primary objective. You've caused the prospect to become curious enough to invite further discussion about the match between their needs and your solutions. This technique actually combines provocative questions with partial information to give potential buyers a glimpse of the value that they could potentially receive. There are thousands of examples, but here are just a few.

| Seller: | *"Mr. Prospect, if our product could increase your company's productivity by 40 to 60 percent, would you want to see a demonstration?"* |

*"With one small change in strategy, we think you
could dramatically improve your return on investment. Would you like me to show you how?"*

*"Other customers have saved lots of money by synchro-
nizing their maintenance contracts. Would you like to
know how much you could save?"*

Talk about glimpses of value! Who wouldn't want to know how to save
money, increase productivity, or improve their return on investment? Ask any
of these questions at the appropriate time and most prospects will absolutely
respond by wanting more information. Now, you have a curious prospect who
is willing to give you their time and attention.

You can also use this technique to identify potential problems and indicate
to prospects that you can provide the appropriate solution(s). That's how I
sell QBS training. Whenever I'm on a conference call with a vice president of
sales, I know that most of them will want to cut right to the chase. That's why
I make it a point to bring up some of their most difficult challenges early. The
conversation usually goes something like this:

Seller: *"One of the biggest challenges sellers face today is penetrating new accounts. Lots of salespeople are leaving
lots of voice-mail messages, but very few prospects ever
call back. To what extent does this happen in your
sales organization?"*

VP of Sales: *"It happens a lot, and it's getting even tougher to
get through."*

Seller: *"I understand. Question Based Selling solves this problem."*

VP of Sales: *"How do you do that?"*

Seller: *"I will address that very issue in just a moment…but
first, let me ask another question."*

VP of Sales: *"Sure."*

Seller: *"Do you find that some newly hired salespeople ramp* *up in a relatively short period of time while others struggle along and sometimes never make it over the hump?"*

VP of Sales: *"Yes. Unfortunately, that happens a lot."*

Seller: *"Question Based Selling solves that, too."*

Now I've got a decision maker who is curious about how I can help him. As a result, he's ready to stay on the call longer to find out more about QBS.

Secret #60 When prospects find out that you may be able to solve their problems, they will become curious and want to know more.

In chapter 9, we will show you how you can use these glimpses to close for a commitment, using Solution Questions. Essentially, a Solution Question is a hypothetical that asks, *"Mr. Customer, if I could show you how to improve your existing condition, would you be interested in taking the appropriate next step?"* This is a wonderful closing technique that can help move your sales opportunities forward.

Newness or Exclusivity

New things are exciting simply because they're new. Exclusive things are enticing because people *always* want to be "in the know." More importantly, no one wants to be left out, as we discussed in chapter 4. Perhaps that explains why prospects and customers have an insatiable appetite for information about new products and upcoming announcements. This gives us another opportunity to engage new prospects (or re-energize old opportunities), by saying:

Seller: *"Mr. Prospect, we've had thirteen new announcements over the last three and a half months, two of which would directly impact your business, and I wanted to see if it would make sense to bring you up to speed."*

If you remember, this is a technique called subsetting. If your new announcements are indeed relevant to the prospect's business, of course it makes sense for them to be brought up to speed. You could make this enticement even more exclusive by offering to share future release plans if the prospect is willing to sign a nondisclosure agreement. How can they know if your product is valuable to their business? The answer is, by engaging in a more in-depth discussion about their needs and your solutions.

Leveraging Momentum

Last but not least, momentum is another very impactful curiosity-inducer sellers can use to capture their prospect's time and attention. We talked about momentum as a strategy back in chapter 4, when we introduced the Herd Theory. If you remember, one of the benefits salespeople gain from leveraging the rest of the herd is credibility. The other was curiosity. If "everyone else" is already moving in a certain direction, prospects *will* naturally become curious as to why, and more often than not, they will want additional information.

One of my favorite applications of the Herd Theory occurs when prospects cut you off in the first few seconds of a sales call to ask: *What's this about?* Rather than being caught off guard by this and fumbling, you might try saying:

Salesperson:	*"Frankly, Mr. Prospect, we solve many of the problems that traditional vendors in this industry have created."*
Prospect:	*"Problems? What problems?"*

When prospects hear that you *solve many of the problems that traditional vendors in this industry have created*, of course they will want to know what the problems are and how you solve them.

Summary

I began this book by saying: *Selling is a creative act.* It's clear that individual salespeople have to differentiate themselves from everyone else who is also competing for the prospect's time and attention. One of the most effective ways to set yourself apart is by leveraging curiosity. If you can make prospects curious, you will penetrate more new accounts, uncover more needs, communicate more value, overcome more objectives, and as a result, your sales results will increase dramatically.

The appropriate curiosity strategy will vary depending on whether you're leaving a voice-mail message, sending an email, or talking directly with the prospect. It will also depend on whether you have an existing relationship or are trying to penetrate new accounts. On one hand, you don't want to be too aggressive. On the other hand, you want to be bold enough to successfully engage potential buyers in a conversation that will lead to real opportunities.

We will explore many of these subtleties and transitions later in chapter 12, when QBS shows you how to "Turn Your Cold Calls into Lukewarm Calls."

For now, realize that making someone curious is not the end of the sales process. Rather, it's just the beginning—curiosity will help you secure the prospect's time and attention in order to give you an opportunity to establish credibility, build relationships, uncover needs, present solutions, and move the opportunity toward a favorable purchase decision.

Chapter 8

ESTABLISHING YOUR OWN CREDIBILITY

Credibility is critical to your success in selling. It's true that people buy from people. It's also true that we inherit all the negative feelings and biases that prospects have against salespeople; and until proven otherwise, most prospects will just assume that sellers have no credibility.

In this chapter, QBS shows you how to establish credibility very early in the sale by "narrowing the scope" of your questions. Then, as you gain the prospect's confidence, we show you how to "broaden the scope" of your questions to engage them in a mutually beneficial sales conversation.

Credibility is not a tangible item. You can't touch or feel it, and you certainly can't pull it out of your briefcase and hand it to a prospective customer. Instead, credibility is an impression that people form about you. It's a sense of trustworthiness, believability, and perceived competence that lets other people know you are able to provide valuable solutions, you deal honestly, and you can be trusted to help them make good decisions.

> **Secret #61** Sellers begin to have credibility when prospects form a favorable impression about their competence and value.

When you are perceived as credible, opportunities to provide valuable solutions will be abundant. Doors will open, and qualified prospects will gladly want to learn more about how your product or service can address their needs. If you are not perceived as credible, however, gatekeepers will hold you at arm's length, conversations with prospective customers will be kept to a minimum, and opportunities to position your product offering will be scarce. That's why gaining credibility has become such an integral part of the QBS methodology.

Back in chapter 6, we introduced the concept of Conversational Layering. There, we explained that to achieve the desired result, sellers must first accomplish certain prerequisite steps in the sales process. We already talked about the first prerequisite in chapter 7—piquing the prospect's curiosity to get their time and attention. As you can see from the diagram, once prospects *want* to engage, and you have successfully secured a forum for selling, the next objective in the sales process is establishing credibility.

Conversational Layering

As we progress through the Conversational Layering Model, we quickly discover that credibility is a prerequisite for building and expanding mutual relationships. In order for a salesperson to have an opportunity to uncover needs, present solutions, and ask for a commitment, prospects must first perceive you as a competent and credible resource. We can take this idea one step further by suggesting that the greater your credibility, the more comfortable prospects and customers will feel, which increases your probability of success. What can you (as a salesperson) do to establish and maximize your credibility early on in the sales process? The answer to this question might surprise you.

Sellers Start with Near-Zero Credibility

When salespeople call on new accounts, prospects begin to form their impressions in a matter of seconds. So, what's a typical first impression? Do you think prospects say to themselves, *Hooray, an eager salesperson is calling! Now I get to talk with someone who wants to show me how they can solve all my problems.* Of course they don't. It's more likely that prospects are trying to figure out the fastest way to get off the phone. First impressions of salespeople are typically not that good, and prospects usually aren't eager to entertain new sales callers for that very reason.

Some people think this sounds negative, but I'm merely being realistic. To illustrate the point, let's try a simple experiment. In your mind's eye, I want you to take a few moments and create a mental list of all of the things you've done in the past thirty days. Include everything from business meetings to answering email, power lunches to eating dinner with your family, and paying bills to watching TV. Once you have compiled a comprehensive mental list, I want you to prioritize it—putting those things that are most important at the top of your list, and those things of lesser importance nearer to the bottom.

Now, where on your list does taking cold calls from salespeople appear? Be honest. For most of us, receiving cold calls from salespeople is at the very bottom—ranking just slightly higher than going to the dentist for a root canal or being audited by the IRS.

Even salespeople don't like receiving sales calls. Isn't that ironic? We make our living trying to penetrate new accounts, yet we are just as cautious and just as reluctant as our own prospects when another salesperson comes calling. Before we even know what they're selling, we turn them away, assuming that they offer little or no value. That's because all salespeople enter the sales process with what I call *near-zero credibility*. Like it or not, we inherit all the negative baggage and prejudices from other sellers who have previously called on an account—and until you prove otherwise, prospects will automatically assume that you have little or no credibility. Consequently, they will assume that you provide little or no value.

> **Secret #62** Salespeople enter the sales process with near-zero credibility.

When salespeople are perceived to have near-zero credibility, prospects are reluctant to engage—which makes it difficult to uncover needs, and even more difficult to provide value. In the American justice system, people are presumed innocent until proven guilty. Salespeople, on the other hand, are presumed valueless until they establish credibility. Don't be offended. Prospects and customers have become increasingly skeptical as the result of their previous experiences with pushy salespeople who were less than honest, or who reneged on promises that were made.

Salespeople these days face an interesting challenge—one that could be compared to the dilemma graduates face when trying to land their first job out of college. Companies want to hire people with experience, but in order to gain experience, college graduates first need to get hired. It's a catch-22. The same is true in sales. Prospects are reluctant to engage unless you are a credible resource, but the only way to establish credibility is to engage the prospect in a productive conversation. Because of this paradox, salespeople who don't get a chance to demonstrate that they are indeed credible miss out on many lucrative sales opportunities. Frankly, without credibility, sellers won't even get a chance to take a swing at the ball.

It's clear that credibility is a prerequisite for building mutual relationships, and salespeople do need to be perceived as credible in order to succeed. So, let's take a look at how you can establish enough credibility to actually challenge the customer's thinking.

Three Ways to Establish Credibility

One of the best options sellers have to establish credibility is to leverage existing relationships. Perhaps you have a friend or acquaintance within a targeted prospect account who would give you a personal endorsement. Or, maybe you already have a business relationship in some other part of the company, and can leverage your contacts there. In either case, personal references are excellent for building credibility with new prospects.

If you already have an existing relationship that you can leverage, then I would encourage you to use it. A credible reference is often worth its weight in commission checks. But where salespeople often struggle the most is establishing credibility in accounts where no relationship currently exists. That's the real challenge salespeople have as they try to create new business opportunities.

Sellers who don't have existing relationships to leverage often try to claim their own credibility. Although it's not a very effective strategy, many sellers are quick to jump into a spiel about how great their company or product is. In an attempt to get prospects to form a positive impression, they blast them with claims of greatness that end up sounding like:

Seller: *"Hi, Mr. Prospect, my name is Johnny Rocket, and I'm the district sales manager for JKL Company, the world's leading provider of intelligent systems. Our track record for success is unmatched in the industry and we pride ourselves on how much we care about our customers. In addition to being the top performing office in the state, we also have the best staff, and I have been the top salesperson for the last five years. Why, I have even accomplished..."*

Claiming your own greatness is a strategy that usually backfires. More often than not, trying to claim credibility causes cautious prospects to mismatch and withdraw even further. I know that I usually tune out whenever an eager salesperson starts telling me how great they are. How about you?

Question Based Selling recognizes that sellers don't always have an existing relationship to leverage. We also assume that most sellers want to avoid the problems that come with claiming their own greatness. That's why we teach salespeople how to earn credibility by asking questions. But not just any questions. We show you how to establish credibility and build relationships by managing the scope of your questions.

Managing the Scope of Your Questions

Scope is the first of three attributes we use to characterize strategic questions in QBS. The other two are *focus* and *disposition*. Every question you ask has a scope, a focus, and a disposition, and how you manage these three strategic attributes will ultimately determine the productivity of your questions, and the quality of the responses you receive.

Scope refers to a question's broadness or narrowness. Are you familiar with the traditional labeling of questions as open-ended or closed-ended? Open-ended questions are broader in scope. They are designed to expand a conversation by getting people to open up and share their thoughts, feelings, and concerns. Examples of open-ended sales questions include:

Salesperson: *"What are your goals for the next five years?"*

"What's the biggest issue you currently face?"

"How effective is your current vendor?"

The scope of these questions is extremely broad, which gives prospects an opportunity to take the conversation in many different directions. Questions can still be open-ended (but much less broad) by probing more specifically. For example, sellers can also ask more specific open-ended questions like:

Salesperson: *"To what extent is growth a factor in your business?"*

"What plans do you have to upgrade your technology?"

"How will the new regulations affect your company?"

Even though these questions are more specifically crafted, they are still open-ended, which means they are designed to get prospects and customers to openly share their thoughts, feelings, and concerns.

Closed-ended questions are traditionally narrow in scope. Rather than trying to get prospects to take the conversation and run with it, closed-ended questions are designed to solicit specific, short-answer responses. Examples of closed-ended questions include:

Salesperson: *"How many users does your system currently support?"*

"Do you own your existing equipment, or lease it?"

"When does your annual maintenance contract expire?"

"Who will approve the final decision?"

In traditional sales training courses, salespeople are taught that open-ended questions are "better" than closed-ended questions, especially when you are trying to penetrate new accounts. On the surface, that seems to make sense; after all, we *do* want prospects to open up.

There's a slight problem with this thinking, however. While we would certainly like prospects to openly share, the vast majority of prospects are reluctant to open up until the person who is asking the question has established some amount of credibility. Consider this: Why would you (or anyone else) choose to openly share your thoughts, feelings, and concerns with someone you didn't yet know or trust—especially with a salesperson whom you assume has near-zero credibility?

> **Secret #63** Open-ended questions are great tools for expanding relationships, but they don't help establish your credibility.

Suddenly, we find ourselves in another catch-22 situation. We want to ask open-ended questions because they are wonderful tools for expanding the conversation and building relationships. But until you first establish some degree of credibility, you haven't earned the right to probe that deeply into the prospect's thoughts, feelings, and concerns.

Putting the Cart before the Horse

First impressions are important. And, prospects will certainly base their impressions on the statements you make. I guess that's why so many salespeople are out there trying to claim their own credibility. But if we look at it from a different angle, it's clear that prospects will also base their impressions on the questions you ask. This realization marks the beginning of another paradigm shift in Question Based Selling.

> **Secret #64** Prospects will form impressions quickly—based on the statements you make, and the questions you ask.

I'm always a little amazed when a cold call starts off with the salesperson saying, *"Hi, Mr. Freese, my name is John Doe, and I'm with Financial Planners of America. What are your financial goals and objectives for the next five years?"*

I don't know about you, but I am reluctant to share my financial goals and objectives with someone I don't know. Even if the caller happened to be the best financial planner on Wall Street, I would still be reluctant to share my personal affairs—because at this point in the call, I don't know anything about John Doe. Instead, I would probably think to myself, "Why should I tell you?" and then quickly get off the phone.

By probing for too much information too soon, this salesperson misses an opportunity with me because he hasn't yet earned the right to ask questions that are so personal. Moreover, asking such broad, open-ended sales questions does little to help his credibility. To me, this salesperson sounds more like someone reading from a cold-calling script than a competent professional offering a valuable service.

> **Secret #65** Prospects are reluctant to answer open-ended questions until the salesperson has proven that he or she is indeed credible.

Sellers can sound less competent by asking the wrong questions (as in this example). But interestingly enough, the opposite is also true. Sellers can raise their prospect's confidence by asking questions that demonstrate high levels of competence and credibility. We will show you how to accomplish this by *narrowing the scope* of your questions.

Narrow the Scope for Maximum Credibility
If you were a patient lying in a hospital bed and a physician came in to check your condition—not your family doctor whom you have known for twenty years, but a specialist who was called in to perform a specific procedure—you would likely begin to form an impression about the doctor's competence shortly after he entered the room, right? Most people would. They would become more

or less comfortable depending on what the doctor said, and more specifically, what he asked. After all, there's no way to know whether this doctor got an A or a C on the final exam in medical school.

How would you react if the doctor came into your room and struck up a conversation by turning on a fake smile and asking, *"So…what are your medical goals and objectives for the next five years?"* Most of us would start to feel a little uneasy. We might even question his competence (or his sanity).

As a patient, I would want my doctor to be the consummate professional. I want him to initiate an intelligent dialogue by asking questions that would bolster my confidence and show me that he knows what he's doing. I would want him to ask if I was allergic to any medications. I would want him to ask questions about symptoms that I've been experiencing and about my medical history. The more specific the questions, the better, since each diagnostic question would raise my confidence that his understanding of the problem would help produce the best solution.

Now let's apply the same principle to selling. Prospects want to know that they're dealing with a competent sales professional, right? (As opposed to someone just following a script.) They want to have confidence that the salesperson can identify potential problems and provide valuable solutions. How can you give them this confidence? One way is by narrowing the scope of your questions—to convey higher levels of competence and credibility.

Ask a Series of Diagnostic Questions

One of the techniques we teach salespeople to initiate their needs development conversation is to simply say, *Can I ask you a couple specifics about _____?* If the prospect is even the least bit curious about who you are or what you can do for them, they will answer *sure*. Now you have earned the right to ask a "couple specifics" about the customer's situation. But rather than starting with one of the traditional open-ended salesy-sounding questions I mentioned earlier, in Question Based Selling, I suggest you use this as your opportunity to establish credibility by asking a series of short-answer, diagnostic questions.

Diagnostic questions are closed-ended and very specific. Because they are intentionally concise, they are easy to ask and easy to answer. Brevity at this stage in a sales conversation is critical because sellers typically have a limited window in which to pique their prospect's curiosity and establish their own credibility. That's why diagnostic questions are such valuable tools. Within the confines of a sales call, sellers can demonstrate high levels of competence and credibility by asking a series of intelligent, diagnostic questions.

When I sold Superservers for NetFrame Systems, for example, I opened almost every sales conversation with the same list of diagnostic questions. It wasn't a trick to get someone to buy something they didn't need; rather it was an effective strategy that differentiated me from all the other salespeople knocking on the prospect's door. I would look for an opportunity to say, *Can I ask you a couple specifics about your current hardware platform?* and then roll right into the following diagnostic questions.

Seller: *"How many file servers do you currently have installed?"*

Prospect: *"We have twenty-two servers downtown and seven in the annex."*

Seller: *"Is your network topology Ethernet or Token Ring?"*

Prospect: *"Ethernet."*

Seller: *"Are you using Microsoft or Novell as your operating system?"*

Prospect: *"Microsoft."*

Seller: *"Version 3.X or 4.X?"*

Prospect: *"We just upgraded to release 4.0."*

Seller: *"How many network segments do you currently support?"*

Prospect: *"Two per server, for a total of fifty-eight."*

Seller: *"And how many users on the network?"*

Prospect: *"We currently have 550 users…but we're growing rapidly."*

If you timed this exchange, you'd see that this series of diagnostic questions took less than sixty seconds. That's a lot of information in a very short period of time. In addition to gathering valuable information about the account, this technique allows me to demonstrate (via questions) that I know something about file server hardware, network topology, operating system software, network infrastructure, and network management.

This is one of the best secrets of Question Based Selling. By demonstrating that you know how to ask relevant and intelligent diagnostic questions, you communicate higher levels of competence, credibility, and value. This automatically sets you apart from other sales callers who either claim their own credibility or sound like they're reading from a script.

> **Secret #66** When you demonstrate an ability to ask relevant and intelligent questions, prospects will automatically perceive a higher level of competence, credibility, and value.

You might think, why doesn't QBS just tell salespeople to ask closed-ended questions? It's because the term "closed-ended" sends a mixed message. For decades, sellers have been taught that closed-ended questions are detrimental to the sales process because they "close down" the conversation. In QBS, I say just the opposite. When a salesperson tries to "open" a conversation by posing the traditional open-ended sales questions too early, very few prospects actually open up. On the other hand, the more credibility you earn by asking diagnostic questions, the more prospects will *want* to engage in more in-depth conversation about their needs and your potential solutions.

Narrowing the scope of your questions is an effective way to establish credibility early in your needs development conversations. Once you begin to establish credibility, you earn the right to *broaden the scope* of your questions to uncover the prospect's true needs—by probing into more depth about their thoughts, feelings, and concerns. We'll talk more about broadening the scope of your questions later in this chapter.

> **Secret #67** If a prospect is curious and believes you are a competent, credible resource, then uncovering needs and presenting solutions is easy.

Crossing Industry Boundaries

Some sales techniques are industry specific—but not this one. This technique applies to virtually every industry because it solves a universal problem. Whether you're selling computers, pharmaceuticals, advertising space, office furniture, financial services, automobiles, insurance, or employee benefits, you are presumed to be valueless until proven credible. Let's look at some real-life examples to show you how salespeople in different industries can establish their credibility using diagnostic questions.

Selling Office Furniture

When I trained the leading office furniture supplier in the Midwest, I was asked to help solve a familiar problem. Although much of their business was in multimillion-dollar contracts with major corporations, the company's sales force was still having trouble overcoming the typical skepticism often displayed toward salespeople. Frankly, they had the very same credibility problem that I described earlier, and asking the same old open-ended sales questions was only making it worse.

In the QBS training, I showed these salespeople how to differentiate themselves by narrowing the scope of their questions. Together we created a list of diagnostic questions specific to their business, and their results were immediate. Now, after they ask, "Can I ask you a couple specifics about _____?" and the prospect says, "Sure," they kick off their needs development conversations with questions like:

1. *Do you currently use systems furniture or free standing?*

2. *Is your office environment traditional or contemporary?*

3. *Do you prefer steel or a wood-grain finish?*

4. *How many office employees are in your company?*

5. *In how many locations?*

6. *Do you own your office space or lease?*

If you sell office furniture to large corporations, the question you really want to ask is: *What's the biggest facilities issue you currently face?* If you start there, however, most prospects will instantly tune you out for all the reasons we've mentioned thus far. But, with a very small investment (usually less than sixty seconds at the beginning of a sales conversation), someone who sells office furniture can quickly differentiate herself by asking a series of diagnostic questions that helps establish their credibility. Doors that were previously closed to this client suddenly started to open up, and their sales organization was able to capitalize on more business opportunities than ever before.

Selling Insurance

Having worked with numerous insurance companies and individual agents, I've seen this technique offer similar benefits to people who sell highly conceptual products like insurance. If that includes you, rather than jump ahead asking the traditional open-ended questions about a client's "goals and objectives," try opening the conversations with a series of diagnostic questions. Next time you meet with a new insurance prospect, first pique their curiosity and then say, *"Can I ask you a couple specifics about your current (_____)?"* It might be as simple as saying, *"Can I ask you a couple specifics about your family situation?"* When they respond by saying, "Yes," you can then ask the following diagnostic questions:

1. *Do you currently have a life insurance policy?*

2. *Was it provided by your employer or did you purchase it separately?*

3. *Is your existing insurance whole life or term?*

4. *How long has your current policy been in force?*

5. *How many people are in your immediate family?*

6. *When was the last time you reviewed your insurance needs?*

In addition to establishing credibility as a competent professional, the technique of using diagnostic questions is designed to make prospects think. Another way to say that is you are earning the right to challenge their thinking. With just a few quick questions, prospects often realize that their family situation *has* changed, their insurance needs *are* different, or they haven't reviewed their existing coverage in quite some time. This paves the way for you, as a competent insurance professional, to further explore those areas where the prospect may have a need.

It Even Works for Car Salesmen

This technique even works for what many regard as the lowest form of salesmanship—the car salesman. I have nothing against the automobile industry, but I think we can all agree that most people tend to picture the "typical" car salesman as pushy or overbearing. But that doesn't have to be the case. Automotive professionals can establish their credibility by asking a series of diagnostic questions just like anyone else. Here's a quick example of how a car salesperson could use this technique to fend off customer skepticism.

Seller:	*"Welcome to ABC Motors. How can I help you today?"*
Prospect:	*(reluctantly)* *"I'd just like to look around, thank you."*
Seller:	*"Have you been to this dealership before?"*
Prospect:	*"Once, a couple years ago."*
Seller:	*"Then I should let you know that we just rearranged our entire inventory. Frankly, we have sold so many cars lately, we had to do something. How the cars are organized is a little confusing right now, but it should help everyone in the long run. Would you like a quick overview to make looking around a little easier?"*
Prospect:	*"Okay, sure."*

- (Pause) -

At this point in the dialogue, the seller has accomplished something significant. By using a question-based approach, he has discovered that the prospect is unfamiliar with the dealership. But rather than jumping ahead and trying to *sell* a car, this salesperson is performing a valuable service by identifying a problem (the prospect's unfamiliarity with the car lot), and then offering to help solve it. When the prospect accepts his offer, the salesperson has an opportunity to engage further—in this case, by asking a series of diagnostic questions to establish credibility and raise the buyer's confidence. You see, car buyers are averse to a salesperson's pushiness, not their competence. So, let's continue the dialogue.

Seller:	*"First, can I ask you a couple specifics about your preferences?"*
Prospect:	*"Sure."*
Seller:	*"Are you more interested in cars or trucks?"*

Prospect:	*"Cars."*
Seller:	*"Would you rather have two doors or four?"*
Prospect:	*"A four-door would be better."*
Seller:	*"Is this car for personal use or business?"*
Prospect:	*"A little of both, but I will definitely be taking customers out in it."*
Seller:	*"Do you prefer sporty or traditional?"* (response)
	"Does engine size matter?" (response)
	"How about trunk space?" (response)
Seller:	*"Here's an idea. What if I show you a few different options to get started, and then you can decide how to proceed from there?"*
Prospect:	*"That would be great, thank you."*

As the salesperson establishes his credibility by asking diagnostic questions, the overall tone of the conversation changes. If this prospect is truly interested in buying a new car, the salesperson is proving through questions that he (or she) can be a valuable resource in the sale—which is very different from the impression people have when a car salesman first approaches with an out-stretched hand and a Cheshire Cat smile.

Use Diagnostic Questions to Open Your Presentation

Diagnostic questions are also useful for breaking the ice in your sales presentations. Sellers often penetrate new accounts through a primary contact and then schedule a presentation for the rest of the committee. Trouble is, you may have established your credibility with your primary contact in the account, but to everyone else on the committee, you are just another salesperson. They don't know you from Adam, which means you again start your presentation with near-zero credibility. You also inherit the baggage of all the other salespeople who have come before. Consequently, presentation audiences tend to assume the worst—that you provide little or no value—until you prove otherwise.

How can you establish credibility with your presentation audiences? The same way you established credibility in the initial sales call—by demonstrating that you know how to ask relevant and intelligent questions. I use this technique every time I kick off a presentation. Knowing that people in the audience who don't know better are going to be skeptical, I want to change their perceptions and I want to change them early in the presentation. So whether I'm the keynote speaker at a national sales meeting or leading a QBS sales training program, I always open my presentation with diagnostic queries like:

Presenter: *"How many people in the audience call on new prospects?"*

"Raise your hand if you leave lots of voice-mail messages."

"Keep your hand up if it's tough to get prospects to call back."

"Do you find that it's difficult to get to the right person?"

By asking questions that people identify with, I am letting the audience know that we're going to be dealing with important issues that are critical to their success. In addition to establishing my own credibility, this technique also helps to pique the audience's curiosity so they'll want to hear more. (We'll talk more about building value in your sales presentations in chapter 15.)

Characteristics of a Diagnostic Question

Crafting effective questions is somewhat of an art, but there are some basic guidelines that will enable you to ask better diagnostic questions and implement this technique in your own unique sales environment.

Start with the Bigger Picture

I like to open with a question that inquires about the bigger picture. Essentially, this paves the way for me to follow up with other more specific diagnostic questions. Going back to the example where I was selling Superservers, the first question I always asked new prospects was, *How many file servers do you currently have installed?* Since NetFrame's bread and butter was reducing the number of file servers a customer had to manage, this question got right to the heart of the matter. If the prospect didn't have any file servers, there was no reason to continue the conversation. If they did have file servers, however, then their response (how many) would lead right into my next diagnostic question, which was: *"Is your network topology Ethernet or Token Ring?"*

> **Secret #68** Starting with the bigger picture allows you to probe more deeply into more specific areas.

The same thing happened when the car salesman asked, *"Are you more interested in looking at cars or trucks?"* Whichever way the prospect goes, the salesperson can easily roll right into the next question, which in the example was, *"Would you rather have two doors or four?"*

Offer Your Prospects a Choice

When an optometrist gives an eye examination, he puts a pair of test lenses in front of a patient's eyes, adjusts the relative strength of those lenses, and then asks, *"Is this better or worse?"* Offering a choice is a diagnostic technique that enables the doctor to zero in on the best solution for the patient.

If you look back, you will notice that many of the diagnostic questions we used in the previous examples offer the prospect a choice. *Is your insurance whole life or term? Is your current office environment traditional or contemporary? Do you own your office space or lease?* Offering a choice makes your questions easier to answer, which is particularly important at the beginning of a sales conversation when you don't yet have the prospect's full attention or their trust.

Variety Is the Spice of Life

Be sure to insert some variety into your diagnostic questions. I say this for three reasons. First, if your questions aren't interesting, it's very difficult to engage new prospects in productive conversation. "Sales robots" don't sound credible, so your questions should be relevant, intelligent, and somewhat interesting.

Secondly, the diagnostic process is a divide-and-conquer strategy. By narrowing the scope of your questions, you are helping to break a large and often intimidating decision down into its component parts. This is a very effective technique because it enables prospects to systematically work through a series of smaller decisions in order to come to the larger conclusion.

> **Secret #69** For most prospects, it's easier to make decisions on smaller components of a sale than to tackle the larger purchase in its entirety.

Last, but certainly not least, mixing up your diagnostic questions gives you multiple avenues in which to explore an opportunity further. In the NetFrame sale, I intentionally asked a variety of questions about computer hardware, network topology, operating system software, and number of users. This opened the door for me to pursue multiple areas where my product could offer a unique advantage.

To Be Perceived as an Expert, Ask Expert Questions

Early in the sales process, our objective is building credibility, to communicate an increased sense of competence and expertise. We're saying you can do this by asking intelligent questions. But I'll let you in on a little secret: you don't have to be an expert to ask expert questions.

A brand-new salesperson can take over a new territory and by the end of their first week on the job sound like a credible expert who's been selling for years. How? By learning what questions to ask and how to ask them.

Experts in every business ask very specific questions at certain times. In fact, they use the same questions in account after account because, while every prospect is different, most have similarities in terms of what they need. Therefore, if you want to sound like an expert, here are some steps you should take. Start by seeking out successful salespeople in your business. What questions do they ask? Make it a point to compile a list of their most frequently asked questions, and then take the time to memorize them. With a few hours of practice, you will be able to rattle off those same questions and convey a similar level of expertise. This does not replace the need to understand your product or industry. I'm simply making the point that perceived credibility isn't just a function of what you know, it's also a function of the questions you ask.

Be Careful Not to Qualify Too Early

Qualifying your prospect opportunities is important, but don't get hung up on trying to qualify an opportunity in the first sixty seconds of the call. That's why I recommend not starting with questions about the prospect's budget, their time frame for making a decision, or anything else that might cause you to sound salesy and/or them to pull back. Once you have established your credibility, and prospects are ready to openly share their thoughts, feelings, and concerns, you will have lots of opportunities to expand the conversation to further qualify the opportunity.

Broaden the Scope to Expand Relationships

Credibility is an asset that does wonderful things for salespeople. Most importantly, it earns you *the right* to then broaden the scope of your sales conversations. But you must be ready to take advantage of this opportunity. As prospective buyers become more willing to openly share, you must be ready to expand the scope of your questions—to find out more about their needs and their motivations for making a decision that will favor your product or service.

> **Secret #70** By establishing credibility, salespeople earn the right to broaden the scope of their sales conversations.

Closed-ended questions are excellent tools for building credibility, but they aren't particularly effective for building relationships. That's because they are too narrow. For example, if you ask a prospect, *Is performance the most important issue in your evaluation?* and the prospect says *no*, then what? Do you guess again, asking, *Is reliability the most important issue? What about cost effectiveness?* In addition to feeling uncomfortable, having to guess puts you in a position of weakness, which is one of the quickest ways for an otherwise competent salesperson to compromise his or her credibility.

> **Secret #71** Closed-ended questions are great credibility-building tools, but you can't build a house if your *only* tool is a hammer.

There's more to broadening the scope of your questions than just reeling off a sequence of open-ended questions. To develop the opportunity, you'll want to ask questions that will challenge the customer's thinking—to uncover and identify needs that can be successfully addressed by your product or service. That's what we'll talk about next in chapter 9. There, you will learn how to escalate the strategic "focus" of your questions in order to expand relationships, uncover needs, and increase the value of your sales conversations.

Summary

Narrowing the scope of your questions can help you establish more credibility than anything else you can do. By asking intelligent diagnostic questions, you let prospects know that you are a cut above everyone else who is also competing for their time and attention. This credibility gives you an opportunity to probe more deeply into their thoughts, feelings, and concerns, so you can uncover more needs and put yourself in a strong position to provide greater value.

Chapter 9

ESCALATE THE VALUE OF YOUR SALES QUESTIONS

To provide solutions, sellers must first uncover a need. That's one of the reasons questions are so important. But needs development is a double-edged sword. We want to successfully identify needs that will fuel the sales process, but we don't want prospects to feel "pumped" for information. In this chapter, we show you how to accomplish both of these goals by escalating the strategic focus of your questions.

"Focus" is the second of three attributes that characterize strategic questions in QBS. In addition to managing "scope," escalating the "focus" of your questions will broaden the customer's needs and increase the value of your sales conversations.

By first establishing your credibility using diagnostic questions, you earn the right to *broaden the scope* of your questions. This allows you to expand relationships and uncover needs. We talked about this in chapter 8. Open-ended questions can be very effective tools for bolstering your sales conversations, but that doesn't mean we want prospects to ramble on and on without direction. This is a hard lesson, and it's one that I learned many years ago as a neophyte salesperson.

I had always been taught it was crucial to get the prospect talking. In theory, that meant asking open-ended questions to build rapport, which would hopefully pave the way for a business relationship. With that in mind, I called on the senior vice president in one of my largest prospect accounts.

The secretary showed me into his office, which was lavishly furnished with mahogany paneling and designer furniture. On the walls were numerous awards, intermixed with original oil paintings. Although I was a little nervous, he seemed quite relaxed and willing to spend time with me. Since this was my big chance, I decided to break the ice by asking a few open-ended questions about his background.

Most people love to talk about themselves, and this executive was no exception. He told me about his college years at Harvard. Then he told me about his two tours of duty in Vietnam. I listened intently—as I had been taught. Forty-five minutes went by and I knew details about his family, his medical condition, where he lived, and his career. I thought it was going well; that is, until the secretary popped in to say, "Your next appointment is here."

> **Secret #72** Small talk might be good for building rapport, but it isn't nearly as valuable as BIG TALK—focusing on key business issues.

We had spent the better part of an hour talking about his life story, but not about his company's needs or my solutions. I had succeeded in getting this senior executive to open up, but I had failed to point the conversation in the right direction. As a result, I missed an opportunity to have a productive discussion about mutual business objectives. I learned that while it is important to ask probing questions, it's even more important to ask the right questions at the right time. This is critical if you want to increase your probability of success and decrease your risk of failure.

Asking the Right Questions

Asking questions to uncover needs is hardly a new idea. There are sixty-seven sales books on my office shelves and all of them say you have to ask questions. In fact, most sales managers and sales trainers will quickly tell you that questions are the key to qualifying new prospect opportunities and identifying buyer motivations. As a result, salespeople go out into their respective territories asking questions in order to create business opportunities that otherwise wouldn't exist.

This is one of the big changes from my first book. The whole notion of uncovering needs is fundamentally flawed. Isn't it true, especially in emerging markets, that some customers don't necessarily know what they need? In which case, trying to uncover needs customers don't even know they have (latent needs) is a flawed strategy. Even if they do understand their needs inside and out, many prospects today aren't willing to share those needs with a salesperson they don't yet know or trust. So much for the idea of uncovering needs.

To me, salespeople need to be thinking about needs development, which is the next generation of the idea of uncovering needs. Needs development is a facilitative exercise that actually challenges the customer's status quo—or, should I say, gets them to think outside the box.

The problem is, asking questions in a random fashion is counterproductive. Questions *are* important, and when used properly, they can absolutely enhance your interactions with prospective buyers and further the sales process. But questions can also kill a conversation. Asking too many questions can make prospects feel pumped for information, and asking questions too aggressively can make them feel as if they're being interrogated.

> **Secret #73** A fine line exists between asking productive questions and "pumping" your prospects and customers for information.

In Question Based Selling, asking questions is *not* a random exercise. We don't just suggest that you go out and ask a bunch of questions. Instead, we've developed a multifaceted questioning toolbox, for leveraging questions in a strategic manner to benefit your current and future sales conversations. Managing the scope of your questions, for example, is important because it establishes your credibility and gives you an opportunity to build relationships. It's equally important to increase the value of your sales conversations by escalating the focus of the questions being asked.

Strategic Questioning Is a Process

The Declaration of Independence clearly states that *all men are created equal*. But it doesn't say anything about the value of strategic sales questions. That's because all questions are *not* created equal in mutual value to the seller and the prospect, and depending on where you are in the sales process, some questions are significantly more valuable than others.

While I do agree that there is a certain art to asking the right questions at the right time, successful questioning is a strategic process—one that goes far beyond telling salespeople to go out and ask a handful of open-ended questions. With Question Based Selling, we characterize this by stratifying the different types of sales questions into four unique categories, according to their mutual value in the conversation.

If you dissect a sales conversation, you will notice that the questions being asked probe to uncover one of the following: either the *status* of the opportunity, an *issue* the prospect may have, the *implications* of that specific issue, or whether a potential *solution* provides value. Because each of these sales questions has a different strategic *focus*, we categorize them as *Status Questions, Issue Questions, Implication Questions,* and *Solution Questions.*

Once we get our head around the four different categories of questions being asked, we must also look at how these questions are being delivered. In

QBS, it is my belief that strategic questions, asked in the proper sequence, can cause prospects to feel more comfortable, in which case they become more open to sharing their thoughts, feelings, and concerns. This becomes important because in the needs-development portion of the sales process we want to gain a detailed understanding of the customer's specific needs.

What's the proper sequence for asking sales questions? I'm glad you asked.

One of our goals in conversations with prospects should be to ask questions that earn us the right to probe further. I say this because it's unrealistic to expect that you will gain a complete understanding of the prospect's needs by asking a single question. Consequently, it makes sense to ramp up your sales conversations by starting out with questions that are easy to ask and easy to answer. That's what we accomplished in chapter 8—asking short-answer, diagnostic questions to establish credibility. We said that these diagnostic questions were intentionally narrow in *scope*. Of course, once you've earned the right to probe further, you'll want to *escalate the focus* of your questions to increase the value of your sales conversations.

> **Secret #74** To increase the value of your sales conversations, you need to escalate the focus of your sales questions.

The diagram below shows each of the four different types of questions escalating in value from *Status Questions* (lowest in value), to *Issue Questions*, *Implication Questions*, and *Solution Questions* (highest in value).

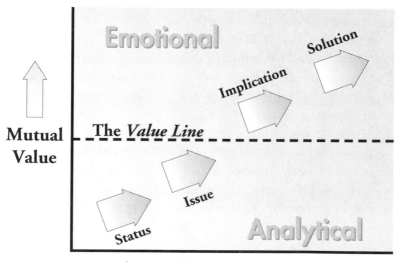

Escalating the "Focus" of Questions

If your objective is to identify the prospect's needs, then *Issue Questions* are more valuable than *Status Questions*. You can't begin to solve a problem until you uncover key issues. Similarly, it's important to identify the implications of an issue in order to justify the need for a solution. And more implications create a greater urgency to find a solution. That's why *Implication Questions* are so valuable. Lastly, *Solution Questions* transition the focus of the discussion from the prospect's needs to the benefits of your solution. This escalation strategy works because asking more valuable questions tends to generate more valuable sales opportunities.

Emotional vs. Analytical

It's important to escalate the focus of your sales questions, because strategic decisions are made more emotionally than analytically. You can see this depicted in the previous diagram, where QBS's escalation model is bisected into two sections: Emotional and Analytical. In other words, after the attorneys, consultants, engineers, and accountants have all submitted their detailed analyses, decision makers still have to "feel" comfortable they are making the right decision in order to pull the trigger. This is where the intangibles we talked about in chapter 1 can make the difference between transacting a sale and losing an opportunity.

> **Secret #75** Most purchase decisions are emotional, where prospects have to *feel* they are making the right decision.

Status Questions and Issue Questions are analytical in nature. On the previous diagram, you will notice that they fall below the *Value Line*, which means they aren't designed to find out what prospects are thinking or feeling. While these questions are great tools for gathering information, escalating the focus of your questions is what enables salespeople to identify the emotional nuances that will ultimately drive a purchase decision.

Implication Questions and Solution Questions are emotional in nature, and as you can see from the diagram, they rise above the Value Line. These are the probing questions that salespeople really want to ask—they help to understand the prospect's thoughts, feelings, and concerns. After all, facilitating an emotionally driven discussion is where you will find out what is actually motivating your prospects to move forward, or what might be holding them back.

Perhaps you are wondering: *If emotional questions are so much more valuable than analytical questions, then why not jump ahead?* We discussed this earlier in chapter 6. Sellers can absolutely jump ahead in the sales process, but doing so only increases your risk of failure and reduces your probability of success. Instead, QBS follows a logical progression. We teach sellers to ask enough Status Questions to earn the right to probe more deeply into the prospect's issues. Once you begin to identify key issues, you earn the right to ask about various implications of the issues that are uncovered. And finally, once you've identified one or more opportunities to solve a problem or satisfy a desire, you earn the right to close with Solution Questions, which essentially ask: *"Mr. Prospect, if our product or service provides a solution for the issues we just discussed, would it make sense to take the appropriate next step?"*

To successfully escalate the value of your sales questions, you must understand the role each type of strategic question plays in the needs development process. I will dedicate the balance of this chapter to communicating those roles.

Status Questions

What is a Status Question? A Status Question is a question that probes for specific pieces of information (facts) that will help reveal the current "status" of a prospect opportunity. Salespeople have been repeatedly taught to ask open-ended questions much too early in their customer interactions. Status Questions should be the starting point in most sales conversations. These initial questions should look familiar, because the "diagnostic questions" we introduced earlier in chapter 8 essentially probed for specific pieces of information about the "status" of an opportunity.

Examples of Status Questions are abundant, but for continuity's sake, let's look at some of the same diagnostic questions we used earlier. After piquing the prospect's curiosity, we asked a series of (diagnostic) Status Questions to establish credibility. For selling Superservers, we asked:

1. *How many file servers do you currently have installed?*

2. *Is your network topology Ethernet or Token Ring?*

3. *Are you using Microsoft NT or Novell?*

4. *Version 3.X or 4.X?*

5. *How many network segments do you support?*

6. *And how many users?*

Each of these questions is designed to uncover information about the "status" of the prospect opportunity. The same was true when we listed a series of diagnostic questions that a life insurance salesperson could ask to establish their credibility. Those questions included the following:

1. *Do you currently have a life insurance policy?*

2. *Was it provided by your employer or did you purchase it separately?*

3. *Is your existing insurance whole life or term?*

4. *How long has this policy been in force?*

5. *How many people are in your immediate family?*

6. *When was the last time you reviewed your insurance needs?*

Once again, these questions are designed to uncover specific facts and information; but because they are narrow in scope, they are very effective tools that you can use to establish credibility. You could try to initiate sales conversations with open-ended Status Questions, but I don't recommend it. Prospects generally aren't ready to open up and give you that much detail until they perceive that a salesperson is indeed credible. Frankly, you'll have lots of opportunities to broaden the scope as you escalate the focus of your questions.

Status Questions Are Low in Mutual Value

Status Questions *do* play a crucial role in sales conversations, but we should invest the time to recognize that Status Questions are lowest in mutual value. What do we mean by that? Ask yourself: how much value does a prospect gain from answering a Status Question? The answer is they get little or no value by answering because they already know the answers to these questions. They already know the status.

> **Secret #76** Status Questions are low in mutual value because prospects aren't learning anything new. They already know the status.

This doesn't mean that we shouldn't ask Status Questions. It simply means that we must recognize that questions that are low in mutual value are merely stepping-stones to more in-depth conversation. It also means you have to be careful not to ask too many Status Questions, as prospects would quickly become bored and impatient with a one-sided conversation. Instead, make it a point to ask enough Status Questions to establish your credibility, and then escalate your conversation on to *Issue Questions*. That's where you will really begin to challenge the customer's thinking and uncover needs that will fuel the rest of the decision process.

Issue Questions

Issue Questions facilitate the first stage of problem solving. They move beyond the status of an opportunity (or the facts), to identify potential issues that are in need of viable solutions. Examples of Issue Questions include:

Seller: *"What's the most significant business issue you currently face?"*

"What would you like to accomplish with this type of product?"

"To what extent is your business growing or changing?"

"What other challenges do you foresee?"

Issue Questions are intentionally broad in scope, because once we have established credibility, we want prospects to openly share. We want to identify potential issues, problems, and desires, but we also want them to expand the conversation by telling us why those issues are important.

To What Extent Is _____ Important?

In almost every sales situation, the template for the first Issue Question I ask is: *To what extent is _____ important?* Just fill in the blank with a relevant issue that's important to the prospect, and you have successfully escalated the focus of your question. Note that unless you have an issue already in mind that's specifically relevant to the customer, you could start by asking: *To what extent is your business (or personal situation) growing or changing?* The reason I open with this particular question is twofold. Asking "to what extent" provides a seamless transition between Status Questions and Issue Questions. It's specific enough to be diagnostic, yet broad enough to generate an in-depth explanation about how the customer is indeed growing or changing. Secondly, change is inevitable in virtually any type of sale. Thus, growth and change serves as a blue-chip starting point because it's always relevant, and the other person will always have an opinion. Whether you're dealing with the CEO of a Fortune 500 company, a spouse, or someone on the lowest rung on the corporate ladder, people will open up and share their thoughts, feelings, and concerns about issues that are relevant and that you might be able to help them address in some way.

> **Secret #77** Asking *To what extent is _____ important?* is a technique that uncovers needs and encourages people to expand their responses.

Asking "to what extent" is also a risk avoidance strategy. I could have simply asked: *Is growth or change affecting your business?* The problem is, prospects could easily mismatch this question because it sounds rhetorical. Of course, growth and change are affecting their business! Rather than risk sounding "canned," I prefer to use the words *to what extent…*

Probe for Gold Medals and German Shepherds

When probing for relevant issues, it is important to remember the motivational differences we talked about in chapter 3. As I explained, while some people are motivated by positive rewards (*Gold Medals*), others are motivated much more by negative aversion (*German Shepherds*). This same concept should also affect the way you probe for and identify potential needs.

The key is asking Issue Questions that probe for both *Gold Medals* and *German Shepherds*. For example, are your prospects more interested in state-of-the-art technology (*Gold Medal*) or eliminating system downtime (*German Shepherd*)? Similarly, you'll want to know if your prospects are more interested in reduced operating expenses (*German Shepherd*) or increasing revenues (*Gold Medal*). These are very different buying motivations. But as we discussed in chapter 3, most prospects are motivated by a combination of *Gold Medals* and *German Shepherds*, which gives salespeople who are willing to probe for both an opportunity to identify twice as many needs.

> **Secret #78** By probing for *Gold Medals* and *German Shepherds*, you have an opportunity to uncover twice as many needs.

Probing for both *Gold Medals* and *German Shepherds* helps salespeople challenge the customer's thinking in a way that will help identify more needs, which gives them an opportunity to provide even greater value, and more easily justify a favorable purchase decision.

Using the Herd Theory to Raise Key Issues

Part of our responsibility as salespeople is helping prospects recognize needs that otherwise wouldn't exist. We talked about turning latent needs into active needs back in chapter 2. Some prospects will respond to your questions with a robust list of issues and concerns. Others will be more reticent, which makes expanding the conversation that much more difficult. If you have ever interviewed a cautious prospect, then you know what I mean.

Rather than pounding away at potential buyers to get them to articulate their needs, you might try leveraging the Herd Theory. Prospects tend to be much more responsive when they find out that other people have similar needs or are already finding value in your solutions. Letting prospects know, for example, that other accounts are also trying to address similar issues like security, management, warranty, support, and product availability gives them comfort. Once you plant the seed that the herd is already moving in a certain direction, in this case, by citing other prospects who have (or have had) certain issues, prospects often recognize that they too have similar requirements.

Urgency Sells!

We know from earlier discussions that complacent people aren't going to buy. They are already satisfied with the status quo, and by definition, the issues that have been raised thus far aren't important enough to justify taking action. The opposite of complacency is urgency, and urgency has the opposite effect on the sales process. The greater the need, the more likely your prospects will feel an urgency to find a solution and make a buying decision.

> **Secret #79** Greater needs cause prospects to feel a greater sense of urgency for finding a solution and making a purchase.

People aren't going to buy just because a problem or a desire surfaces as an issue. Rather, they buy when these issues become detrimental enough, or opportune enough, to justify a purchase. That's why it's critical to uncover the implications of issues that get raised, by asking *Implication Questions*.

Implication Questions

Once a prospect acknowledges an issue as being important, salespeople must probe further to understand specifically *why* the issue is important. When I was selling computer systems, for example, system downtime was often an important issue—one that most people wanted to avoid. But *why* was it important? Was it because end users would complain every time the system went down?

Was it that downtime prevented the company from entering new orders or servicing its existing customers? Was management getting upset? Was downtime costing the company money? If so, how much money?

Implication Questions are designed to get prospects to think about the effects of an issue on their business or in their personal life, because it's the implications that will ultimately justify the decision. Did you do your homework assignment from chapter 2, and build a repository of issues and their related implications? If so, asking implication questions is how you can emotionally transition your sales conversations from just probing about the facts and information (using Status and Issue Questions), to really understanding the emotional drivers that will occur if a pending issue isn't properly addressed.

Here's a quick example of an Implication Question.

Seller:	*"What would happen if your computer system went down and was unavailable for the entire day?"*

Imagine the responses you might get. When you ask Implication Questions about issues that are important to your prospects, they will explain vividly why their issues are critical. But you shouldn't leave it up to your prospects to think of all the reasons to buy your product or service. Invariably, they will fail to raise some key points that could help justify your solution. Perhaps they will name two or three implications out of the ten on your list. Well, who is going to bring up the rest? You are, because it's critical for sellers to proactively bring up implications in order to raise the prospect's awareness to even greater heights. More implications will tend to make their issues larger, which creates a more urgent need for a solution. Are you getting it? Identifying a broader range of issues and implications is your opportunity as a salesperson to be a more valuable resource to your prospects and customers.

Seller:	*"Have you ever calculated how much money every hour of unscheduled downtime is costing your company?"*
	"How does system downtime affect your customers?"
	"How does management feel about recent system problems?"
	"What would happen if your data was lost completely?"

As more and more implications are identified, prospective buyers will begin to feel a greater sense of urgency to find a solution. Wouldn't you rather they have five, ten, or even twenty reasons to make a purchase decision in your favor, instead of only one or two? Literally growing the need through strategic questioning is the value of Implication Questions in the needs development process.

> **Secret #80** The more implications you uncover, the easier it is for prospects to justify a favorable purchase decision.

Although system downtime was the sample issue we expanded upon in the previous example, the same technique applies whether you're selling medical supplies, real estate, financial services, advertising space, pharmaceuticals, or life insurance. It also applies to each and every issue that gets raised. By probing further into more specific implications, you are essentially asking, *"Mr. Prospect, if (issue) becomes a problem, what effect will that have on the different areas of your business (or personal situation, or both)?"*

Issue Questions & Implication Questions Work Together

To increase the value of a sales conversation, QBS teaches sellers to initiate the needs development conversation with Status Questions, using the technique of asking a series of short-answer diagnostic questions. This is an effective strategy because asking relevant questions about the status of the customer helps establish your credibility and earns you the right to ask more in-depth Issue Questions. The underlying concept is sound. Once customers perceive you as a valuable resource, you earn the right to escalate the focus of your questions to identify a broader range of needs. It's like graduating from high school in order to move onto bigger and better things.

The relationship between Issue Questions and Implication Questions is different. Rather than uncovering a bunch of issues and then moving on to ask about the implications of those issues, a back-and-forth strategy is more effective. This includes focusing in and asking a series of Implication Questions to expand on each one of the prospect's issues as they get raised. This process is depicted by the graphic on the right.

To uncover needs in QBS, we use a simple formula. Every time you uncover an issue, you should probe further by asking at least three Implication Questions to understand the prospect's true thoughts, feelings, and concerns about that particular issue. You will want to know how each issue affects their business or how it might impact them personally. The objective of this technique is to expand the issues as they get raised, so prospects will feel a greater sense of urgency to find a solution and ultimately make a decision. This back-and-forth methodology also helps you accomplish the objective of identifying multiple facets of an issue, and gives your prospects multiple reasons to move forward in the sales process.

Once you have successfully expanded an issue, the process repeats. Uncover another issue, and then expand it by uncovering three more implications of that issue. There's no need to make this difficult. To uncover the first issue, you simply ask, *"To what extent is (Issue 1) important?"* When it's time to move on to the next issue, simply ask, *"What about (Issue 2)? To what extent is (Issue 2) important to your business?"*

Does it make sense to raise every possible issue and every corresponding implication to each and every prospect you meet? The answer clearly is no way! But, it's a good rule of thumb to think in terms of 3 × 3 for your initial sales conversations. If you raise three issues and three corresponding implications of those issues, you will be ahead of the game.

Use Global Questions to Develop the Need

What I'm describing is a process of building relationships by enriching and deepening your needs development conversations. Facilitating a valuable needs development conversation is really how you build rapport with potential customers. We want to ask questions that make people feel comfortable enough to openly share their thoughts, feelings, and concerns, but not so many questions that prospects feel *pumped* for information. That's where *Global Questions* come in.

What's a Global Question? Basically, a Global Question is a way to say, *"Tell me more."* But since we don't have the right to "command" prospects and customers what to do, it's always better to use the global questioning technique.

Examples of Global Questions include:

How do you mean?	*And then what?*
How so?	*Like what?*
What happened next?	*How does that work?*

You'll notice that with Global Questions, there is no subject within the question itself. That's because the Global Questions are designed to expand the context of the existing conversation. For example, to expand a comment or statement your prospect makes, you simply respond by asking *How so?* or *What happened next?* Using this technique, you are essentially paying them a compliment by showing you are interested in what they said or what they have asked. Essentially you are inviting them to *please continue.*

Global Questions are easy to deliver, and they are some of the most productive questions you will ever ask—especially if you are trying to encourage prospects to open up and talk about the emotional aspects of a problem or an upcoming purchase decision. To illustrate, suppose you wanted to find out just how important the issue of security was to a prospect's business. Then, you might ask:

Seller:	*"To what extent is security important to your business?"*
Prospect:	*"Security is very important."*
Seller:	*"How do you mean?"*

The salesperson in this example uses a Global Question to probe further and find out why the prospect feels security is important. In a real-life conversation, you can actually feel the tone of a conversation shift when you show additional interest. What's more, Global Questions are extremely practical—much more so than having to concoct a sophisticated-sounding question every time you want to probe for additional information.

You might be surprised to know that the single most effective question I used as a salesperson, and still use today, is the Global Question, *"How do you mean?"* This question is effective because it's extremely nonthreatening. When you ask, *"How do you mean?"* people automatically open up. In fact, whenever you use this Global Question, you can expect two to five paragraphs of additional information from prospects, customers, coworkers, or anyone else—which is a pretty good return on investment for having used only four words. Even though this question is "grammatically challenged," it is one of the most effective ways to find out what people are thinking and feeling.

> **Secret #81** Asking, *"How do you mean?"* will give you great insight into what other people are thinking and feeling.

Be careful, though. Asking, *"How* do you mean?" is very different than asking, *"What* do you mean?" *"What* do you mean?" causes some people to get defensive. When people feel that their opinion is being challenged, they tend to close up—which is counterproductive in a sales conversation. We can absolutely challenge the customer's thinking, but there's no need to pick a fight. This may seem like a trivial distinction, but the difference between "what" and "how" could mean the difference between a budding relationship and a lost opportunity.

Focus on Your Areas of Strength

Using strategic questions to uncover and help identify a prospect's needs gives you tremendous latitude in directing your sales conversations. This is an important point because very few products enjoy superiority in every area, and you will want to focus your conversations on those areas where you provide the most value. For example, if your competitive advantage is quality, you will want to find out *to what extent* quality is important to the prospect. Likewise, if your competitive strength is providing cost-effective solutions, you'll want to find out *to what extent* your prospects are interested in saving money. I'm not suggesting that you should avoid other issues. I'm merely suggesting that it never hurts to tip the scales in your favor by focusing on your areas of strength.

Solution Questions

Solution Questions are valuable closing tools. After you've uncovered your prospect's needs and the implications of those needs, Solution Questions are used to secure the next step in the sales process. This is how you change the focus of your sales conversations from a discussion of issues, and the implications of those issues, to a discussion about the benefits that will come from choosing the right solution.

Solution Questions help balance your sales conversation. On one hand, we want to increase the prospect's sense of urgency. (That's why we use Implication Questions—to make the issues raised seem larger.) On the other hand, we don't want prospects to feel so overwhelmed by the magnitude of a problem that they divert their attention elsewhere. Instead, we want them to be excited about solving the problem. That's where Solution Questions come in. They help prospects recognize that positive emotions like satisfaction and relief are just around the corner from their current levels of frustration, pain, or desire.

What are Solution Questions supposed to look like? I'll illustrate by creating a quick example. Let's say that during your initial meeting with Mr. Jenkins, the assistant director at one of your largest prospects, you successfully uncover several issues and the implications of those issues. You feel that you can offer some real solutions, so to move the opportunity forward, you might ask a Solution Question like:

Salesperson: *"Mr. Jenkins, if this is what you need and that's what we do, would it make sense to schedule a time to get the appropriate people together in front of a piece of paper to map out your options, the impact on your business, and the associated costs?"*

What's the appropriate next step? That depends on what you're selling. The next step might be a technical meeting with a certified engineer or a presentation to the decision committee. Perhaps it would make sense to schedule an executive meeting. Me, I like to suggest that *we schedule a time to get the appropriate people together in front of a piece of paper to map out your options, the impact on your business, and the associated costs.* Note that whenever you're going to "map out" your options, people tend to take the meeting much more seriously, they block more time, and they tend to invite more important people.

Whatever the next step in your sales process is, Solution Questions are excellent closing tools that use the potential value of your offering to secure the prospect's commitment to engage further.

> **Secret #82** Solution Questions motivate prospects to move forward by focusing their attention on solving the problem.

Solution Questions are also great qualifying tools. If your prospect is not willing to move forward, then something's wrong. After all, why would a qualified prospect willingly participate in an in-depth discussion about their issues and the implications of those issues, but then not want to hear more about your solutions?

Make the Next Step Their Idea

Prospects don't want to be "told" and they certainly don't want to be pushed. It's always been my belief that buyers cannot be forced to take the next step in the sales process, so there's little point in trying to push them. As we said in chapter 5, the harder you push, the harder your prospects and customers will push back. That's why it's smart to make closing their idea.

In chapter 7, QBS introduced you to one of the fundamental principles of engagement. We said that prospects who are curious will want to engage, while prospects who are not curious won't. This same principle applies when asking Solution Questions. If your prospects are indeed curious, they will *want* to find out more about how your solutions address their specific needs. How can you make prospects curious? By asking Solution Questions that give prospects *a glimpse of value* for how they can improve their existing condition.

Another Opportunity to Be Creative

Solution Questions are usually hypothetical. Essentially, you're posing a question to your prospects that asks, *If we can show you how to solve your outstanding problems, would you like to know more about the solutions we offer?* Another way to get prospects to focus on benefits rather than problems is to ask them to visualize the perfect solution. You can easily accomplish this by asking them Solution Questions like:

Seller:	*"Mr. Prospect, in your mind, what would the ideal solution to this problem/issue look like?"*

–or–

Seller:	*"If money was no object in your decision, what would you do to solve this problem?"*

One caution: be careful not to ask Solution Questions too early in the needs development process. The reason? You have to get prospects to open up before you can close. Solution Questions end the discovery process because they dangle your potential solutions out in front of a prospective buyer, asking *Would you like to know how our products or services can add value?* Asking Solution Questions too early puts you at risk, because you will end up moving forward before you have uncovered enough needs and implications to justify a favorable decision. (Of course, this is a moot point if you properly develop the need before dangling your solutions.)

Summary

Asking sales questions isn't without irony. Faced with the pressure and anxiety that often accompany a sales call, inexperienced salespeople sometimes panic when prospects seem standoffish or reluctant to answer Status Questions. Not wanting to upset the prospect further by asking even more questions, sellers jump prematurely into their sales pitch. In the strategic sale, this is a mistake because it's impossible to present valuable solutions without first developing the need.

What these sellers fail to realize is that important prospects appreciate being asked important questions. They want to talk about their issues, problems, and concerns, because they need valuable solutions. Once you understand this, you can literally watch prospects perk up as you escalate the focus of your questions, thereby raising the value of your sales conversations.

> **Secret #83** Prospects are motivated to respond when they recognize that by helping a salesperson, they're actually helping themselves.

People love to talk about themselves. They also love to talk about issues that are important to them. Using the techniques and strategies we outlined in this chapter, you can help prospects satisfy their own needs by engaging them in more productive sales conversation. It's truly a win-win situation.

Chapter 10

HOW TO SOLICIT MORE ACCURATE FEEDBACK

Disposition is the third attribute that characterizes strategic questions in QBS. It refers to the tone of your questions. Most sales questions are delivered with a certain degree of positive hopefulness, because the salesperson is hoping to receive a positive response. But just the opposite happens, as "hopeful" questions are more likely to induce caution, which generates less information and less accurate responses.

In this chapter, you will learn how to solicit more open, honest, and accurate feedback from your prospects, customers, friends, and coworkers—by neutralizing the disposition of your questions.

Early in the sales process, prospective buyers are cautious and reluctant when responding to questions, mostly because the salesperson hasn't yet earned enough credibility to gain their trust. Later on in the sale, prospects may still be cautious and reluctant when responding to questions—but now it's because they don't want to say something that would either jeopardize their negotiating position or be detrimental to their relationship with *you.*

This creates a problem for salespeople, because prospects who are cautious or reluctant aren't likely to provide open, honest, and accurate feedback. Rather than tell you exactly how they feel, they tend to hold back. The net result of being on the receiving end of sketchy or incomplete information is that it's difficult to know where you stand in the sale. Thus, your ability to manage the sales process is significantly impaired.

Accuracy Is the Objective

Accurate information is one of your most valuable assets in selling. It's critical to know exactly where the prospect stands and what else needs to occur to complete the transaction. Accurate information is also important because if a transaction is not going to happen, you want to know so you can refocus your efforts on something else that's more productive.

It's always valuable to know about things that are going well, but it's critical that salespeople know when something is wrong. Particularly in the strategic sale, many of the decision factors that will influence the outcome of a sale are constantly in a state of flux. Sometimes, a sale will take a turn for the better. Other times, problems are brewing within an account, and it's imperative that the salesperson know exactly what's happening. In Question Based Selling, we've adopted the premise that the only way sellers can effectively manage a sale is to recognize and become aware of potential problems or issues as they arise.

How can sellers be aware of potential problems when they occur? It would be easy to suggest that salespeople should just ask their prospects for an updated status. But guess what? Most prospects are reluctant to share bad news with an eager salesperson, and most salespeople aren't particularly good at asking for it anyway.

> **Secret #84** Prospects are reluctant to share bad news, and most sales-people aren't particularly good at asking for it.

Unfortunately, when sellers don't have complete and accurate information, they sometimes blame the prospect, thinking that customers should be more forthright. In QBS, we take the opposite tack. Instead of blaming potential buyers, we find that the quality of the information you receive is more a function of the questions you ask. To show you what I mean, let's take a look at what happens when a salesperson asks "hopeful" questions.

Do You Ask Hopeful Questions?

Asking questions in sales can be a risky proposition—particularly the hard questions, where salespeople are trying to qualify an opportunity or secure a prospect's commitment to move forward. What if the prospect says no or *We're going to purchase your competitor's product*? What if they raise an objection you can't resolve? With the potential for bad news lurking on the other side of every question, probing the status of an opportunity can be an intimidating task.

Let's be honest. Most salespeople don't want to hear bad news. They don't

want to find out that an opportunity may be slipping away or that their investment in time, effort, and energy may have been wasted.

> **Secret #85** The risk of failure and the possibility of hearing bad news makes the "hard" questions in sales very difficult to ask.

As a result, salespeople who are averse to hearing bad news tend to bias
their questions toward the positive. Rather than probing for information, they
probe for positive information. And rather than soliciting open, honest, and
accurate feedback, they deliver questions with a positive tone, hoping to avoid
an unfavorable response. It's as if they're saying, *"Mr. Prospect, please spare my
feelings by telling me what I want to hear."*

For example, if a salesperson was trying to close an important deal by the
end of the month, he might ask: *"Mr. Prospect, are we still in good shape to
complete this deal by the end of the month?"* Notice that this salesperson is not
asking for bad news. Rather, he is very specifically asking if the sale is still "in
good shape."

Another salesperson might come at it from a different angle by saying,
"Our solution looks really good, doesn't it?" Or, *"Are you happy with the information we've provided thus far?"* Some might even ask: *"Are you as excited as we are
about entering into a business relationship?"*

These are all "hope-filled" questions. You can literally feel the hopefulness
in the wording of the question, and the way in which it's delivered. In each of
these questions, the salesperson is obviously hoping to hear a positive response.
They are hoping to be *"in good shape"* to complete a sale by the end of the
month. They are also hoping that their solution *"looks really good,"* and that the
prospect is *"happy with the information"* that has already been provided. The
last salesperson is even hoping that the prospect is *"as excited as they are"* about
entering into a business relationship.

> **Secret #86** Salespeople who bias their questions positively are hoping that prospects will tell them what they *want to hear.*

In QBS, we say these questions are positively *dispositioned.* This means they
have a built-in tone that is biased toward the positive. People ask positively
dispositioned questions when they are hoping for good news or when they are
feeling some risk. You can even watch someone who asks a positive question
bob their head up and down with a certain puppy-dog hopefulness, as if to
encourage the other person to give a more positive response.

Do you ask hopeful questions? If so, you are limiting the value and depth of the responses you will receive from whomever you ask.

The fact that salespeople are reluctant to ask for bad news is understandable—after all, who wants to invite trouble, especially when things seem to be going well? But have you ever thought about why prospects are reluctant to share? It's one of the great ironies of selling. When a prospect senses that you are hoping for good news, they are more likely to respond cautiously and diplomatically, rather than openly and honestly. As a result, you end up getting incomplete and less accurate information.

Being the Bearer of Bad News

No one likes to deliver bad news, particularly when the message being conveyed is not what the other person wants to hear. For example, suppose you are invited to your friend Linda's house for dinner. After a five-course meal, it's obvious that Linda is very proud of her accomplishment as a hostess, but you thought the food was terrible. If, at the end of the evening, Linda, in her most hopeful tone, asks, "How was everything?" would you be completely honest? Really? Most people wouldn't, because we would not want to hurt Linda's feelings. Frankly, we would rather sidestep the issue, make up something, or even tell a little fib, because it's very difficult to be totally honest when you know that the whole truth is not what the other person wants to hear.

> **Secret #87** Most people would rather sidestep a difficult issue, or make up a convenient excuse, than be the bearer of bad news.

Prospects are often faced with this type of situation when they are dealing with an energetic salesperson whose livelihood depends on hearing good news. It's very possible that the prospect will not be ready to complete a transaction by the end of the month. Perhaps the budget was cut, or the company is leaning toward a competitor's product. Whatever the reason, if bad news is brewing, prospects are reluctant to share when they know it's not what the salesperson wants to hear.

Salespeople Don't Handle Rejection Well

In addition to protecting our delicate egos, prospects have also learned (through experience) that many salespeople don't handle rejection well. When an opportunity seems to be headed south, rather than thank prospects for their time and graciously bow out, salespeople are trained to persist. I remember listening to a sales training CD set early on in my career where the trainer's motto was, if you're going to lose a sale, you might as well go down in flames.

Almost every prospect you call on has had to deal with a salesperson who wouldn't take no for an answer. *What do you mean you're not going to buy our product? I've worked on this deal for months! Let's schedule another presentation or meet with the committee again.* When the prospect turns them down, the seller goes over their heads, calling their boss or anyone else who will listen. As a result, prospects have been conditioned to play it close to the vest, rather than sharing their thoughts and concerns with an overzealous salesperson who might go berserk at the first sign of rejection.

Soliciting Open, Honest, and Accurate Information

Soliciting feedback from your prospects and customers isn't difficult. What's difficult is soliciting open, honest, and accurate feedback. This means knowing the total picture, which includes positive information as well as any potential problems, pending bad news, or constructive feedback.

The question is, if problems or issues are brewing in one of your prospect accounts, do you want to know about it? If the answer is yes, then a small adjustment in strategy will make it okay for prospects to openly share both good news and bad. As a result, you'll receive more open, honest, and accurate information.

> **Secret #88** If you want open, honest, and accurate responses, then you need to make it okay for prospects to openly share.

How can salespeople make it okay for prospects to openly share? The answer is, by neutralizing the disposition of your questions. Rather than asking hopeful sales questions with the hope of receiving a more positive response, this QBS technique of neutralizing the disposition of your questions will enable you to have more productive sales conversations by replacing hopefulness with accuracy.

Neutralize the Disposition of Your Questions

Neutralizing the disposition of your questions is easy. Simply offer the prospect a choice to respond either positively or constructively. For example, in an earlier illustration the salesperson asked, *"Mr. Prospect, are we still in good shape to complete this deal by the end of the month?"* As is, this question is biased with a certain positive hopefulness that encourages prospects not to share openly and honestly. To ensure a more productive response, I would much rather neutralize the disposition of this question, by asking, *"Are we still in good shape to complete this deal by the end of the month, or do you think something might cause it to be delayed?"*

By repositioning the tone of the question, I am giving this prospect a chance to agree that either yes, we are in good shape to complete the deal by the end of the month, or no, something might cause it to be delayed. In essence, I have invited the prospect to share the whole story, which includes good news as well as any potential problems or concerns.

This technique can be applied to everyday life. Whether you're posing questions to your prospects, your boss, or even to your spouse, you will get a more accurate response if you give them the opportunity to answer either positively or constructively. Below are some sample neutral questions.

To a Prospect: *"Ms. Prospect, would it be possible to meet later in the week…or would that put a burden on your schedule?"*

To Your Spouse: *"Honey, do you feel like making dinner tonight…or is that too much to ask after a long day with the kids?"*

To Your Boss: *"Would it be okay for me to take a week's vacation during the holidays…or no?"*

As you may be noticing, neutral questions are not hopeful in their delivery, nor do they urge a more positive response. Instead, neutral questions are designed to solicit open, honest, and accurate feedback by making people comfortable enough to share their true thoughts, feelings, and concerns.

Introducing the Negative

A question is neutralized when you introduce the negative. This is not a defensive strategy, however. In fact, it's just the opposite. By asking prospects for both good news and bad, you take the pressure off by inviting them to give you an honest response. It's a terrific way to let people know that you are a professional who is more interested in dealing with the actual needs of your customers, rather than someone who's just pursuing his or her own interests.

Neutralizing the disposition of your questions is also easier than you might think. Just add four letters (*o, r, n, o*). By appending the phrase "*or no*" onto the end of any positive question, you automatically invite the other person to share both good news and bad. Perhaps you noticed this technique just now, in the example where the employee asked, *"Would it be okay for me to take a week's vacation during the holidays...or no?"*

Introducing the negative into your sales questions doesn't guarantee a favorable response. That's fine, because we're not trying to manipulate prospects into saying yes. The truth is, you may *not* be in good shape to get the deal by month-end, or it may *not* be okay to take vacation during the holidays. But, the only way to know exactly where you stand is to have a complete and accurate status—and neutralizing the disposition of your questions *does* guarantee more open, honest, and accurate information.

> **Secret #89** Having an accurate read on your sales opportunities gives you a strategic advantage over your competition.

Competent professionals aren't afraid of hearing bad news, and they don't ask questions positively, hoping to generate a more favorable response. Instead, they would rather deal with important business issues by introducing "the negative" as an integral part of their questioning strategy, as opposed to beating around the bush with a less direct approach.

The Emotional Rescue

Critics of this technique could argue that "neutralizing" the disposition of your questions gives the prospect an "out." I disagree. I would argue that most prospects already have an out. Unless you represent a monopoly, the people you call on are well aware they are under no obligation to buy from you.

But consider this. We have already talked about neutral questions, and how they make prospects feel more comfortable about sharing *bad* news. Neutral questions are good because they give sellers a chance to discover any problems or issues that may be brewing within one of their prospect accounts. When *good* news is brewing, however, it's a whole different story.

People are reluctant to share bad news when they know it's not what the other person wants to hear. On the other hand, sharing good news makes people feel great. So guess what happens when you neutralize the disposition of your questions? Actually, two things happen. First, if there are any problems brewing, you will find out about them. Secondly, if there's good news, prospects will not only share the good news, they will be emphatically positive. In QBS, we call this reflexive behavior the *emotional rescue*.

By definition, the emotional rescue is a mismatch. But rather than asking positive questions and having prospects push back against the positive, you can leverage the negative disposition of your questions to let those same prospects rescue you. Let's take an example. Earlier, we rephrased a sample closing question (and neutralized its hopefulness) by asking: *"Are we still in good shape to complete this deal by the end of the month, or do you think something might cause it to be delayed?"* If this deal is truly at risk of being delayed, the neutral disposition of this question invites the prospect to share any bad news. We talked about this already. But if the opposite is true, and you are indeed in "good shape" to get the deal, prospects will quickly rescue you by saying: *"No, no…everything is fine! The order is being approved. Don't worry. I'm all over it."* I don't know about you, but this is the kind of emotional support I like to receive from prospects.

> **Secret #90** Inserting the negative into your sales questions causes positive responses from prospects to become emphatically more positive.

Talk about irony! For all this time, people have been asking hopeful questions in the hopes of receiving a more positive response. Lo and behold, exactly the opposite happens. When you insert "the negative" into your sales questions, people will jump to your emotional rescue.

Test it out for yourself. Walk up to someone and say, *Excuse me, but am I interrupting?* Then listen carefully to see how they respond. More often than not, they will rescue you saying, *No…no, it's okay. I was just getting ready for an appointment. What can I do for you?*

You will see this technique used throughout Question Based Selling, particularly in chapter 12 when we talk about contacting new prospects. I use it all the time. Whether I'm calling a business contact or a friend, I always open the call off by saying, *"Hi, Jim, this is Tom Freese. Did I catch you at a bad time?"* Notice the disposition of my question. There's a high probability that Jim will rescue me by saying, *"No…no, this is fine. What's up?"* As you will see later when we talk about calling new prospects, you must be purposeful in your opening before asking if it's a bad time.

Of course, Jim might say, *"Tom, I'm sorry, but this is not a good time. I've got a bunch of people in my office."* That's good information to have because if Jim is truly busy, blindly plowing ahead with the call would have created an awkward situation for both of us. I'd rather know right off the bat that it's a bad time, so I can ask, *"When should I call you back?"* When Jim gives me a time to call back, now I have an appointment.

The emotional rescue is *not* a manipulation tactic to get people to buy something they don't need. And please, don't even think about approaching your prospects and saying, *"You don't want to buy any of this junk, do you?"* in the hopes that they will rescue you. That is *not* how this technique works.

Neutralizing the disposition of your questions is a strategy for making people feel more comfortable. It takes the edge off and makes it easy for prospects and customers to respond openly, honestly, and accurately. It also makes the "hard" questions easier to ask, because when you know you are going to get a more productive response, your risk (in asking) is significantly reduced.

> **Secret #91** By making it easy for prospects and customers to respond, the "hard" questions become much easier to ask.

It all boils down to one simple question: Would you rather have prospects and customers invite you in or hold you at arm's length? In other words, since we know that mismatching is an instinctive behavioral tendency, would you rather have prospects pushing back against the positive in your questions, or rescuing you from the negative? I would much rather be rescued, and therefore, invited in—which is why I neutralize the disposition of my sales questions.

Humbling Disclaimers

Using *humbling disclaimers* is another way to get prospects to openly share. What's a humbling disclaimer? A humbling disclaimer is an assertion that precedes a statement or question with the purpose of injecting humility and procuring a more productive response. That's a mouthful, I know.

Would you agree that humility is a very attractive human quality? Sellers can leverage this quality by neutralizing their questions, using humbling disclaimers to lower the prospect's defenses. Examples of humbling disclaimers include:

Salesperson: *"I'm not sure how to ask this, but…"*

"Without being too forward, can I ask about…"

"At the risk of getting in trouble, would you mind if…"

"I don't want to ask the wrong thing, but…"

Humbling disclaimers give other people in the conversations a chance to rescue you before you even deliver the question. Again, I encourage you to test it out for yourself. In your next sales call, when you want to ask about something delicate in nature (like the prospect's budget), simply precede your question with a humbling disclaimer. Something like: *"I don't mean to push, but can I ask you about the budget for this project?"* Before you even make it to the real question, your prospect will be reassuring you, saying, *"No…no, it's okay… you can ask about the budget."* Bingo!

> **Secret #92** Humbling disclaimers give other people an opportunity to "rescue" you before you even deliver the question.

Humbling disclaimers also help to soften your questions. Besides making prospects feel more comfortable, humility lets them know that you are not just another high-pressure salesperson who won't take no for an answer.

Being Humble Doesn't Mean You Should Apologize

When you make a mistake, in life or in business, you should apologize. But you should not have to apologize for doing your job as a salesperson. I make the point to distinguish between using humility as a conversational tool and apologizing unnecessarily.

One of my former office mates used to begin every sales call with an apology. He would start off the call by saying, *"Hi, Ms. Prospect, my name is Jeff, and I'm with XYZ Company. I'm really sorry to bother you, but I wanted to see if I could get just a few minutes of your time to talk about…"*

Prospects tend to form their impressions very quickly, and opening your sales calls with an apology is not the message you want to be sending. If you want to be perceived as a competent professional, then it's important to act like one, which does not include begging, groveling, or doing anything else that will reduce your credibility or disparage yourself as being unimportant.

Asking the Hard Questions

As the sale progresses, you will come to a crossroads where it's time to ask the prospect if they are ready to move forward. Asking closing questions are essential to making deals happen; but for those salespeople who do not want to hear bad news, closing questions can be very difficult to ask.

We'll talk more about closing the sale in Part III of the QBS methodology. For now, I want to make the point that hopeful questions are especially counterproductive when you are trying to close sales. When you are nearing the end of the sales process, you must know exactly where an opportunity stands. That's why I always make it a point to ask questions in a way that invites the prospect to openly share. Here are some examples of closing questions that I would be likely to ask:

Seller: *"Is it a fair question to ask your impression?"*

"Mr. Prospect, are we at risk of losing this business?"

"If you were the salesperson on this account, what would you be doing differently?"

By inviting prospects to openly share, you may find out that you are *not* in good shape to get the sale. Some people view this as bad news. To me, it's an opportunity to make a conscious decision about how best to proceed, either by addressing the outstanding issues, or cutting your losses and reallocating your selling resources elsewhere.

You can also use "the negative" to smoke out any issues or objections that are preventing an opportunity from moving forward. As we said earlier, some prospects are reluctant to share their problems and concerns, especially with a salesperson. That's why I ask questions like:

Seller: *"Something is holding you back, isn't it?"*

"Is it just me, or is something bothering you about this proposal?"

"What other concerns do you have, if any?"

Negative dispositioning allows salespeople to be very direct without being overly aggressive. This is a quality your prospects (and your sales manager) will greatly appreciate. Even you will be amazed at the openness and the value of the responses you receive.

Ask Prospects to Predict the Outcome of the Sale

Another way to find out where you stand in the sale is to ask your prospects to predict the outcome of the sale. Essentially, you invite them to become part of the process by helping to accurately assess the status of an opportunity. But rather than revert to the "hopeful" approach, it's much more productive to ask questions that will produce open, honest, and accurate responses, questions like:

Seller: *"Mr. Prospect, my boss keeps asking when this sale is going to close. I would much rather be accurate than optimistic, so should I tell him that we are in good shape to complete the deal by the end of the month, or should I tell him not to get his hopes up?"*

"Realistically, what are the chances your management will approve this deal before year-end?"

"If you were a betting man, would you say this deal is getting ready to close, or would you say we're at risk?"

All of these are great trial closes, and unless a prospect is intentionally stringing you along, they will come forward with information that will tell you exactly where you stand in the sale.

Also Good for Building Champions

Neutralizing the disposition of your questions also serves as a great tool for developing internal champions. There are people out there who will love the solution you have proposed. But since most prospects have not had any formal sales training, they won't know how to position the value of your product or service to others who also need to sign off on the decision. Before their boss or someone else on the decision committee puts them on the spot, you may want to ask some of the tougher questions to see how they respond. This will tell you how much additional coaching they might need. For example, I always make it a point to ask questions like:

Seller: *"What will you do if your boss says the price is too high?"*

"What if someone on the committee wants to delay the project?"

"What if they ask about different maintenance options?"

If your champion has the answers to these questions down pat, this exercise will boost their confidence. But if they hesitate, you can work with them to reinforce key points that support a decision for your offering.

Secret #93 Negative dispositioning gives sellers an opportunity to see how well champions will handle the "tough" questions.

Summary

Competent sales professionals aren't afraid of hearing bad news, and they don't ask positive questions in the hopes of receiving more positive responses. Instead, they want to know exactly where they stand in the sale in order to know what else needs to occur to complete a transaction. That's why complete and accurate feedback is so important. By learning how to neutralize the disposition of your questions, you will solicit more accurate responses from prospects and customers. Not only will this boost your sales and your confidence, it will give you a strategic advantage over your competition—who are all out there asking a ton of hopeful questions.

Part Three

Implementation:
Putting Methods into Practice

Part 3 of *The Secrets of Question Based Selling* is where the rubber meets the road. Thus far in QBS, we've talked about strategies for increasing your probability and reducing your risk; we've given you the tools to engage more prospects in more productive sales conversations; and we've shown you how to manage the *scope, focus, and disposition* of your questions. Now, it's time to take an in-depth look at the QBS sales process to see how a question based approach can help you penetrate new accounts, get to the right people, build value in your sales presentations, and ultimately close more sales.

Strategic questions play an important role in the implementation of the QBS methodology. In addition to piquing interest, establishing credibility, and uncovering needs, strategic questions are powerful tools that can be used to navigate the sale. They put you in control of the sales process by allowing you to set the pace, content, and direction of your conversations. They also help you find out where you stand in the opportunity so you can determine what else needs to occur to bring the sale to fruition.

Come with us now as we show you how to implement QBS techniques and strategies into a proven sales model that will enable you to put this methodology into practice.

Chapter 11

NAVIGATING THE SALES PROCESS

To achieve your goals in the profession of selling, you must have a proven and repeatable sales model that produces consistent results. Your model must lead qualified prospects and customers through the decision making process, and it must effectively lead them toward the desired result.

In this chapter, we introduce you to the QBS sales process. As a proven and repeatable sales model, the QBS approach will show you how to accomplish your goals using the most powerful tool in sales—the strategic question.

I have always believed there's no such activity as selling. Salespeople don't just walk into their offices in the morning, sit down at their desks, and begin to "sell." While it is true that we do tend to wrap everything in our daily routines together under the heading of selling, we make the point in Question Based Selling that selling is not an activity…it's a process.

You can't just start selling. You can, however, initiate sales calls to generate qualified leads. You can also solicit referrals, send correspondence, and call new prospects to engage them in productive conversations about what they might need. And, as an opportunity progresses, you can work with prospects to demonstrate solutions, handle objections, justify the purchase, and consummate mutually beneficial transactions.

From a methodology perspective, there is a huge difference between selling and identifying the specific sales steps, activities, and events that need to occur in order to motivate qualified buyers to move forward in the sales process and toward the desired result.

> **Secret #94** In QBS, "selling" is not an activity...it's a process.

Without exception, the most successful salespeople are the ones who follow a consistent and repeatable process model. Rather than just trying to "sell" a product or service, they take the time to identify each of the component steps that will ultimately lead to a successful sale, and then they organize those steps into a proven success formula that's both easy to understand and easy to implement. Now the question is, what should your specific sales model look like?

The Evolution of a Sales Process

To get our arms around the desired sales process, we must first identify the component steps that are necessary to have a successful interaction with a qualified prospect. If this were a live QBS seminar, I would grab a marker and ask you (the audience) to help me compile a typical list of sales steps onto a flip chart. Here's a list that was created during a recent QBS program.

Identify Leads	Follow-up	Demonstration
Qualify	References	Site Visits
Initial Meeting	Handle Objections	Negotiate
Presentation	Proposal	Close

After identifying the components of the sales process, the simplest way to organize these steps is chronologically. This creates a linear sales model.

The linear model is one way of representing the sales process. It gives salespeople a mental image of the events and activities that must occur, and the order in which they occur, from the beginning of the process to the completion of a sale. The diagram below depicts a linear sales model.

Particularly in the strategic sale, a linear sales model loses some of its luster once we begin to realize that it's only two-dimensional. Essentially, it's a sequential list of sales events and activities plotted against a time line. While this does help to identify possible next steps, a linear model does not prioritize the importance of individual events. It also does not account for the fact that prospects are different and every sales situation is unique.

Another way to characterize the sales process is to make the presentation of value the central event. The typical salesperson feels most comfortable when talking about the value of their product or service, so it's easy to gravitate to the idea that presenting features and benefits is the watershed event in the sale. Of course, this changes our image of the sales process from a linear model to one that revolves around a central event (as pictured). But in most strategic sales, the presentation of value is not the most important event. It's just one of many steps that must occur for an opportunity to move closer to a mutual business transaction. In fact, you'll find in Question Based Selling that the *Presentation* phase of the sales process doesn't require nearly as much time, effort, or resources as the *Interest Generation* phase or the *Closing Steps* phase.

Introducing the QBS Sales Process

As the sales process continues to evolve, we recognize that it's important to identify each of the component steps in the sale, but it's also important to consider the issue of resource allocation—where to spend your time, effort, and resources to maximize the greatest return on your effort. In QBS, we give consideration to these factors by taking a more holistic view of the sales process and breaking the larger sale down into three distinct phases. These phases are *Interest Generation*, *Presentation*, and *Closing Steps*.

Successfully engaging new prospects, presenting solutions, and closing sales is not as easy as one, two, three, however, and we certainly don't want to trivialize or oversimplify the strategic sale. That's why the QBS process model includes two other unique characteristics: an hourglass-shaped outer shell, and an embedded sales funnel. By characterizing the sales process in this way, QBS gives salespeople a blueprint that's generic enough to implement across a wide range of industries and customer scenarios, yet specific enough to implement with consistent and repeatable success.

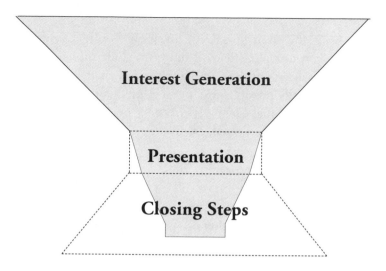

The hourglass shape represents the distribution of effort in each of the three phases in the QBS sales process. Unless you're selling a pure commodity, the majority of your time, effort, and resources will be spent in the *Interest Generation* and *Closing Steps* phases. It sometimes takes months of positioning and persistence to break into a brand-new prospect account and get them to agree to sit through a sales presentation. It can be just as time consuming to work with prospects following the presentation to justify a purchase and bring it to closure.

The *Presentation,* on the other hand, is usually a one-time event. Granted, there are larger sales that will require more than one presentation, but it's still a pass-through event. And while it's a very important event, the presentation itself usually represents a much smaller investment in time, effort, and resources than the other two phases of the sales process. Most salespeople spend only a small fraction of their time delivering presentations compared to all the time they spend generating interest and closing sales.

> **Secret #95** Most of your invested sales effort is spent generating interest and moving prospects forward toward closure.

In addition to its hourglass shape, the QBS sales process also features an embedded sales funnel. No matter how well a territory is organized, sellers cannot escape the fact that selling is ultimately a numbers game. A large pool of targeted accounts will yield some lesser number of qualified opportunities; then, depending on your qualifying criteria, the actual number of prospects who are ready, willing, and able to make a decision will naturally funnel down to an even smaller number of closable transactions.

This narrowing of opportunities doesn't mean you're doing a bad job. It simply means that not every prospect you call on is a qualified lead. Some prospects won't have needs. Others won't have the money, the authority, or the sense of urgency to make a buying decision. Put it this way. If you succeed in selling to every prospect you call on, your price is either too low or you're not calling enough people—Macro Economics 101.

This funneling effect creates an interesting phenomenon with respect to resource distribution. In the top of the funnel, in the *Interest Generation* phase, the amount of effort invested (by a salesperson) is diluted across a broad number of prospect opportunities. At the bottom of the funnel, roughly the same amount of sales effort is concentrated on a smaller number of qualified deals. This means a salesperson's invested effort *per prospect* increases dramatically as an opportunity moves forward in the sales process. This is particularly significant later in QBS when we talk about moving opportunities toward closure and securing the prospect's commitment to buy.

Moving the Opportunity Forward

Whether a prospect enters the sales process on their own or you initiate contact via a sales call, it's up to you to pique their interest and keep them engaged. I make the point about keeping them engaged because very few strategic sales are consummated during the initial conversation. It's rare that a prospect becomes so interested that they make a purchase decision on the spot. It's more likely that prospects who become interested will want more information. They'll want to see a detailed presentation or talk with customers who are already using your product or service.

But engaging potential buyers is only the beginning of the journey. We must also move them forward in the sales process. This means that we must generate enough interest in Phase I (*Interest Generation*) to move qualified prospects on to Phase II (the *Presentation*). Once we are in Phase II, we must accumulate enough value to motivate them to move forward into Phase III (*Closing Steps*).

> **Secret #96** Sellers must accumulate enough value to get their prospects to *want* to move into the next phase of the sales process.

Phase I: Interest Generation

Everything that happens at the beginning of the QBS sales process is designed to generate interest—to pique the prospect's curiosity and get him or her to want more information about the value you offer. That's why we call it *Interest Generation*. In Phase I, prospects enter the sales process as the result of interest generation activities like initial sales calls, trade shows, seminars, mass mailings, and special promotions. The initial phase of the QBS sales process is represented by the top of the embedded sales funnel.

Our objective in Phase I is simply to generate enough interest to move potential buyers onto Phase II. How do you generate interest? The three ways we have discussed so far in Question Based Selling include: making prospects curious (chapter 7), establishing credibility (chapter 8), and uncovering needs that fuel the prospect's sense of urgency (chapters 3 and 9). We also showed you how to leverage the Herd Theory in chapter 4 to increase your ability to motivate prospects to *want* to move forward.

Since our objective in Phase I is motivating prospects to "want to" move forward into Phase II, one might view Phase I as the least important part of the sales process. Don't let yourself fall into this trap. Your success in sales will likely be determined by your ability to pique the prospect's interest, uncover needs, and establish credibility—all of which occur in Phase I.

> **Secret #97** Salespeople who are the most effective in Phase I typically have the largest pipelines and the greatest sales results.

Phase II: The Presentation

People often think of the sales presentation as a formal event, but it doesn't have to be. Depending on the product, some sales are geared more toward a one-on-one presentation—like when an insurance agent sits down with an individual prospect to discuss a new policy. In most corporate sales, the presentation is usually accompanied by some degree of pomp and circumstance to make an impact on the audience and to differentiate the message.

The presentation is the pivot point of the sales process. Once you have generated enough interest to get prospects into Phase II, the sales presentation is your opportunity to educate them on the value of your solutions so they will want to continue into Phase III (*Closing Steps*).

Phase III: Closing Steps

Phase III of the sales process is where buyers and sellers come together to agree on the terms and conditions of a sale, and wrap up the business transaction. In QBS, we take the position that you can't force prospective customers to buy a product or service they don't really want. Instead, they must conclude the value of your product or service is great enough to justify its cost. How prospects arrive at this conclusion is often determined by what transpires after the sales presentation.

The steps required to close a sale will depend on the opportunity. Some buyers will want proof—references or testimonials that support the suppositions and key points made during the presentation. Other prospects, especially those who focus on the monetary aspects of a decision, might be more interested in seeing financial projections that will justify the purchase.

Ultimately, your objective in Phase III is closing the sale. That means securing the prospect's commitment to choose your product or service. While this sounds straightforward, it's a little ironic that your ability to close sales in Phase III usually depends on how effective you were at generating interest in Phase I, and presenting your solutions in Phase II.

Who Controls the Process?

As much as you might wish it would, the sales process does not move forward by itself. It needs a catalyst—someone who can control the process and make sure opportunities are headed in the right direction.

Who controls the sales process? The answer to this question depends on what you believe. Some people choose to believe the customer is always right. They rationalize that since the customer has the need, the budget, and the authority to make a decision, they should be in control of the sales process.

While I do agree that customers ultimately control their own destiny, I will argue that it's problematic to assume they should control the sales process. Here's why. If you assume that *the customer is always right*, then you have to assume they already know everything about your product or service. You also have to assume that they fully understand their own problems and know how best to proceed in addressing them. If this were truly the case, why would anyone ever need a salesperson? Obviously, these assumptions are incorrect. Not only that, assuming that the customer is always right leaves salespeople in the undesirable position of having to ask what hoop to jump through next, rather than leading prospects through the sales process toward a mutual exchange of value.

> **Secret #98** If you believe the old saying *the customer is always right*, you forfeit your opportunity to add value in the sales process.

Expecting customers to control the sales process itself opens a salesperson up to significant risk. If the buyer is inexperienced and doesn't know how best to proceed, your opportunity can quickly get off track. If you are dealing with an experienced buyer, relinquishing control of the sales process invites them to concoct a long list of to-dos and action items that may not move you any closer to making a sale. In either case, you don't want to put yourself in a position where the prospect tells you to jump, and then you have to ask, *"How high?"*

When Larry Dawson first started selling communications equipment to small and medium-sized businesses in the Southeast, he didn't want to be perceived as too aggressive. Some of Larry's accounts were candidates for upgrading their existing systems. Others were first-time buyers. But because Larry was timid about taking control of the sales process, he asked questions like: *"What would you like me to do next?"* He put himself at the mercy of prospective buyers, many of whom wanted to find out just how high Larry was willing to jump. Here's how some of Larry's conversations went:

Larry:	*"What would you like me to do next?"*
Prospect:	*"Well…first, I need a list of twenty local references who all have the exact configuration that you proposed."*
Larry:	*"Twenty? Are you sure you need that many?"*
Prospect:	*"Yes! …And I want you to prepare a detailed cost justification document to present to our board of directors.*
	"…And I also want your proposal broken down by cost center and resubmitted by this Friday.
	"…And I need a detailed price list showing the maximum discounts we can expect.
	"…And I want a document that shows how your solutions compare to other competitive products.
	"…And…and…and…and…and…"

Like many other sellers who have tried this approach, Larry had good intentions. He wanted to be attentive to the prospect's needs and responsive to their requests. The only problem is, by asking the prospect to control the sales process Larry extended an open invitation for them to create a long list of action items that will have him chasing his tail for weeks.

Buyers *do* need direction from salespeople. At the very least, they need clues that will show them how best to proceed. As a salesperson, you're the expert. You have the skills and experience to help identify potential problems and you can give prospects a vision for how those problems can be addressed. So rather than asking prospects: *"What would you like me to do next?"* it's critical that salespeople take a proactive role in the sales process, helping lead prospects through those steps that must occur to successfully complete a transaction.

> **Secret #99** Buyers need direction from sellers, or at the very least, clues that will show them how best to proceed.

In reality, prospects don't always understand their own problems, and they certainly don't always know how best to proceed in addressing them. Moreover, every prospect is different, and every sale is unique. That's where you (the salesperson) have an opportunity to add value—by taking a leadership position and helping prospects uncover needs, investigate alternatives, and evaluate the benefits of your proposed solutions.

The Paradox of Control

Suggesting that salespeople should control the sales process creates another interesting paradox. As you know, sellers don't have the right to *tell* prospects what to do. But as we just explained, it is not particularly effective to ask prospects what should happen next. Effective salespeople can, however, control the process by leading prospects toward the desired result using questions strategically, rather than trying to push your own agenda forward with statements.

> **Secret #100** Top performers control the sale using questions, while average performers let themselves be controlled by the sales process.

Asking questions enables you to manage your sales conversations in much the same way a handheld remote allows you to control your television or DVR. If you would like to know the status of one of your prospect's account, simply ask a question that solicits accurate feedback (as discussed in chapter 10). If you want to expand the discussion, ask a question that broadens the scope of the conversation, or solicits additional detail about specific implications (chapter 9). To switch topics or further clarify a point, you can easily change the focus of a conversation by transitioning from issue to implication questions. We could go on and on looking at examples. The point is, questions are strategic tools that enable you, the salesperson, to control your conversations and more effectively navigate the sales process.

Using Questions to Soften Your Suggestions

You can't just *tell* prospects they need to see a presentation, but you can absolutely *ask* them if they would like to know how other customers have increased their revenues and decreased their expenses by using your product or service. Likewise, you can't just *tell* prospects to check references or escalate a recommendation to the appropriate decision maker, but you can certainly *ask* them if it makes sense to act on these suggestions as the next appropriate step in the process of evaluating your potential solutions.

Questions are valuable tools for managing the sales process because they soften your suggestions. This enables salespeople to be more assertive without making prospects feel pushed or pressured.

Secret #101 Questions allow sellers to offer ideas and raise aspects of a decision that prospects might not have otherwise considered.

The idea of leading prospects through the sales process using questions has a wide range of positive implications. Suppose, for example, that several key people involved in the decision were unable to attend your recent sales presentation. Given the level of competition, you realize that educating everyone is critical to maintaining a leadership position in the account. Instead of demanding more time for education, why not ask a question that leads your prospect toward the desired result? You could ask:

Salesperson:	*"Mr. Prospect, several people on the committee were not able to attend last week's presentation. Does it make sense for us to educate these people, too—so they will be up to speed when it's time to review the details of our proposal?"*
Prospect:	*"Yes, that probably would make sense."*
Salesperson:	*"Could we schedule a follow-up event to include those who were unable to attend the first presentation?"*

After the salesperson in this example raises a problem, he states the benefits of solving the problem, and then asks a question that suggests how best to proceed. This seller is controlling the sales process by making valuable suggestions, even though the buyer still has the final say in whether they wish to move forward with the salesperson's advice. It's another win-win situation.

How Strategic Questions Work

Asking good questions has always been an integral part of selling. As we have shown you, asking strategic questions at the right time is the most effective way to establish credibility, gather information, and uncover needs. Well-crafted questions can definitely help move opportunities forward in the sales process. But while sales trainers (and sales managers) are quick to stress the importance of questions, they often ignore the stress caused by asking them.

Since I started studying questions and their effect on the strategic sales process, I've discovered an interesting phenomenon. Some salespeople, particularly those with limited experience, are timid about asking questions. They worry their questions will be viewed by prospects and customers as a sign of weakness, as if *having to ask* indicates their lack of intelligence or capability. Think about it this way: have you ever felt stupid or inadequate because you didn't already know something and had to ask for help?

This creates one more interesting paradox. Salespeople need to ask questions to establish credibility, gather information, and uncover needs. We've talked about this at length already. But if questions make them feel inadequate or incompetent, then *having to ask* could actually undermine their credibility by demonstrating a lack of knowledge. *Huh? I guess I don't get what you're saying? Do you mean if they have to ask, they appear less credible? Shows their feelings?* Can you see the dilemma?

This paradox confuses salespeople about the role of questions in the sales process, which leads us to consider, are questions putting salespeople in a position of weakness or a position of strength?

He Who Asks the Questions Has the Power

Make no mistake: asking questions puts the "asker" in a unique position of strength. No matter how squeamish you might feel about asking, questions ultimately drive every conversation you ever have. In fact, rather than feeling nervous about asking questions, Question Based Selling helps salespeople realize that *he who asks the questions holds the power* in the conversation.

Here's a little anecdote to show you what I mean. Suppose you are diligently working at your desk, when someone suddenly knocks on your office door. *"Come in,"* you say, not expecting anyone in particular. Much to your surprise, in walks the President of the United States, followed by an entourage of government officials and Secret Service agents. The president greets you with a hardy handshake, and you graciously exchange pleasantries.

After the initial shock of the situation, you pull yourself together long enough to realize that you have the opportunity of a lifetime—a chance to talk with the President of the United States. But rather than trying to impress him with something you could say, you decide to ask a question.

Fortunately, your brain happens to be "on" that day, and despite all the hoopla, you deliver a wonderfully articulated question, one that even impresses the Secret Service agents milling about the room. Upon hearing your question, the President pauses for a moment to collect his thoughts, and then begins to respond.

Here's my point. At the very moment in time when the President of the United States begins to respond to your question, who is answering to whom? In this case, the President of the United States, arguably one of the most powerful people in the world, would be answering to you. At that point, you have control of the conversation because *you* are the one who asked the question.

> **Secret #102**   He who asks the questions has the power in sales conversations.

Asking questions puts you in a desirable position with respect to your sales conversations, too. It puts you in control. By asking questions, you can control the subject of your sales conversations. You can also control the pace and depth of the conversation, depending on what questions you choose to ask and how you ask them.

If your prospects are asking all the questions, then they are controlling the sales process. Does that mean it's bad for prospective buyers to ask questions? No, not at all. In Question Based Selling, we want prospects to be interested and curious, enough so that they will ask for additional information. But, you can still maintain control of your conversations by using the QBS technique of answering a question with a question.

Answer a Question with a Question

When someone asks me, *"How much do you charge for QBS training?"* I always answer their question with a question of my own. I say, *"Which QBS program are you interested in?"* Now, who's controlling the conversation? Answer? Whoever asked the last question—in this case, me.

Some people might argue that answering a question with a question is a deflective strategy, a method of dodging the original question in the hopes of redirecting the prospect's attention onto something else. That's not the case in Question Based Selling, however. Rather than dodging the prospect's questions, we are simply trying to find out what they really want to know, and *why*, so we can know how best to respond.

Secret #103   When people ask questions, it's important to know *why* they're asking in order to know how best to respond.

There are countless examples of this. One of your prospects might ask, *"What advantages does your product have over other solutions?"* Instead of jumping into an explanation of features and benefits of your product or service, I would recommend asking, *"How familiar are you with our products?"* This gives you a chance to find out whether they simply want more information, or are challenging your proposal—which would dictate two very different responses.

The easiest way to find out why a prospect is asking a question is to respond with a Global Question. We first introduced this technique back in chapter 9. A Global Question is designed to get the other person to elaborate on something they've said, or asked. Essentially, Global Questions allow you to say, *"Tell me more."* Try it. The next time one of your prospects or customers asks you a question, ask them back, *"How do you mean?"* Odds are, they'll provide a lengthy narrative, which will give you valuable insight about how best to position your response. Using Global Questions to understand the prospect's perspective is a valuable strategy, whether you are responding to inquiries at the beginning of a sale or handling objections at the end.

The only caveat is that your questions must first pass the *Four-Year-Old Test*. It may be cute when little Johnny at the family picnic incessantly asks, *Why? … Why? … Why?* But it's a lot less cute when a professional salesperson asks a mindless barrage of questions. The moral is: don't sacrifice quality for quantity. Every question you ask should add value in the conversation by uncovering additional information, or clarifying something that's already been said.

The Second Law of Thermodynamics

In addition to controlling the sales process, salespeople must also ask questions to gather information. It's part of qualifying an opportunity, uncovering needs, and understanding the competitive environment. To accomplish these objectives, however, information must flow freely and easily from the buyer to the seller.

In high school physics, many of us learned (and some even remember) the Laws of Thermodynamics. If high school physics does not happen to be fresh on your mind, the Second Law of Thermodynamics states that energy flows naturally from high concentrations to low concentrations (from hot to cold, for example). To demonstrate this phenomenon, open a window in the middle of winter. Heat will automatically escape from the higher concentration inside your home to the lower concentration outside.

The same principle applies to sales conversations. If you humble yourself long enough to show prospects that you don't know everything, you may be surprised to see how readily information flows from the person who has it (the prospect) to the person who wants it (the salesperson). How can salespeople humble themselves? One way is to use humbling disclaimers, saying things like *"I'm confused"* or *"Am I missing something?"* followed by a summary of the key points you want to better understand. The message is simple; if you are willing to ask for help or admit that you don't already know everything, people are quick to offer assistance. Contrast this with the perceived arrogance of someone who positions himself as a know-it-all. Of course, prospects are going to clam up, because they will feel like they are in a position where they cannot contribute any value.

Ironically, the flow of information from high concentrations to low is initiated by silence. If you want other people to respond productively, you have to be willing to ask questions and then clam up. The resulting silence creates a natural vacuum in the conversation, and this vacuum automatically puts the onus on the other person to contribute a response.

> **Secret #104** After a salesperson delivers a legitimate question, the flow of valuable information is often initiated by silence.

Unfortunately, silence sometimes makes salespeople very uncomfortable. As a result, they tend to jump into the conversation to fill the silence with words—usually a product dump. You must resist this temptation, however, because if you don't fill the silence with noise, your prospects will fill it with valuable information.

Summary

The most effective salespeople in every industry are the ones who realize that one of their greatest assets is their ability to find out information they don't already have. Even the most knowledgeable sellers still have to ask questions, because every prospect is different and every sale is unique. Once we understand that questions allow us to control our own destiny, we can now shift our focus to weaving the various QBS techniques together into a cohesive strategy—starting with executing the initial sales call, which is what we will cover next in chapter 12.

TURNING COLD CALLS INTO LUKEWARM CALLS

Nobody likes "cold calls." Salespeople don't particularly like to make them, and prospects don't particularly like to be on the receiving end. Nonetheless, sales is partially a numbers game, so sellers must contact new prospects to uncover potential sales opportunities. Cold calling has been the primary way to do that.

But who says your initial sales calls have to be "cold"? By applying the QBS techniques that we have introduced thus far, you can leverage curiosity, credibility, momentum, and a greater sense of value to "warm up" your sales calls and significantly enhance your results.

Most selling opportunities begin with a sales call. While some potential buyers might just show up on your doorstep because they have already recognized an opportunity to improve their existing condition, most won't. And when they don't show up on their own, it's your responsibility to initiate contact and create business opportunities that otherwise wouldn't exist.

Initiating contact can be a difficult challenge, however. Whether it's on the telephone or in person, sales callers who are either trying to introduce a new idea or unseat an existing vendor relationship are constantly barraging decision makers. Even if prospects wanted to entertain every sales call that came in, there's simply not enough time in the day to do so.

As a result, the average success rate when contacting new prospects is very low, typically between 2 and 5 percent, and getting smaller. That means out of every hundred sales calls, the average performer can expect to generate only a small handful of opportunities. The other 95 to 98 percent of these sales calls end in rejection—which, as we talked about earlier, makes it that much more difficult for sellers to stay motivated.

Secret #105   Show me a salesperson who says they *like* making cold calls, and I'll show you someone who would really rather not.

If you already have an existing relationship you can leverage, or some other entrée into a targeted prospect account, your probability of success will likely increase significantly. Having an "in" relieves much of the tension, anxiety, and nervousness that accompanies an initial sales call. If you don't already have an existing relationship, however, the alternative is cold calling—contacting potential buyers to introduce yourself, your company, and your product in an attempt to create a spark of interest that will challenge the status quo (their current thinking) and make them want to engage further.

Nobody Likes Cold Calls

Most prospects view a cold call as an unwelcome interruption rather than a valuable use of time. We have to realize that key decision makers at important prospect accounts are already busy with meetings, events, and managing their daily business. So when the telephone rings and the third or fourth overeager salesperson in the last hour dives headfirst into his or her spiel, most prospects are neither excited nor impressed.

The problem with cold calls is, they're *cold*. When a prospect picks up the telephone or answers the door, and they don't know you from Adam, they are naturally reluctant to engage. It's a predictable reaction. Remember, we said earlier that salespeople begin the sales process with near-zero credibility? Therefore, if prospects aren't yet curious, and you don't already have a relationship to leverage, it's not surprising that many of your cold calls will be ill-received.

Nonetheless, the initial sales call is a watershed event in the QBS sales process. If the first contact goes well, you will have an opportunity to engage new prospects in productive sales conversation. This starts you down the path toward understanding their needs and positioning your solutions. If the initial sales call goes poorly, however, you're out. That's the bottom line. That's also where Question Based Selling comes in—by showing you how to increase your probability of success when making these initial sales calls. Read on!

Warming Up Your Cold Calls

Early in my own sales career, I made countless cold calls. "Smiling and Dialing" we used to call it. With a prospect list and a telephone, I held onto the belief that persistence was the key. So I called each of the prospects on my list, again and again, assuming they would be impressed by my tenacity. But my results were mediocre at best, and I became more frustrated with every call. As it turned out, the prospects I was pursuing were getting frustrated as well.

The people I called weren't as impressed with my persistence as I had hoped. Instead, it was more often the case that they were put off by it. I was doing everything I could to penetrate the account and schedule an appointment, while they were doing everything they could to get off the phone. Every call was a battle and I was obviously losing the war. Something had to change.

What changed was my approach to the initial contact. Since my cold calls didn't seem to be working, it didn't make sense to continue with the same old strategy of blindly lobbing calls into prospective accounts. Once I realized the "coldness" of my initial contacts was causing the problem, I decided to change my approach to increase the "warmth" of my sales calls. That's when my results significantly increased.

How can you increase the warmth of your sales calls? That's what the rest of this chapter is about. You will learn how to increase the effectiveness of your calls by applying the QBS methodology to pique the prospect's curiosity, establish your own credibility, understand the customer's needs, build relationships, and secure the prospect's commitment to take the next step in the sales process.

> **Secret #106** When calling new prospects, the rule of thumb is: the "warmer" the call, the greater its probability of success.

Contacting new prospects is just as important now as it ever was. But that doesn't mean your initial sales calls have to be cold. Instead, QBS teaches salespeople how to make "lukewarm" sales calls. After all, you only get one chance to make a first impression, so it might as well be a good one.

A Microcosm of the Sales Process

In chapter 11, we introduced the QBS sales funnel that broke the sales process down into three component phases. While our ultimate goal is closing more sales, you must succeed in each of the smaller component phases of a sale (generating interest, uncovering needs, and presenting solutions), before you can ask prospects for their commitment to buy. Succeeding in each of these areas of the process will lead to accomplishing the desired outcome, which is the sale.

The same is true in the initial sales call. If your objective on the call is getting an appointment or securing some other commitment to engage new prospects in the sales process, then you must first pique the prospect's interest, identify their need(s), and let them know that you provide valuable solutions. Your calls must also be purposeful, relevant, valuable, and credible in order to earn the right to get into more depth. In that sense, lukewarm calling is a microcosm of the larger sales process.

In QBS, we use a divide-and-conquer strategy to break the initial sales call down into its component parts. Perhaps you've heard the old saying that the best way to eat an elephant is one bite at a time. We make the same argument here. The best way to consistently succeed in the initial sales call is to execute the call one step at a time. That means accomplishing a series of smaller objectives to achieve the larger goal.

> **Secret #107** In the strategic sale, the larger goal of making the sale is achieved by accomplishing a series of smaller successes along the way.

The lukewarm sales call that we will describe throughout the rest of this chapter has four unique stages: *Introduction*, *Discovery*, *Value Proposition*, and *Closing on Next Steps*. This model serves as a blueprint for conducting the actual call and for qualifying the opportunity. Does the prospect have a need? Do they have a sense of urgency? Do they have the authority to make a decision? Who else needs to be involved? This blueprint should look familiar because it works in conjunction with the Conversational Layering Model we introduced earlier in chapter 6. This model is versatile enough to apply in virtually any sales situation, yet specific enough to implement with predictable results.

The 4 Stages of a Lukewarm Sales Call

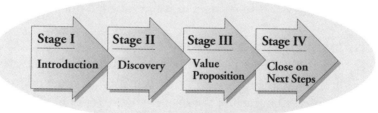

Stage I — Introduction
Stage II — Discovery
Stage III — Value Proposition
Stage IV — Close on Next Steps

Sometimes people ask if it's really necessary to have such a detailed strategy for the initial contact. The answer is no, it's not. Anyone can make cold calls, as it takes almost no skill whatsoever to transform a large number of sales leads into a very small number of prospect opportunities. But if you want to significantly increase your sales results, you will have to improve the quality of those calls, in order to penetrate significantly more new accounts. That's what we will show you how to accomplish in this chapter. By understanding how each component of the lukewarm call works, you will be able to engage more prospects in more productive sales conversations.

STAGE I

Introduction

The telephone rings and your prospect answers. For salespeople, this is the moment of truth—the beginning of the initial sales call, where the butterflies in your stomach must all fly in formation to allow you to speak the right words. Whether the prospect picks up the telephone or answers the door, it's time to execute, and it's do or die.

The lukewarm sales call begins with the *Introduction* stage. Although the *Introduction* is the shortest of the four stages, generally lasting only fifteen to forty-five seconds, it's a mistake to discount the significance of an effective opening. Our objective in the *Introduction* stage is very straightforward. We are simply trying to get one foot in the door in order to secure a few minutes of the prospect's time and attention. While this may sound easy, experienced salespeople are keenly aware that the beginning of the initial sales call is one of the highest hurdles in the sales process. In reality, salespeople know that it can take thirty, forty-five, or even sixty *minutes* to uncover needs and communicate value, but once the prospect realizes you are a salesperson, it's more likely you only have thirty, forty-five, or sixty *seconds*. Cautious prospects form their impressions very quickly, and as a salesperson, you aren't likely to get a second chance. Therefore, how you choose to manage this window of opportunity will likely determine whether your call ends abruptly or you succeed in getting that foot in the door.

> **Secret #108** Very few sales are consummated during the initial sales call, but this is where many sales opportunities are lost.

The first stage of the lukewarm sales call (*Introduction*) is divided into three sub-steps. Each of these component steps and their effect on the successful execution of your initial sales calls is explained below.

Identify Yourself and Your Company

When you contact new prospects over the telephone, you may get put through to their voice-mail system. When this happens, I recommend using one of the curiosity strategies that was outlined earlier (in chapter 7) to generate a return call. If you are able to pique the prospect's curiosity using voice mail, then they will call you back. If the prospect answers the phone directly, however, it's critical you identify yourself and your company right up front. Here's what that might sound like:

Seller: *"Hello, Mr. Prospect, my name is Jane Whitman, and I'm with Pharmacon Products Corporation."*

The salesperson in this example is straightforward and to the point. Not bad. She identifies herself and her company, but rather than trying to open with some clever line or juicy enticement, she lets her prospect know (up front) who they are dealing with.

She could enhance her introduction with a few small but important changes. Titles are unimportant at this stage, but letting prospects know what your role is can be very valuable. The fact you are on a team is also good, because customers like to be supported by a team rather than a rogue individual. Attaching these details to the opening of your calls gives prospects a sense about the nature of the call. This is particularly effective when prospects wouldn't otherwise recognize you or the name of your company. Here's an example of what that sounds like:

Seller: *"Hello, Mr. Prospect, my name is Jane Whitman, and I'm with Pharmacon Products Corporation. I'm on the customer service team that works with pharmaceutical suppliers in the tri-state area."*

Notice here that the added tagline is attempting to create relevance with the customer. People just want to have a sense of who you are. As I mentioned when talking about voice mail, just saying: *"Hello..., my name is ..., and I'm with ...,"* is not enough information if this is a first-time call. Are you the president, a customer service rep, or from the accounts payable department? Instead of making them guess, I simply add a tagline that identifies me to them, such as: *"I'm on the customer service team that works with pharmaceutical suppliers in the tri-state area."* Now at least they have a sense of who they're dealing with. It also creates built-in relevance, particularly if a customer thinks to themselves: *"Hey, we're a pharmaceutical supplier in the tri-state area, so this call might be relevant to me."*

Not only should your words be straightforward, but your physical conduct should mirror that as well. If you happen to meet a prospective buyer in person, look them in the eye, extend your hand, and confidently state your first and last name. Prospects will follow your lead. They too will reach out their hands and reciprocate by saying their first and last name. Now, you have automatically put yourself on a first-name basis with the potential buyer.

The beginning of a sales call is typically not a good time for small talk, however. Opening with questions like, *"How are you today?"* or *"How's your day going?"* may seem nice, but you might as well say: *"I'm trying to get you to like me so I can sell you my product."* Remember that many other salespeople are also calling and asking how the prospect is doing. So this is a good time to be purposeful rather than fake or overly friendly. Keep it real and to the point. There will be lots of time for chitchat once you establish yourself as a credible resource.

Associate to Create a Sense of Familiarity

After you identify yourself and your company, it's important to let the prospects know *why* you're calling. But that doesn't mean jumping ahead into a litany of generic-sounding features and benefits like the traditional sales approach. Here's how that could sound:

Seller: *"Hello, Mr. Prospect, my name is Jane Whitman, and I'm with Pharmacon Products Corporation. I'm on the customer service team that works with pharmaceutical suppliers in the tri-state area. Our company prides itself on maintaining the highest quality standards in the industry. We have the best products and the best service, and I would like to have an opportunity to solve all your problems with our valuable solutions."*

This may sound good to the salesperson, but to the prospect, it sounds more like Charlie Brown's teacher: *"Mr. Prospect, our company prides itself on …wah…wah…wah. We have the best…wah…wah…wah, and I would like to have an opportunity to talk with you about…wah…wah…wah."* As we pointed out earlier, if this is what your prospects hear, they will no doubt respond by saying, *"No thanks, we already have enough…wah…wah…wah."*

A salesperson should have a valid and purposeful reason for calling, one that piques the prospect's interest so they will want to engage further. While many initial sales calls are indeed "cold," QBS's lukewarm calling strategy is intended to lower the prospects' defenses by creating a sense of familiarity (an associative reference) that indicates you have already made it past the gatekeeper.

> **Secret #109**   Prospects are more likely to engage and share information
> with a salesperson who is already "plugged in."

Have you ever noticed that it's easier to find a new job when you already have a job? Likewise, it's easier to get a date when you already have a boyfriend or girlfriend. We can draw a similar parallel when trying to penetrate new prospect accounts. It's much easier to get to the key person if it appears that you are already engaged in the account. You can create this sense of familiarity (to warm up your sales calls) by leveraging any number of techniques introduced earlier in Question Based Selling, including *Personal Endorsements, Associative References, Herd Momentum,* and *Glimpses of Value.* Keep in mind that we're still in Stage I of the lukewarm sales call, where the introductory portion of the call typically only lasts between fifteen and forty-five seconds.

Personal Endorsements

Chip Graddy sells financial services for Northwestern Mutual Life on the Gulf Coast of Florida. During his first few years with the company, his sales results skyrocketed, and he became one of the company's top producers. Chip's success is largely attributable to his ability to leverage personal endorsements. Chip has mastered the use of mutual contacts to create a sense of familiarity and warm up his initial sales calls. Here's a sample dialogue:

Chip:	*"Hi, Steve, this is Chip Graddy of Northwestern Mutual Life. Did Fred Thompkins let you know I'd be calling?"*
Prospect:	*"I think he mentioned it."*
Chip:	*"Fred is a good friend of mine, and he's also a client. He speaks very highly of you and suggested that you would be a great person for me to get to know. Do you have a few minutes?"*

Chip knows that first impressions mean a lot. If the endorsement comes from a credible source, most prospects will take a few minutes to talk with you—if for no other reason than respect for their friendship with the person who gave the referral. This technique can do wonders for your credibility, and it's also a good way to pique the prospect's curiosity.

Associative References

Some sales trainers are adamant about calling the decision maker first. You have to get to the right person, they insist! That means cold calling some very important people. Personally, I would rather have a valid reason for calling than give key decision makers the impression I'm just another telemarketer. So in Question Based Selling, we take a different approach with these calls.

We talked about this earlier in chapter 7. Rather than starting with the highest-level decision maker, you can initiate a dialogue with purchasing, marketing, or some other area of the business first. This gives you an opportunity to create an *associative reference*. Now, when you call the high-level decision maker, your opening sounds less like a sales call and more like someone who's already plugged into the account. Here's an example:

> **Salesperson:** *"Hi, Ms. Prospect. My name is Don Smith, and I'm with XYZ Company, I'm on the office automation team that works with manufacturing accounts in Dallas. Ms. Prospect, I just got off the phone with Doris in purchasing…and I have a question. Do you have a minute, or did I catch you at a bad time?"*

Most prospects will probably take this call for two reasons. First, the salesperson in this example is making it easy for the prospect to engage. After giving a valid reason for the call, the salesperson is only asking for "a minute" of the prospect's time. Everyone can spare a minute. Secondly, this approach is designed to pique the prospect's curiosity by leveraging an associative reference. In this example, if the prospect wants to know what's up with Doris in purchasing, then you will surely get some time and their attention. Remember, at this point in the call, you're just trying to get a foot in the proverbial door.

Herd Momentum

Another way to warm up your sales calls is to use *herd momentum*. You've heard the phrase "guilt by association." The Herd Theory gives salespeople an opportunity to establish *credibility by association*—by letting prospects know that "everyone else" already seems to be moving in a certain direction.

> **Salesperson:** *"Our products are currently being used by companies like Delta Air Lines, IBM, General Motors, Lanier Worldwide, Bank of America, Monsanto, Lockheed Martin, Citicorp, International Paper, HP, FedEx,*

> *Coca-Cola, Westinghouse, and the federal govern-*
> *ment…just to name a few.*
>
> *On Tuesday, May 17, we are hosting a seminar to*
> *demonstrate how we have already helped these and*
> *other customers solve some of the challenges that tradi-*
> *tional solutions have created."*

As prospects become curious about what the rest of the herd is doing, salespeople have an opportunity to engage them in a more in-depth discussion. This helps transition the conversation into the next stage of the lukewarm sales call: *Discovery.*

Secret #110 Associative references won't close the sale, but they can give you an opening to execute a strategy that will.

Glimpses of Value

You can also warm up your sales calls by giving prospects a *glimpse of value.* This early in the call, you haven't earned the right to challenge the customer's thinking or ask lots of questions. But you can absolutely dangle a few enticing benefits out in front of your potential buyers to see if they would like to hear more. Some people call it "selling the sizzle, not the steak." Here are some examples:

Seller: *"Would you like to know how to significantly reduce your cost of goods sold with one simple change in strategy?"*

—or—

"If we could increase your revenue by 45 percent, would you be interested in hearing more about our new products?"

One of our best clients first opened their doors in 1991 as a network services company based in the Silicon Valley. They have since enjoyed explosive growth in the United States and around the world. One of the strategies they used very effectively to penetrate new accounts was dangling a glimpse of value in front of their prospects. They would say:

Seller: *"Give us your most difficult networking problem, and if we can't solve it within a mutually agreed-upon time frame, our time and effort will cost you nothing."*

For those decision makers who were wrestling with a host of technical problems, this was an extremely valuable offer. Who wouldn't want to resolve their most difficult networking issue? Frankly, the salesperson for this company was putting the prospect in a position where they had nothing to lose and everything to gain. The salesperson, on the other hand, used this strategy to gain an opportunity to penetrate and qualify many more new accounts. This positioning also gave them a way to expand the engagement by demonstrating real value in terms of on-site expertise, technical capability, and measurable performance increases.

Use Humbling Disclaimers to Minimize Your Risk

To some degree, making sales calls is a matter of personal style, but I use one QBS technique in particular at the beginning of almost every call. I open with a humbling disclaimer (see chapter 10). Whether I'm calling new prospects or existing customers, I identify myself and my company, state my purpose of the call, and then ask: *"Did I catch you at a bad time?"*

Some salespeople are reluctant to ask this. They worry this question gives prospects an easy out. But as we stated earlier, your prospects already have an "out." Prospects and customers are well aware that they don't have to buy from you. Frankly, they don't even have to take your calls.

Asking if it's a "bad time" actually puts a salesperson in a very strategic position. The person you're trying to reach might be on another call or in the middle of a meeting, in which case, they'll respond by saying, *"Yes, this is a bad time. I have several people in my office."* But you mustn't despair. If a prospect truly is unavailable, you wouldn't have secured their time or attention, no matter what you said. But asking if it's a bad time gives you an opportunity to follow up with: *"When should I call back?"* In most cases, the prospect will name a time when they expect to be more available. Now you have an appointment.

What happens if you ask, *"Did I catch you at a bad time?"* and your prospect says, *"No…no, this is fine. What can I do for you?"* Prospects are often quick to rescue you by inviting you to please continue. This gives you exactly what you wanted—a mini-invitation to proceed with the call. In addition to being polite, this approach is extremely respectful of the prospect's situation, which increases the likelihood that they will give you a few minutes. Just don't forget to state your purpose for the call before asking.

What if the Prospect Asks: "What's This About?"

Be careful. With first-time prospect calls, asking the question *Did I catch you at a bad time?* too early carries some risk because you are essentially asking for a commitment (of time) before the prospect even knows why you're calling. You might have called a prospect who is quick to jump in and ask, *What is this about?*

This question instantly puts sellers on the defensive. Understandably, the prospect is trying to cut to the chase to decide whether the call is a valuable use of time or just another nuisance. Unfortunately, salespeople who get intimidated tend to jump ahead into their elevator pitch. That usually sends the call into a tailspin, because sellers cannot effectively present a solution without first uncovering a need.

Sellers can minimize this risk by first legitimizing a reason for calling as part of their introduction. For example:

Seller: *"Hi, Mr. Prospect, my name is John Smith, and I'm on the communications team that works with commercial accounts in central Illinois. I was hoping to catch you for a minute to discuss (insert legitimate reason for calling). Did I happen to catch you at a bad time?"*

This phraseology is direct but also down-to-earth and considerate of the customer's time. You are basically saying that you only want a brief window of time to talk about (whatever your reason is for calling).

Even so, if a prospect asks, *"But what's this about?"* you simply respond by restating the purpose of the call, *"Well, Mr. Prospect, we've figured out how to solve a series of very specific business problems that many customers in your industry currently face, and I wanted to see if it would make sense for us to have a conversation."* Very few prospects will pass up the opportunity to ask, "What problem do you solve?" That's what you're hoping for. Now you have another mini-invitation to engage the prospect further.

The Transition into Stage II (Discovery)

In Stage II of the initial sales call, the direction of the call changes—from introductory mode to an information-gathering mode. The transition between Stages I and II is where sellers often lose control of their calls, however. In many cases, salespeople have been taught to press on whether the prospect wants to or not. QBS takes the opposite approach. Rather than trying to force the conversation, we recommend putting yourself in a position of having earned the right to engage further and uncover the prospect's needs in Stage II.

The easiest way to set up this transition between the *Introduction* and *Discovery* stages is to ask one of two questions. After you have identified yourself and your company, and you have communicated your reason for calling, simply ask: *"Are you the right person to talk with about...?"* If you are selling office equipment, for example, you would ask, *"Are you the right person to talk to about upgrading your office equipment?"* If you sell surgical supplies, you would say, *"Are you the right person to talk with about medical supplies?"*

Their answer is either going to be, *"Yes, I am the right person,"* or, *"No, I'm not."* If the person on the phone is not the "right person," this does not mean you have failed in the call. Many times, the wrong person will go out of their way to help put you with the right person. When they do, you have a terrific opportunity to leverage a new associative reference by saying:

Seller: *"Hi, Mr. Prospect. I just got off the phone with Joe Sandler in the Minneapolis office, and he said you would be the right person to talk with about _____. Did I catch you at a bad time?"*

If, on the other hand, your prospect concedes that he or she is indeed the right person, you automatically gain their implied permission (another mini-invitation) to proceed into the *Discovery* stage of the call.

> **Secret #111** Whenever someone agrees they are the *right person*, you automatically earn the right to probe further.

The other question you can ask to set up the transition between Stages I and II of the initial sales call is: *"How familiar are you with ABC Company?"* This is different than asking, *"Have you heard about...?"* or *"Are you familiar with ABC Company?"* Asking prospects one of those questions is problematic because if they say, *"Yes,"* they have essentially shut the door on your opportunity to educate them further. If instead, you ask prospects how familiar they are with your company or products, very few will claim absolute knowledge. That gives you an opportunity to educate them.

"Can I Ask You a Couple Specifics About...?"

The most effective way to transition your calls from Stage I (*Introduction*) to Stage II (*Discovery*) is to simply say to your prospect: *"Can I ask you a couple specifics about ____?"* There is only one time in all of Question Based Selling that I recommend exact wording, and this is that one time. Why? Because this is one of those questions that elicits a predictable response. When you say, *"Can I ask you a couple specifics about _____?"* 99 percent of the people you ask will automatically say, "Sure." Now you have earned their permission to proceed.

> **Secret #112**   By securing your prospect's permission to proceed, you can expect more productive responses to your probing questions.

Some sales trainers might argue that it's unnecessary to ask prospects if you can ask them a "couple specifics," but I haven't met a customer yet who didn't appreciate the gesture of my seeking their permission to proceed. In fact, securing a mini-invitation to ask a series of diagnostic questions not only earns you the right to proceed, it's also a terrific way to eliminate some of the nervous tension that's often present at the very beginning of a sales call.

What If the Prospect Asks You a Question?

Prospects sometimes try to put salespeople on their heels by asking a question of their own at the beginning of the call. But guess what? We want prospects to ask questions. We want them to be curious, and we want them to desire additional information about the solutions we offer. If your prospect asks a question, don't be nervous. Be excited, and let their question be your invitation to engage them further in a discussion about their needs and your value.

Congratulations! You have made it past the most difficult part of the initial sales call (Stage I). By piquing the prospect's interest and securing their permission to proceed, you now have an opportunity to ask questions to establish credibility, and, most importantly, to "discover" potential problems or desires that will fuel the sales process moving forward. That's why Stage II is called *Discovery*.

However, because it's still early in the call, you must resist the temptation to start spewing features and benefits. Until you know more about the prospect's needs, you cannot effectively position the value of your solution. Hence the importance of asking good discovery questions.

Narrow the Scope for Credibility

Having earned the right to ask questions, now let's ask ourselves, what's the best way to proceed in the call? You could start by asking some of the more traditional broad or open-ended sales questions, like *What are your goals and objectives in the next three years?* or *Can you tell me a little about your business?* These are certainly good questions, but if you remember back in chapter 8, the more effective approach is the QBS one where you open with a series of short-answer, diagnostic questions that establish your credibility. Again, realize that salespeople begin the whole process with near-zero credibility, so *narrowing the scope* of your questions allows you to earn high levels of competence and credibility, which differentiates you from the couple of dozen other salespeople who are also trying to penetrate the same account.

> **Secret #113**   Prospects who don't like cold calls will gladly open up once you differentiate yourself as a competent professional.

By demonstrating your ability to ask a series of short-answer, relevant, and intelligent questions, prospects will automatically assume you might be able to add value in those areas. Diagnostic questions also help uncover information that will qualify the opportunity. If you sell employee benefits packages to large corporations, for example, you might ask the following series of diagnostic questions:

Seller: *"Can I ask you a couple specifics about your employee benefits program?"*

1. *How many employees does your company currently have?*

2. *What percentage of your workforce receives health benefits?*

3. *Does your existing health plan offer HMO and PPO options?*

4. *What about life insurance, disability, and dental coverage?*

5. *Who is your current benefits provider?*

6. *When is your benefits contract up for renewal?*

If you sell computer equipment and supplies, you might ask:

1. *Is your I/S environment centralized or distributed?*

2. *What's your current network operating system?*

3. *Are you using version 3.X or 4.X?*

4. How many end users do you support?

5. Do you develop your own software or buy applications?

In QBS, we recommend you work through a series of five or six diagnostic questions as you lead into needs development. These questions let prospects know that you *do* understand something about their specific business. Using this technique enables you to establish credibility quickly, which is critical because it's still early in the call. Of course, once you establish credibility, something magical happens. Curious prospects who believe that you are indeed credible begin to open up. They start to share information, and they ask to hear more about your products and services.

Broaden the Scope for Relationships

Narrowing the scope of your questions helps establish your credibility, so you can then *broaden the scope* of your questions to uncover needs and start building relationships. As a reminder, effective probing is more than just asking a bunch of open-ended questions. You also need to escalate the focus of your questions to raise the value of your sales conversations.

Escalate the Value of Your Questions

We made the point in chapter 9 that some questions are more valuable than others. We showed you how to escalate the *focus* of your questions to increase their intrinsic value in the conversation. This process begins with Status Questions, which probe the "status" of the opportunity. Status Questions are diagnostic in nature—they allow you to initiate conversation, gather information, and most importantly, establish your credibility. Status Questions are easy to ask and easy to answer, which makes them a good starting point in the initial sales call. But as we pointed out, prospects have a limited tolerance for Status Questions because they are lowest in mutual value. Your prospect already knows the status. Therefore, you will want to ask just enough Status Questions to establish your credibility in the call. Then you can escalate the focus of the conversation by asking Issue Questions and Implication Questions that challenge the customer's thinking in order to identify key business issues and the implications of those issues.

Issue Questions don't have to be complex, and they don't have to test the intellectual depths of your prospects to be effective. In fact, it's best to keep it simple, using one of the most effective QBS questions: *"To what extent is _____ important?"* Just fill in the blank with a relevant business issue and you can very effectively probe the needs of any prospect in any industry.

> **Secret #114** The most effective way to uncover prospect needs is to simply ask: *"To what extent is _____ important?"*

Prospects don't respond well to rhetorical questions, so stay away from questions like, *"Is quality important?"* or *"Is cost important?"* Of course quality and cost are important! Instead, you want to understand *why* these issues are important. Asking "to what extent" is valuable because it helps uncover implications that justify a favorable decision later in the sale. For specific examples of Implication Questions, you might want to refer back to chapter 9. But just like we talked about, unless you have a better opening, asking, *"To what extent is your business (or personal situation) growing or changing?"* is a great starting point.

Expand Responses with Global Questions

Some prospects will take the ball and run with it, giving you lengthy and in-depth responses to all your questions. With other prospects, you will have to work a little harder to get them to open up. That's where Global Questions are particularly useful.

Global Questions were introduced earlier as tools for expanding your sales conversations. They help reduce the risk that prospects feel you are asking too many questions or probing too deeply. Essentially, Global Questions offer a very polite and respectful way to say, *"I'm very interested in what you just said… so could you please tell me more?"*

Some of the most common Global Questions include:

"How do you mean?"	*"And then what?"*
"What else?"	*"What happened next?"*
"Like what?"	*"How so?"*

Global Questions offer a compliment to the prospect's ego because you are letting them know you are interested in their opinion, and you would like them to please continue. This attentiveness is likely to generate a significant amount of additional input from qualified buyers.

Clarifying Vague-onyms

Another technique you can use to expand your sales conversations is to clarify any what I like to call *vague-onyms*. What's a vague-onym? You probably know what synonyms are—different words that have the same meaning (*big* and *large*). Homonyms are words that sound the same but have different meanings (such as *there* and *their*). Antonyms are opposites, like *up* and *down*. So what's a vague-onym, besides being a QBS-invented concept? The English language is highly interpretable, so a vague-onym is a word or phrase that is so vague it's impossible to know what the other person really means without receiving additional information.

Sales managers tear their hair out when salespeople use vague-onyms to report the status of an account. Statements like *The deal is going to close very soon* make sales managers have to follow up with *What do you mean by soon?* Trouble is, in many cases, the salesperson is just telling the sales manager what the prospect told them. A similar lack of information exists whenever prospects say things like *Your product costs too much* or *Quality is one of our biggest concerns.*

Vague-onyms simply don't give you enough information. How soon is "soon"? For some prospects, soon might mean by the close of business on Thursday. For others, soon might mean a couple of months, or it might signal that a prospect is having trouble overcoming a budget problem or some other obstacle in the sale. And while we're at it, how much is "too much," and what does a prospect mean when they say that quality is one of their "biggest concerns"?

The *Discovery* stage of the initial sales call is a good time to clarify vague-onyms as they come up. Clarifying them right up front gives you an opportunity to better understand the prospect's needs and their buying motivations. For example, if a prospect says, *We have recently experienced significant problems,* you should ask for clarification with questions like: *What kind of problems? What do you mean by significant? When did these problems occur?* (Although perhaps not in a rapid-fire delivery!) Here are a couple of other examples where the salesperson has an opportunity to clarify vague-onyms:

Seller: *"Mr. Prospect, you mentioned that you were look-ing for some creative solutions. What did you mean by creative?"*

"When you said you want your new computer system to be easily expandable, what specifically did you mean?"

Because English is a colloquial language, the people who use vague-onyms usually know exactly what they mean. But you don't, and there is danger in assuming you do. What does this mean for salespeople? It means that you should assume nothing because everyday words and phrases can have very different meanings, depending on the context in which they are used and the biases of the people involved.

> **Secret #115**   The meaning of everyday words depends on the context in which they are used and the biases of the people involved.

This idea of clarifying vague-onyms makes some salespeople nervous because they don't want prospects to think they aren't listening. On the contrary, clarifying the prospect's vague-onyms gives you an opportunity to demonstrate that you actually were listening so intently you want to understand exactly what the prospect meant by what they said. It also gives you an opportunity to probe further by asking additional questions.

The Transition into Stage III (Value Proposition)

The objective of Stage II is information gathering. We want to identify enough needs to fuel the sales process moving forward, and we want prospects to feel comfortable enough to openly share. Once you have accomplished these goals, it's time to transition the call into Stage III (*Value Proposition*).

Stage III of the lukewarm sales call is your opportunity to convey the value of your product or service. But it's important to recognize that just because you are ready to present value doesn't necessarily mean your prospects are ready to listen.

How can you make sure your prospects are ready to listen? The answer is by making them curious enough to want more information about how your product can address their specific needs. Prospects must *want* to be educated further. Therefore, to successfully transition the call into Stage III, the easiest way is to keep it simple, by asking, *Would it make sense for me to take a minute and bring you up to speed on our products?* Prospects who were willing to share their issues will surely want to hear more about the solutions you offer. Now you have another mini-invitation to proceed in the call.

STAGE III

Value Proposition

Stage III of the lukewarm sales call is the *Value Proposition*. This stage marks the beginning of your opportunity to educate qualified prospects. It's also where you'll start to build value in your product or service offering.

For people who sell over the phone in a telemarketing capacity, Stage III of the initial sales call becomes the product presentation. When a prospect is interested and they have a need for what you sell, this stage of the call is your opportunity to communicate the value of your solutions. You will learn more about positioning value in chapter 15, "Building Value in the QBS Presentation."

In most strategic sales, the initial sales call is just the first step in a longer process, and it wouldn't make sense to try to close the sale over the phone, or at a trade show, or at a lead generation seminar. Instead, in this call you should be trying to secure a commitment from the prospect to participate in the next step in the sales process, whether that's a meeting, a presentation, a proposal, or a product demonstration.

Provide a Thumbnail Sketch

Top performers in sales are masters of their message. When they have an opportunity to give a full-blown presentation, they provide a complete and detailed account of how their product or service works, and they explain how their proposed solution will address the prospect's needs. These complete presentations can last anywhere from thirty minutes to a couple of hours. When the customer has limited time, however, a top performing salesperson can effectively overview the same basic value message into a *thumbnail sketch*—typically lasting three to five minutes.

Positioning value in Stage III of the lukewarm sales call is somewhat of a balancing act. We want to give potential buyers enough information to get them excited about our solutions, but we also want to leave some "meat on the bone" so they will have a reason to engage further.

> **Secret #116** Providing too much information, too early in the process, makes it way too easy for prospects to say, *"No, thanks."*

The initial sales call typically offers a limited time window in which to communicate your value proposition. To be successful, you must be clear, concise, and impactful. Brevity counts. Tom Peters makes this point in his book, *The Pursuit of WOW*, where he says that given the pace of today's business environment, successful business people should be able to articulate their entire value proposition in twenty-five words or less. Can you do that for the product you sell?

Put Your Best Foot Forward

I like to think of Stage III as a brief "infomercial." It's your opportunity to rave about the value of your product or service. By letting prospects know you can solve their problem or significantly improve their existing condition, you cause them to want more information; and when they want to know more, it's easy to schedule the appropriate next step—an on-site meeting or a product presentation.

> **Secret #117** Salespeople can rant and rave about their products without sounding arrogant. They sound arrogant when they start ranting and raving about themselves.

The goal in Stage III is to put your best foot forward. Essentially, you want to match the value of your solutions to the needs you uncovered in Stage II. You also want to position both the *Gold Medal* and *German Shepherd* aspects of your offering to maximize your opportunity to motivate prospects. Once you get prospects interested, you will have an opportunity to substantiate your claims of value in a more detailed presentation.

Another Opportunity to Leverage the Herd

The Herd Theory can be used very early in your sales calls to pique a prospect's interest, and it can also be leveraged in Stage III to communicate value. Because prospects are naturally cautious, the Herd Theory gives them a sense of comfort, knowing that many other customers have already blazed the trail to success using your offering.

Seller:	*"Mr. Prospect, you mentioned you wanted to increase the efficiency of your business while reducing expenses. I'm not surprised to hear you say that, because that's what other customers like Exxon, IBM, AT&T, Bank of America, Norfolk Southern, General Electric, Westinghouse, Southern Railroad, Ford, and Coca-Cola are already doing."*

Whether it's at the very beginning of the sales process or later on, the Herd Theory is a momentum play. The fact that everyone else is already moving in a certain direction implies that something about your offering must be valuable. Now the question is, do your prospects want to know more? If so, then it's time to move on to Stage IV of the call.

STAGE IV

Close on Next Steps

As in the larger QBS process, once you have successfully generated interest, identified the customer's issues and implications, and communicated value, it's time to close for a commitment. In the lukewarm sales call, closing means securing a mutual agreement to then move on to the appropriate next step(s) in the sales process.

Stage IV is much more than just scheduling additional events, however. It's also an opportunity to manage your prospect's expectations and expand the scope of engagement to include other people who may play a role in the final decision. Additionally, Stage IV of the lukewarm sales call is a good time to begin developing potential champions—people who will help ensure that subsequent sales events go well.

So, how do you close the initial sales call? Let me show you.

Seller:	*"Mr. Prospect, I can go on and on telling you about the value of our product…but here's the problem. There's no good way to show you how the product actually works over the telephone. That's why, with most customers, we set up a (meeting, demo, or presentation) so you can understand how our product will address your specific issues. Would it make sense to get the appropriate people together in front of a piece of paper to map out your options, the impact on your business (or personal situation), and the associated costs?"*

This closing dialogue incorporates a number of strategic phrases. Two of the most critical occur in the very first sentence:

Seller:	*"Mr. Prospect, I can go on and on talking about the value of our product…but here's the problem."*

Notice that the salesperson interrupts his own Stage III value proposition to let the prospect know that he could go *"on and on."* The salesperson's implication that there is so much more to say about the product entices prospects to want to learn more. But instead of going on and on, the seller raises the problem of not being able to do everything over the telephone, and sets up his actual close.

Seller:	*"There's no good way to show you how the product actually works over the telephone."*

The salesperson here is essentially saying that a different venue is needed to satisfy the prospect's desire for additional information. This is a reasonable conclusion, since very few products can be adequately explained via telephone. This positioning actually adds to the salesperson's credibility, because the seller is now helping the prospect solve a problem by working with him or her to figure out how best to proceed. This lays the groundwork for the salesperson to suggest an alternate path.

Seller:	*"That's why, with most customers* [using the Herd Theory], *we set up a meeting, demo, or presentation*

so you can understand how our product will address
your specific issues."

Once again, we're closing with a familiar phrase—asking prospects if they "want" to know how "our product" can address their "specific issues." The salesperson is basically suggesting that unless there's a better way, the prospect should take the direction that we already know is productive. *"Would that be valuable?"*

What If the Prospect Says Yes?

If the prospect says yes and accepts your invitation to take the next step in the sales process, then you have accomplished the primary objective of the initial sales call. But don't get all giddy and hang up, because there's still some work to be done to properly close the call.

> **Secret #118** The prospect's acceptance of your offer to engage further marks the beginning of your sales effort, not the end.

Closing the call is your opportunity to secure the prospect's commitment. It's also your opportunity to set the prospect's expectations so that the next step in the sales process is destined to succeed. To ensure your success, make it a point to help prospects think through the logistics of subsequent events, and work with your contacts in the account to expand the audience to include other key players. Also, to help your champions look good in front of their peers and their manager, I encourage you to cover the following points before wrapping up the call.

Ask: Who Else Needs to be Involved?

Most strategic sales involve more than one person in the account. For sellers, that means the person you originally contacted may not be the person who ultimately signs off on the purchase. Particularly if your next step in the sale is a presentation, you want to expand the audience to include everyone who will have a role in the purchase decision. Some salespeople just assume the right people will automatically show up at the next event. This is a mistake. Instead, you should make it a point to ask, *"Who else needs to be involved?"* We will talk more about getting to the right person, and getting the right people involved in chapter 13.

Seller: *"Would it make sense to get the appropriate people together in front of a piece of paper to map out your*

> *options, the impact on your business (or personal situation), and the associated costs?"*

Now you're firing on all cylinders. Decision makers ultimately want to know three things—their options, the impact on_____, and the associated costs. And, if you are offering to get in front of a piece of paper and map this out for the customer, you're playing right into that desire. That's when they tend to schedule more time on the calendar, and invite more important people.

Scheduling the Actual Event
The best time to schedule potential next steps is before you get off the phone, presumably while you're closing the call. Be sure to pick a date far enough into the future to allow everyone to synchronize their calendars, but not so far off that prospects will say, *"Can you refresh my memory on why we scheduled a meeting?"* It's also important to avoid dates that conflict with regularly scheduled staff meetings, the decision maker's vacation plans, or a national holiday.

Offer a Range of Dates
Most sellers work closely with their internal champions to schedule the next step—a product presentation, for example. Once you select a tentative date, the champion goes off to see if that date works with their boss and other members of the decision committee. When multiple people are involved, there is often a scheduling conflict. So, your champion comes back and says, *"We need to choose another date."* You pick another date, somebody else has a conflict, and you end up playing calendar Ping-Pong, as you try to schedule against a moving target.

Going back and forth to accommodate everyone's schedule can be a frustrating experience for your internal champions, such that it can dampen their enthusiasm. To avoid this, try offering a range of date options. If you want to schedule an event in April, for example, let your prospect know that as of right now, you are available on April 9 and 10, or any time the following week. This gives your champion an opportunity to target a range of dates and hopefully eliminates much of the back-and-forth hassle. Be sure to let your champion know that you need an answer ASAP, so you can work around other clients. It's a nice way to give them first choice, but this positioning also creates a sense of urgency because they realize you can't be expected to hold multiple tentative dates open indefinitely.

What If the Prospect Says No?

QBS's lukewarm calling model increases your probability of success, and it also decreases your risk of failure. By the time you make it to Stage IV in the call, scheduling the next step in the sales process is usually a foregone conclusion. Very few prospects will become curious in Stage I, share their needs in Stage II, listen to your thumbnail sketch in Stage III, and then not want to hear more about the solutions you offer. If you are going to be rejected, it will usually occur much earlier in the call. Nonetheless, prospects at this stage might still say, *"No, thanks."* In that case, my advice is to look for a reason to re-engage at some point in the future, rather than persist until the prospect gets upset, and the longer term opportunity goes down in flames.

Nobody likes being rejected—we've talked about this several times. Most salespeople would rather move on to some other task than dwell on the negative after a prospect says no. But just as we learn from our successes, there is also an opportunity to learn from rejection.

It's critical to understand why your prospects are saying no. If you are having difficulty in the initial moments of your calls, then you may want to revisit your curiosity and credibility strategies. If prospects seem to be losing interest after you provide a thumbnail sketch, you may want to reevaluate your positioning strategy. In either case, I have always encouraged salespeople and sales managers to actively track their losses, because we often learn more from failure than we do from success—and one small adjustment in your approach might become the differentiating factor in your very next sale.

Summary

I no longer make cold calls, and I recommend that you don't either. In addition to being universally despised, cold calls usually produce unimpressive results. To succeed in sales, however, you still must be able to penetrate new prospect accounts and create business opportunities that otherwise wouldn't exist. That's exactly what you will accomplish with a little creativity and some solid techniques—to "arm up" your sales calls and significantly improve your sales results.

Chapter 13

GETTING TO THE "RIGHT PERSON"

The question of who to target in your sales opportunities is an ongoing debate in the world of sales training. Some sales trainers say it's better to start high in the organization and work downward. Others feel it's better to start lower and work your way up the decision-making ladder. In either case, the key is getting to the right person—the one who can actually make a buying decision.

In this chapter, we'll talk about the best place to start, but more importantly, we will show you how to get to the "right person" once you penetrate the account.

So far in this book, we have talked about many different aspects of the strategic sale. We've talked about uncovering needs and positioning value. We have also introduced numerous strategies and techniques for generating prospect curiosity, establishing your credibility, leveraging momentum, and soliciting more accurate feedback. All of these things can significantly enhance your sales effectiveness, but only if you are dealing with the right person in your prospect and customer accounts.

Identifying the "right person" within your targeted prospect accounts is easier said than done. Every sale is unique, and the person (or people) who will actually make the decisions varies from opportunity to opportunity. In some accounts, the president of the company will take a hands-on approach and want to be intimately involved with every aspect of the decision. In other accounts, senior managers will delegate decisions to much lower levels of authority.

Earlier in my career, when I was selling Hospital Information Systems, the chief financial officer always played a role in the decision, because he or she would ultimately have to sign the check. But between hospitals, the CFO's role in the sale varied dramatically. Some CFOs became personally involved with everything from identifying the evaluation criteria to negotiating the terms and conditions of a contract. These CFOs were the true decision makers. In other hospitals, the CFO would assemble a committee to represent the different hospital departments in a formal evaluation process. The committee would then submit a recommendation back to the CFO for approval. Were the people who served on these committees decision makers? You bet. Even if they didn't actually sign the check, their opinions and recommendations were integral to the final decision.

Corporate culture plays a big role in how buying decisions are actually made. So does the personality profile of the person who has the authority to make a purchase. While some people choose to micromanage every decision, others are willing to solicit input from, or delegate responsibility to, other people. For example, some marketing executives will only trust their own instincts when evaluating a proposed advertising campaign, while others will rely heavily on input from others to evaluate an idea or make a decision.

> **Secret #119** While some prospects micromanage every decision, others are more likely to solicit input from, or delegate responsibility to, someone else.

Away from the corporate environment, how decisions are made still depends on the individual prospect. Real estate agents can certainly attest to this. With some prospective couples, the husband clearly has the greater influence and will ultimately determine the outcome of the sale. In other situations, it's the wife who will make the buying decision. In many cases, the husband and wife will each influence certain parts of the decision. The husband might have greater influence when it comes to the yard and structure of the house, while the wife may be more concerned about closet space, bathrooms, and decor. I'm not trying to be sexist here. I'm merely pointing out that different people make decisions differently.

What does this mean for salespeople? It means that sellers can no longer assume they know who will actually make the decision in any given account. Just because the vice president (or the husband) was the decision maker in the last sale doesn't mean it will happen that way in the next.

Top-Down or Bottom-Up

It's easy to assume the decision maker in a corporate sale must be the person with the greatest power. That usually means the person with the biggest title or the one who is highest on the organizational chart. In addition to controlling the purse strings, they also have the authority to determine priorities and set direction. Typically, the higher you go in an organization, the more authority the person you call on will have.

This idea that you'll find greater decision-making authority at the top of the organization has made it fashionable to train salespeople on using a top-down approach—contacting the very top officer in a company first. Some sales trainers base their entire strategy on making the "top officer" the central figure in the sale. While that may be good in theory, it's often impractical because the top officer isn't always the person who will most influence the decision.

If you sell copiers to small businesses, for example, it absolutely makes sense to "call high," because the owner or principal of the company is usually the only one with the authority to make a buying decision. Likewise, if you sell pharmaceuticals or medical supplies, you should call on doctors directly for the same reason. But if you are selling copiers, and you want to penetrate large corporate accounts like Westinghouse or Coca-Cola, does it really make sense to initiate the sales process by calling the CEO? Of course not. In such a large account, there are many layers of decision-making authority and starting too high ends up being a low-percentage play.

I'm not against calling "high" in new prospect accounts. The fact is, I have closed numerous sales that began with the very important top officer in a company. Top-down selling does work. But I have also sold millions of dollars' worth of products and services in prospect accounts where the opportunity started with someone much further down in the organization. This has led me to conclude that bottom-up selling works too.

> **Secret #120** Some of the most exciting sales opportunities begin with someone other than the very important top officer.

When contacting new prospects, there are some definite advantages to calling high. But there are also some risks. Understanding both the benefits and the risks will help you determine how best to proceed when penetrating new accounts.

The Benefits and Risks of Calling High
The most significant benefit of calling high is power. If someone high in the organization likes what you have to say, they usually have the power to set up a meeting or schedule a presentation. They also have the power to make sure the right people are in attendance. And, if the "big kahuna" likes what you have to offer, they ultimately have the power to pull the trigger on a purchase.

Calling high can also create some powerful associative references—an idea that we first introduced back in chapter 7. If you contact someone high in the organization, and they refer you to someone lower, you can leverage your new associative reference to say, *"I just got off the phone with Mr. Peterson (vice president of finance) and he suggested I contact you. Do you have a minute?"* This gives you a very nice opening to initiate a productive dialogue with the "right person."

Ted Ranft, who sells professional services in Philadelphia, has been very successful using a variation of this technique. Ted targets someone high in the organization, knowing full well that his call is going to be intercepted by the voice-mail system. Then, Ted leaves a detailed voice-mail message, followed by this request, *"Can you, or someone on your staff, please call me back?"*

Senior managers are very busy people, and they are always looking for ways to delegate action items. By wording his message this way, Ted is actually inviting the senior manager to forward his voice mail on to someone else—presumably, a subordinate. As a result, Ted almost always receives a return call. If your boss forwarded a message and asked you to follow up, wouldn't you return the call? This technique is effective because it leverages the power of someone at a higher level to help the salesperson penetrate new accounts.

> **Secret #121**   High-level contacts have the authority to make a decision, or the ability to bring together the people who can.

What are the risks of calling high? Actually, there are several. While high-level contacts typically have greater decision-making authority, they are significantly more difficult to reach. As you get higher in an organization, the gatekeepers tend to become more stringent. They have to be tough, because people in positions of authority are being pulled in so many different directions. They are also being bombarded with sales calls. Even if you succeed in getting past the gatekeeper, the senior manager you're calling may be so far removed from the details they don't recognize the existence of a problem. Consequently, they wouldn't see a need for your solution. And even if they do recognize the problem, high-level managers simply cannot afford to personally involve themselves in each and every decision their organization makes.

Another risk of calling too high is political fallout. If a senior executive doesn't see a need for your product or service, or they are already pursuing another solution, they can quickly kill your opportunity by saying, *"No thanks."* Sure, you could still call someone lower in the organization, and you may even succeed in penetrating the account, but you will eventually have to come back to the big boss who has already said no.

If a high-level executive *does* like your offering and agrees to take the next step in the sales process, you may face a different challenge—the risk that lower-level people in the organization will resent you for circumventing their authority and going straight to the top.

The Benefits and Risks of Calling Low

There are advantages to calling low in an organization as well. The biggest advantage is lower-level people tend to be more accessible. This doesn't mean they aren't busy. It just means they are more likely to pick up the telephone when you call or be available to meet with you. This is a tremendous advantage for salespeople. Before I meet with a corporate executive, for example, I try to talk with someone lower in the organization first. This gives me a chance to do some reconnaissance work and collect valuable information about their current business environment. People at lower levels typically have more time for details, and they're almost always closer to the problems that need to be solved.

Calling low in an organization also gives you an opportunity to develop internal champions. We know most people like to look good in front of their peers and their management, so if we can garner the support of people at lower levels, we can leverage them as advocates to help take our value messages higher in the organization. It will always be true that internal champions have more credibility than a salesperson who's just trying to break into a new account.

Lower-level contacts also make good associative references. Call it reverse name-dropping. It can be a very effective, for example, to leave a voice mail with a senior manager saying, *"Mr. Prospect, my name is Tony Simpkins, and I'm with Unified Systems, Inc. I just got off the phone with Frank in distribution—and I have a question. When you get a chance, could you please call me back?"* Most high-level managers will return your call because they'll want to know what's up with Frank in distribution.

Calling low is not without risks, however. Perhaps the greatest risk is being told by someone at a lower level of authority not to call anyone else in the organization—particularly not their boss. Now you're blocked. You could ignore this mandate and call their boss anyway, but then you risk losing the support of a potential influencer, champion, or coach. Of course, if you heed their advice, then your proposal might not ever get the visibility it needs to be seriously considered.

> **Secret #122** The greatest risk of calling low is being blocked by someone who doesn't have the authority to make a decision.

Another risk of calling too low is that people at lower levels of authority may not see the bigger picture. If their sphere of influence is limited to certain job functions, they may not be in the loop on decisions regarding the company's strategic direction or the timing of an upcoming purchase. As a result, calling too low can result in incomplete or inaccurate information. Even if your contacts are aware of the bigger picture, it's very possible that you could threaten their security. Perhaps you will expose a weakness in their current job performance. Or, your product's ability to enhance productivity (or reduce overhead) might eliminate their job altogether. Needless to say, people who feel threatened are less than helpful, and they might even try to sabotage your selling efforts.

Strategic Decisions Usually Involve Multiple Players

One single person often makes purchase decisions for smaller items. For example, when a transaction involves products like cosmetics, radios, shoes, books, or office supplies, the actual buyer rarely needs someone else's approval in order to make a purchase. But when you are selling high-end solutions to corporations or even to someone personally, it's a different story. Very few large decisions are made by one single person.

Strategic decisions usually involve multiple players. Of course, we are talking about decisions that will impact multiple areas of a business over an extended period of time. To go back to an earlier example, purchasing a hospital information system is a very strategic decision, one that affects doctors, nurses, patients, employees, hospital administrators, and in some cases, the entire community. Similarly, when companies purchase database software, employee benefits packages, telephone switches, consulting services, manufacturing equipment, or commercial real estate, they are making strategic decisions that will have far-reaching effects on their businesses.

Strategic purchases are more complex, because each of the participants in the decision has their own agenda. Nurses who evaluate hospital information systems, for example, want user-friendly clinical systems that will enable them to provide better patient care. Department managers want system capabilities that reduce their administrative workload. Meanwhile, the "ever frugal" accounting department may be satisfied with fewer bells and whistles, in order to reduce the acquisition cost of the system. At some point, the hospital's decision committee will assimilate all of this input, weigh it against the decision criteria, and make a recommendation.

When multiple players are involved, it's unwise to focus on any one individual in the hope that they alone will determine the outcome of the purchase.

Instead, we want to focus on everyone who can influence the outcome of the decision. This includes *decision makers, influencers, executive sponsors, champions, coaches, informants,* and *anti-champions.* In order to help you identify who's who in your prospect accounts, here's a profile of each major player in the strategic sale.

The Decision Maker

As I said earlier, the decision maker in a prospect account can be difficult to spot. In many cases, the person who signs the check will also make the decision. Other times, the person who signs the check has delegated the decision to someone else. And, it's also true that some people *claim* to be decision makers even though they are not.

In simplest terms, the decision maker is the person in the account who will ultimately "pull the trigger" on the decision to purchase. They have the authority to accept or reject your proposal, and they are held accountable for the decisions they make. But just as no man is an island, few decisions are made in a vacuum. Most decision makers solicit input from other sources. In doing so, they are influenced by the opinions, biases, and recommendations of people around them.

> **Secret #123** Not everyone can *pull the trigger* and make a decision, but lots of people can *pull the plug* on your opportunity to sell.

As salespeople, we definitely want to target the decision maker within our prospect accounts, but we also want to work closely with those people who will influence the outcome of the purchase decision.

Influencers

Influencers are the people that have the decision maker's ear. While influencers can't actually make the buying decision, they can definitely affect the outcome of a sale by providing input and information that will sway the decision one way or another. That's why they're called "influencers."

These people are important to identify because of their effect on the opinions of other people within the account. Especially when a committee is issuing a recommendation, influencers can garner the votes of other people to create an even more powerful voice in the final decision.

> **Secret #124** Key influencers are able to *influence* opinions and create a very powerful voice in the final decision.

One caution, though. Don't be fooled into believing that the most vocal participants in a decision have the greatest influence. It's quite possible that the person who sits quietly and listens carefully wields the biggest sword. Sellers also have to be aware that influencers can affect the outcome of an opportunity in more than one direction. A key influencer who likes your product or service can help you immensely, while an influencer who either dislikes your offering, or supports some other alternative, can negate your sales efforts from inside the account.

The Executive Sponsor

When the top officer in a prospect account makes a decision, that means the decision maker and the executive sponsor are one and the same. But as we discussed already, larger companies have to delegate decision-making authority because the very important top officer cannot spare the time to be intimately involved in every purchase.

Most delegated decisions have an executive sponsor—a senior manager who doesn't actively participate in the detailed evaluation, but does approve the final decision before the purchase takes place. The executive sponsor is generally the ranking officer in the part of a business most directly impacted by an impending decision.

It's very difficult to sell an executive sponsor without first securing the support of the decision maker and any key influencers. In fact, executive sponsors usually don't like a top-down sales approach. That's because they rely on the diligence and expertise of their subordinates to investigate potential solutions and present the best alternative. It is valuable, however, to find out as much as you can about the executive sponsor, so you can appropriately package your solution for easy approval.

Internal Champions

One thing that separates top salespeople from the rest of the masses is their ability to develop internal champions. An internal champion is someone in the account who wants your product or service offering so much that they are willing to go to bat for you within the organization to help secure a favorable decision.

Internal champions become your inside salespeople. They are the ones who are willing to support your proposal and fight to overcome objections that get raised. They usually have an emotional stake in the solution, and in many cases, they want the sale to happen as much as the salesperson does.

How do you build internal champions? The answer is by making your victory in the sale their victory as well. Champions are people who have something to gain if your product or service is selected and something to lose if it is not. For salespeople, the trick is figuring out who will benefit if your proposed solution is chosen.

Let's remember that these internal advocate relationships are developed. Very few of your prospects have ever attended a sales training course. Therefore, they most likely will need guidance to sell your solutions internally. But one thing is for sure: internal champions *do* want to look good in front of their peers and their manager. So, it's to your advantage to teach them how to effectively position your proposal. This is an investment that can pay you back many times over, as your internal champions become an extension of your own selling efforts. One other point: the more authority your champions have, the greater impact they will have on the outcome of a decision.

Coaches

Coaches won't fight for your solution like an internal champion would, but they can absolutely give you valuable advice and direction about how best to proceed in the sale. Ultimately, coaches want you to succeed in the sale, but they are not in a position to actively promote your proposal.

Your coach may be someone who is directly involved with the decision, or your coach could be an independent third party working in the account. At NetFrame Systems, for example, we often partnered with third-party leasing companies to finance the sale. Not surprisingly, we shared information and coached each other about how to succeed in the account. Other vendors and outside consultants can also be valuable coaches. In reality, it's amazing how much coaching you can receive if you are just willing to ask for help.

Informants

Some people can assist you in the sale, even if they are not in a position to champion your solution or coach you on how best to proceed. We call these people informants. What they can do is provide you with valuable insight or information that will help you plan your next move. As an example, administrative assistants and executive secretaries make great informants, although it's remarkable how many salespeople just blow these people off as being unimportant. You should try to develop relationships with informants, because they often have valuable information that will help you more effectively navigate the sale. They may know something about your competition or about the status of the budget. They may also know when the decision maker will be back in his office or what's on the agenda for the next staff meeting.

Informant relationships are based on trust. Hence, the more credibility you establish with a potential informant, the more information you will receive.

Indifferents and Anti-Champions

There are other people in the sale who aren't decision makers, influencers, executive sponsors, champions, coaches, or informants, but who are still important to know and understand. These people fall into one of two categories: "indifferents" or "anti-champions."

People who are indifferent couldn't care less about the outcome of a decision. Either they're not impacted by the purchase, or they are too busy fighting other fires to dedicate any emotional bandwidth to your sales cycle. Trying to cultivate a relationship with someone who is indifferent could have some long-term benefit, but you should definitely limit your investment of time, effort, and resources in the shorter term.

Anti-champions are the people you have to watch out for. They are the ones who will speak out against your proposed solution, whether they favor a competitive offering or just want to maintain the status quo. How much time should you spend with anti-champions? Some sellers attempt to turn them around by proving that their proposed solution is indeed superior. I usually don't waste any time on that. If they are truly anti-champions, direct confrontation just fuels additional debate and disagreement. Instead, my strategy is to try to neutralize the anti-champion's negative influence by getting them to agree that both solutions could be viable options. Then, once they agree that my solution is indeed viable, I work through my internal champions to position my proposal as the best alternative.

> **Secret #125** The best way to neutralize an anti-champion is to get them to agree that both solutions are viable alternatives.

Knowing Who's Who in the Decision

When a salesperson first calls on a new account, they may know a few names and titles, but until they actually engage the prospect, it's impossible to know who's who in the decision-making process just by looking at the facade of a building. As we've said, every prospect is unique, and just because someone played an important role in your last sale doesn't mean a person at the same level will be a key player in the next.

The actual decision maker might be the president of the company. Perhaps a vice president, director, regional manager, supervisor, or a technical analyst will make the decision. In some cases, an on-site consultant will make the decision. Identifying the actual decision maker is only part of the puzzle, however. To maximize your effectiveness, you must also identify the other key players, including influencers, potential champions, coaches, informants, executive sponsors, and anti-champions.

In a complex sale, the director of operations may choose your product after being influenced by several key department managers. But when the recommendation is presented to the company president (the executive sponsor), suddenly there is resistance from the internal auditor—your anti-champion in the account—who is more familiar with a competitor's product. When you sell complex products to large corporations, any number of political and economic subtleties can affect the outcome of a decision. But one thing is sure: anyone who doesn't understand the value of your product or service will ultimately vote against it. That's why it's critical for salespeople to understand how decisions are made and who needs to be involved in them.

> **Secret #126** Anyone in an account who doesn't understand the value of your product or service will ultimately vote against it.

How can salespeople know who needs to be involved in a decision? By asking questions that will not only reveal the key players, but also their role in the evaluation, selection, and approval process for your proposed solution. That's why I always make it a point to ask the following questions:

Seller: *"Are you the right person to talk with about _____?"*

If this sounds familiar, it's because this was one of the initial questions we posed in the lukewarm sales call in chapter 12. It's a great question because you are asking the person to either accept responsibility for a particular function of the business, or refer you to someone else.

Seller: *"Who else needs to be involved in the discussion?"*

Since most strategic decisions do involve multiple players, it's critical to find out who else will need to be involved in the decision. To reduce the risk of getting blocked by someone lower in the organization, I purposely phrase the question this way. Even if my contact wants to limit access to other people in the account, this phrasing will usually produce a response that lets me know who the key players are, in addition to giving me some valuable information about how decisions are typically made.

Seller: *"Who will ultimately sign off on the purchase?"*

This question will usually identify the decision maker and the executive sponsor. It may also initiate a discussion about the various steps a recommendation must go through to be approved.

Seller: *"Is there anyone who might oppose this proposal?"*

Who knows…you might be able to smoke out any anti-champions early enough to neutralize them. At the very least, using this question will help you identify potential opponents to your proposed solution.

Probe for Champions and Coaches

In addition to finding out who fills the various roles in a decision, I also want to find out whether the person I'm talking to would be willing to help me as a coach or a champion. It can be a little awkward to come right out and ask, so I use the following questions to give prospects an opportunity to let me know where they stand in the sale.

Seller: *"How do you feel about the proposal that's on the table?"*

Essentially, you are asking the prospect how they plan to vote. Those people who oppose your solution will either be antagonistic or tight-lipped. Prospects who support your offering, however, will often step forward with some valuable information and opinion about where your proposal currently stands in the evaluation process, and how you should proceed in the sale.

Seller: *"How would you handle this situation if you were in my shoes?"*

People love to give advice. We talked about this in chapter 11. If you are willing to ask, it's amazing how much help you can receive. Personally, I have always contended that your best coach in the account is the person on the other end of the telephone. Virtually anyone in the account can be a valuable coach. In addition to knowing the status of the sale, they also know the political climate within the account. Anyone and everyone can help you in some way, if you are just willing to ask.

> **Secret #127**   When making calls, your best coach in an account is the person on the other end of the telephone.

The Best Place to Start

Question Based Selling doesn't advocate a top-down approach *or* a bottom-up approach. Instead, we take the position that, in the vast majority of new prospect opportunities, it's virtually impossible to know how decisions are made until you actually penetrate the account.

So, rather than trying to guess who the "right people" are, I recommend that sellers target multiple contacts within their prospect accounts. Where it's appropriate, call prospects at a high level, even if your chances of getting through are somewhat limited. But you should also pursue lower levels too, in an effort to build grassroots support for your product or service. Then, once you get in (at whatever level), you can leverage your contacts within the account to identify the right people, uncover needs, build internal champions, and move the sales process forward.

Cross-Reference Information You Receive

One of the challenges sellers face when talking to more than one person within an account is receiving conflicting information. Because people tend to view things differently, you are likely to receive different information from a high-level manager than you would from a technician. It's easy to assume that people in positions of authority are always right, but we have to be careful not to discount the value of the information we receive from other sources. When you do receive conflicting information, it's important to find out which version of the truth is correct. In QBS, we call this cross-referencing.

Cross-referencing is a questioning technique that's designed to validate the accuracy of information you receive. Essentially, you pose the same questions to different contacts within the account and then compare their responses. If the information you receive from two or more sources is consistent, that information is probably accurate. However, if the information you receive from different sources does not match, then further investigation is required. Chances are good one of the answers is accurate—you just don't know which one until you do some follow-up.

> **Secret #128** When multiple people give the same response, the information you are getting is probably accurate.

Cross-referencing gives you an invaluable opportunity to uncover some of the political subtleties within your prospect accounts. Using this technique, you can discover who is likely to help you make a sale, and who is likely to lead you down a dead-end path. This knowledge will help you more effectively position your solution and navigate the sales process.

Summary

Getting to the right person in your prospect accounts is critical to your success in sales. So is understanding all the different influences that will affect the purchase decision. Whether you're selling computer systems, medical supplies, life insurance, financial services, manufactured goods, or employee benefits, every account is unique, and different people will take on different roles. Your job is to successfully identify those people who will affect the decision, so you can effectively manage the outcome of the sale. Once you know who's who in the decision, the next step is getting them involved in the sales process, so you can build value in how you position your solutions. Strategic positioning is what we'll talk about next.

Chapter 14

RE-ENGINEERING THE ELEVATOR PITCH

Ready for a curve ball? What if I told you that how most salespeople position the value of their products and services is exactly the opposite of how customers make purchase decisions? If that is true, you'd have a decision to make about how you want to be perceived by your target customers. The question is, would you be ready and willing to adjust your approach?

Before we talk about specific presentation techniques, we must first examine the strategy for matching your value to the customer's needs. So far, we have talked about needs development and expanding your value proposition. Now we need to put it together into something other than a standard elevator pitch.

Companies often spend millions of dollars trying to craft next generation messages to "arm" their respective sales forces with a more impactful elevator pitch. Then they hire me—and I show up and tell the client that starting with an elevator pitch puts the salesperson in an extremely weak position.

> **Secret #129** Opening with an elevator pitch about the company or product puts a salesperson or sales organization in an extremely weak position.

The phrase "elevator pitch" is a colloquialism that characterizes the statements salespeople use to open their conversations with prospective customers. The reference comes from the visual one would get if you suddenly found yourself in an elevator with the key decision maker at one of your important prospect accounts. As soon as the decision maker pushes the button for the twelfth floor, you essentially have a small window of time in which to say something that would hopefully be impactful enough to get the prospect's attention. This type of situation occurs at the beginning of every sales call and product presentation as well. Knowing that prospects are quick to form impressions, salespeople feel a similar pressure to say something impactful that will grab and hold the prospect's attention.

Starting your sales calls or presentations with an elevator pitch is problematic, however, as I pointed out in chapter 2. Why is the traditional elevator pitch such a problem? Let me explain with a real-life scenario that occurred shortly after I began training salespeople. Several months had gone by when my office assistant received a call from IBM World Headquarters. As it turned out, the vice president of Eastern operations for IBM had heard about Question Based Selling from another QBS client, and his administrative assistant was calling to schedule a conference call with me, so her boss could find out more about the training programs we offered.

A call was scheduled for the following Tuesday afternoon. As I dialed into the appropriate number at the prescribed time, I was immediately put on hold into one of those automated conference-calling forums. Honestly, I was a bit nervous. As you might imagine, IBM was a lucrative prospect for a sales trainer like myself. After nervously waiting for several minutes, the VP came onto the conference call and was as nice as he could be. He apologized for being a few minutes late and then jumped right into his purpose for calling.

"Tom, I've heard great things about Question Based Selling and the programs you deliver," he said. *"We have a new initiative at IBM to modify our strategic sales process, and based on the recommendations of several colleagues, QBS seems like it could help us transition our sales teams. Therefore, Tom, I've got the next forty-five minutes on my calendar blocked off so you can tell me all about Question Based Selling."*

Now, let me pause the story for a moment. Do you think that opening is what a sales trainer like myself would want to hear from the vice president of Eastern operations at a very large prospective client like IBM? The answer is, yes, absolutely! Besides having already heard positive feedback from another QBS client, he was, in essence, giving me a red carpet invitation to tell him all about Question Based Selling.

My ego started to swell and the natural tendency would have been to jump right in and start "telling" him about QBS and all the wonderful things we could do for his sales teams. The urge to brag on our programs and client accomplishments was huge. Isn't that how most salespeople begin their presentations—with some form of elevator pitch or information dump?

Fortunately, I held back, because I have learned that starting with the elevator pitch is the quickest way to commoditize your value proposition.

Secret #130   Starting with the elevator pitch is the quickest way to commoditize one's value proposition.

What Impression Do You Want Prospects to Form?

When you first engage a new prospect, what percentage of them do you suppose start forming an initial impression of you and your company the second you open your mouth? The answer is 100 percent. Literally everyone you talk with will start forming an impression of you from the very beginning of your sales conversations. The question is, what impression(s) do you want prospects and customers to form about you?

With respect to sales training, I figure most sales VPs have experienced plenty of training programs over the years—some good, and others not so much. It's also safe to assume that whatever I say about the QBS methodology will likely be compared to the impressions they have formed as a result of previous sales training experiences. Knowing this to be the case, I definitely didn't want to start spewing buzzwords and worn-out phrases that would make me sound just like the rest of the sales training establishment.

With an interested prospect who admittedly had already heard positive things about the QBS methodology, I could have jumped right into my pitch about Question Based Selling. After all, I am fully convinced that what I teach is very different from traditional sales methods. But even though I didn't succumb to the urge to do just that, I would like to show you what the QBS elevator pitch might have sounded like and let you judge for yourself. Who knows, you might be duly impressed. Maybe you'll even stand up and salute when you hear it. On the other hand, you might find that the standard elevator pitch (for QBS) sounds very similar to what every other sales trainer would say about their training programs. Therefore, I invite you to imagine yourself listening objectively in order to form your own impression and we'll see what happens.

Sample QBS Elevator Pitch: *"After seventeen years in the trenches of corporate sales and management, I developed a high-end sales methodology called Question Based Selling, and now I teach salespeople all over the world how* *to be more effective in penetrating new accounts. I help people uncover needs, increase the buyer's sense of urgency, build internal champions, shorten the sales process, increase the size of their sales forecasts, close more deals, handle objections, increase margins, maintain market share, be proactive versus reactive …blah…blah…blah…blah."*

Isn't this what every sales trainer says about their programs? You know it is! Everyone who offers sales training talks about pipeline generation, penetrating new accounts, handling objections, and closing sales. And you can be sure they all make similar claims of superiority that sales executives have heard many times before. Consequently, when prospects hear the same old pitch, it's logical to assume they might form the impression that, *"Hey, this person sounds just like everyone else."* Rather than differentiating myself, leading with the solution commoditizes your value because you sound no different than anyone else who's in a similar business.

If the company you represent sells high-value products or services, you don't want to sound the same as everyone else. Instead, you want to differentiate your solutions, your company, and most importantly, yourself, causing prospects to form the impression that, *"Hey, this person sounds very different (and potentially more valuable) than everyone else!"*

SPA vs. PAS Positioning

Back in the 1980s and early '90s, a paradigm shift occurred in the marketplace, where sales leaders began to recognize that it was more lucrative to focus on selling a total solution as opposed to just selling individual product features. As a result, sales conversations began to shift from being product-oriented to more solution-oriented, even though the company itself or the products being offered hadn't really changed. Particularly in large accounts, proposing an entire suite of products and services offered the mutual benefit of providing fully integrated solutions for the customer and big fat commission checks for the seller. Solutions, solutions, solutions…it was all about selling solutions. Ever since, the word *solutions* has become one of the favorite "linguistic condiments" of marketers everywhere. Especially when preceded by the phrase "leading provider of," such as claiming to be "the leading provider of solutions," those words are regularly used to enrich the headlines on everything from corporate web pages to press releases and product literature.

Selling solutions continues to be a good business strategy in the current economic climate, though sellers must recognize that the playing field has changed with regard to the use of industry buzzwords. If you want to be seen as customer-centric, then the focus of the sales conversation should no longer revolve around your solutions. Instead, customers in every industry are much more focused on addressing their own problems, issues, and concerns than they are in hearing yet another sales pitch.

> **Secret #131** Customers are much more focused on addressing their own problems, issues, and concerns than they are in hearing your sales pitch.

Even so, sellers naturally gravitate to what I would characterize as an *SPA approach* when positioning their company, products, and even themselves. SPA is how most salespeople have been conditioned over time to sell themselves and their products. We start telling about our solutions (S), in the hopes that the conversation will naturally transition into a more in-depth discussion of the customer's problems (P). Then, later on in the conversation or sales process, we assume customers will inevitably consider how our proposed solution stacks up against other alternatives (A). Hence the abbreviation, S-P-A.

After much study and having worked with literally thousands of salespeople, I have concluded that the reason sellers gravitate so naturally to an SPA approach is because it's easier to start a conversation by talking about what we do know (our solutions) than what we don't know (the customer's problems). Maybe it's fortunate that we've finally reached the point where the theory behind this notion of "selling solutions" can be called into question and more carefully examined. As an example, let me show you a couple of logic problems with the traditional SPA positioning model.

Let's start by asking: What do you suppose is more important to the typical customer when you first engage—their problems (P) or a salesperson's solutions (S)? From my vantage point, it's clear that the vast majority of customers are much more focused on their own problems, issues, goals, and objectives than they are interested in hearing a sales pitch. Thus, it no longer makes sense for a customer-focused salesperson to open his or her presentation with a data dump of detailed product information (S), rather than focusing on the customer's problems (P).

Nonetheless, salespeople are quick to do exactly this, as countless training seminars and sales courses still espouse the value of sellers opening with a perfunctory elevator pitch about their products and services, in the hopes of securing the prospect's attention. I'm sure some of you will think to yourselves, "I don't do that." And maybe you don't. But to prove how prevalent SPA is among sellers today, try this experiment. Next time you deal with a salesperson of any kind, make it a point to ask them, "Can you tell me about your product?" Then, check your watch. Time them to see just how long they ramble on about themselves, their products, or their company, before they realize they have absolutely no idea what you might need, or why you even asked the question.

What's the alternative to SPA? Well, the answer will reveal itself if we apply some deductive reasoning. In order to even have an opportunity to provide solutions, one must first be able to identify the customer's problem or problems (P). To the extent that selling is about helping people accomplish their goals, objectives, issues, and concerns, then whatever advice and direction a salesperson ends up providing should be prescriptive in nature, and not just a data dump.

We agreed earlier that it's important to be customer-focused, right? Well, if we consider customers are much more interested in their own problems (P) than a salesperson's solutions (S), and we recognize that sellers must be able to identify a problem in order to provide valuable solutions, then wouldn't it make more sense to adjust your sales strategy in order to follow more of a *PAS approach*?

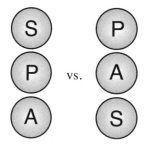

PAS is not only a more effective positioning strategy; it also represents the logical thought process most people use to make decisions every day. Case in point: in order for a customer to purchase your product or service, the decision maker at some point must think to themselves, *Because I have this problem (P), which the alternatives (A) don't solve as effectively, that's why I am going to choose to purchase or implement this particular solution (S).*

Essentially, every value-based decision that you or your customers make is arrived at using PAS logic. Whether you are considering the purchase of a new computer, car, house, or even a new outfit, the underlying decision process is essentially the same. Because you have a problem (P), that the alternatives don't solve as effectively (A), you are going to choose this particular solution (S).

For example, have you purchased a digital camera in the last few years? If so, let me take a guess at the thought process you used to make that decision—and I don't even know you personally. Regarding the digital camera, at some point you said to yourself, *Because I have this problem (a need to take great pictures) (P), which the alternatives (my current camera, my movie camera, buying a disposable camera while on vacation, or taking no pictures at all) (A) don't solve as effectively, I will choose to buy this new digital camera (S).*

The underlying logic is universal, and it doesn't matter how complex the purchase. When a hospital administrator chooses between multiple suppliers from which to purchase medical equipment, the decision maker in the hospital must conclude the following: *Because we have certain goals, objectives, issues, concerns, wants, needs, desires, or problems (P), which the alternatives (other suppliers) (A) don't solve as effectively, that's why we are going to procure these solutions (S) from this particular vendor.*

As an added bonus, the underlying logic of this new PAS positioning model has a hidden benefit. Simply put, you bond with people by focusing on what's most important to them—their goals, issues, needs, concerns, desires, and problems (P)—as opposed to whatever is most important to you—your solutions (S). This especially makes sense in the selling arena, because in order to communicate the value of your product or service, you must first have something to build value against. Bonding with prospective buyers on what's most important to them is also strategically significant, because that's what allows them to begin to trust you.

> **Secret #132**   Bonding with prospective buyers on what's most important to them is significant, because that's what allows them to begin to trust you.

You Bond with People on Their Problems

Having good intentions is not the issue. Sellers who lead with their solutions are doing so in the hopes of engaging prospective customers in more in-depth discussions about their needs. After all, uncovering potential problems is what ultimately creates sales opportunities. But leading with your solutions, in order to get into a discussion of the customer's needs, follows an illogical progression. Besides the fact that an elevator pitch filled with industry buzzwords and phrases is so easily commoditized, positioning your solution first makes no sense. Prospects don't have needs because a salesperson happens to offer a potential solution.

To communicate the value of your product or service, you must first have something to build value against. Therefore, rather than trying to bond with potential customers on your solutions, you will create many more opportunities to provide value if you bond with them on their problems, issues, and concerns. To illustrate this point, let's go back to my conference call with the vice president of Eastern operations from IBM. If you remember, having heard good things about Question Based Selling, he invited me to tell him about the QBS Methodology. But rather than opening with a sales pitch hoping to get him excited about my solutions, I did just the opposite. In fact, here is how my initial conversation with this IBM sales executive actually went. Frankly, this is how most of my sales calls for QBS training go.

First, since it's always nice to hear positive feedback from previous client events, I thanked him for his positive comments about my sales training programs. Then I responded to his request for information by saying, *"I would be happy to tell you all about Question Based Selling. Can I ask you a couple specifics about your sales team so I can give you relevant information?"*

Of course, he said, *"Sure."* This is that one time in QBS that I recommend exact words to secure a mini-invitation from the customer. With one simple question, I have instantly transitioned the conversation out of "presentation mode," and into *Discovery.* This creates a perfect opportunity for me to ask questions that will help identify potential needs (as we talked about in chapter 8). Again, practicing what I preach, I started with a series of diagnostic questions—a QBS technique that enables sellers to establish credibility early in the dialogue.

TF:	*"How many people do you currently manage?"*
VP:	*"Approximately 300."*
TF:	*"Does that include Systems Engineers?"*
VP:	*"No, we have another 65 SEs."*
TF:	*"Do you currently leverage an inside sales organization?"*
VP:	*"Actually, two. One of our inside sales teams is in the Northeast, and the other is in Atlanta."*

TF:	*"Are most of your people centralized in regional sales offices or spread out in virtual offices?"*
VP:	*"We have several regional offices, but many of our salespeople are transitioning to a virtual environment."*

Once the conversation was appropriately kicked off with a series of relevant diagnostic questions about his sales team, I switched gears with my questions to focus on needs development (chapter 9), in order to bond with this prospect on his specific problems (P). Let's continue the dialogue.

TF:	*"Well, let me ask you this. Do you have salespeople out in the field trying to penetrate new accounts, making lots of sales calls and leaving lots of voice-mail messages, but not being called back?"*
VP:	*"We absolutely do! Penetrating accounts at a strategic level is a big challenge for us."*
TF:	*"Question Based Selling will solve that!"*
VP:	*"Really?"*
TF:	*"Yes…and, since we're talking about your goals for the training, let me ask you about something else. Do you find that with newly hired salespeople, some ramp up in a very short period of time while others struggle along and sometimes never make it over the hump?"*
VP:	*"Yes. Ramping new salespeople up is another challenge."*
TF:	*"QBS solves that too."*
VP:	*"How?"*

Suddenly, the conversation we were having was very different than it would have been had I opened with the standard elevator pitch. Already, I had identified a couple of big concerns and he was inviting me to educate him on how we could help address those issues.

> **Secret #133** You bond with prospects by focusing your attention on their problems, not on your solutions.

After raising some key business challenges, you earn the right to engage decision makers (like this VP) in a productive conversation about their needs and your solutions. Bonding with prospects on their problems is also the key to broadening the sale by creating many opportunities for you to provide value. Let me show you what I mean.

Expand Your Opportunity to Provide Value

This is where our earlier discussion about issues and implications gets applied to the actual customer conversation. If the products and services you sell offer numerous benefits, then you will want to give qualified buyers multiple reasons to buy from you. That's why it is important to challenge the customer's thinking and broaden the scope of your sales questions to include a variety of different areas where your products and services can add value. Remember that while we want to bond with prospects on their problems, we also want to increase their sense of urgency by expanding their needs and giving them many reasons to move forward with a purchase. Expanding their needs also expands your value proposition, which increases your probability of success in making the sale.

What problems do *your* prospects and customers face? In technology sales, for example, customers consistently encounter business issues like reliability, manageability, and upgradability in their daily routines. If you sell manufacturing equipment, issues like inventory, cost containment, or time-to-market might be areas of interest for potential customers. If you sell financial services, then business issues like timely reporting, margin requirements, or the institution's track record might be in the forefront of your customer's mind.

Whether you sell medical supplies, telecommunications services, consulting, or durable goods, you can easily build a list of key business issues that typically drive decisions in those selling environments. But as I said earlier, key business issues like reliability, manageability, upgradability, inventory, cost containment, time-to-market, reporting, margin requirements, and a company's previous track record usually aren't the driving force behind strategic decisions. While issues like these are often the focus of the typical elevator pitch, they are usually not what drives the actual purchase decision. Instead, it's the implications of the problem and the corresponding benefits of your solution that drive most buying decisions. Sound familiar? Back in chapters 2 and 9 we explained that the implications of a problem are the underlying hot buttons that cause problems to be important to your specific customer.

Suppose You Sold Water Pumps

To show you how implications can expand your opportunity to provide value using the PAS model, here's a simple exercise I use when delivering "live" QBS training programs. For the next few minutes, let's suppose you work for a company that manufactures and sells water pumps. Your target market is homeowners who have flooded basements, as the result of bad weather or a pipe that unexpectedly bursts. And let's say your company offers a solution that can pump the water out of the client's basement. Note: For the skeptics who are thinking, "I don't understand how an example about selling water pumps can help me," I invite you to buckle your seat belt, as this exercise may radically change the way you interact with prospects and customers in the future.

Back to our example, let's suppose that you received a qualified lead and tomorrow, you and I are going to call on this new prospect who has a flooded basement. Before we actually go on the sales call, however, let's spend a few minutes strategizing together about how we want this call to go. We would certainly want to be on the same page when we got in front of the customer, and strategizing in advance will give us an opportunity to "arm" ourselves with a broader list of implications that will enable us to expand the prospect's needs and increase their sense of urgency for making a decision.

The first step in our strategy session would be to identify the customer's problem. Given the scenario I just described, it's relatively obvious what the prospect's problem is—they have water in their basement. Seems simple enough, doesn't it? Be careful, though. Many sellers hear about a problem in their sales calls and jump immediately into their value propositions, saying, *"Hey, let me tell you about my pump!"*

But guess what? People don't buy water pumps because they have water in the basement. They buy water pumps because of the potential implications that could arise as the result of having a flooded basement. There's a difference.

To strategize about potential implications, I ask you this question: Why might water in the basement be a problem for this customer? While there is no way to know a customer's specific hot buttons before we actually meet them, we can absolutely prepare ourselves in advance of the call by identifying potential implications might impact their decision. Therefore, if we worked together to create a top ten list of potential risks homeowners face as a result of having flooded basements, we might end up with a list of implications like the one on the following page.

Water in the basement could...

1. ...cause structural damage to the home.

2. ...damage personal property.

3. ...create a mildew or odor issue.

4. ...present health or safety risks.

5. ...affect other systems in the house (AC, electrical, etc.).

6. ...likely create a huge inconvenience.

7. ...present an insurance hassle.

8. ...increase stress within the household.

9. ...reduce the homeowner's property value.

10. ...end up costing the homeowner lots of money.

This list of implications represents the driving force behind the purchase of every water pump. Think about it this way. If a prospective buyer isn't concerned about things like structural damage, property damage, health risks, odor, their time, stress, insurance, and costs, then you probably won't sell them a pump. But, to the extent you can lead the conversation toward these potential implications, you can significantly expand the prospect's sense of urgency by giving them multiple reasons to buy from you.

Two Common Mistakes

To put this in perspective, let's jump out of our hypothetical strategy session and fast-forward to tomorrow's sales call—and think about what might actually happen when we meet the prospect face-to-face.

Knock-knock. When the homeowner answers the door, we first introduce ourselves by saying, *"Hi, my name is Tom Freese, and this is my assistant, (your name), and we're with XYZ Water Pump Company. How can we help?"*

The prospect responds saying, *"I've got a flooded basement."*

This is where the person with a traditional sales mentality hears a problem they can fix and has an intense urge to jump right into their value proposition, by saying, "Let me tell you about our pumps!" Of course, the value proposition at this point in the sale would take the form of an elevator pitch where the prospect would hear some well-rehearsed rhetoric that sounds like *blah...blah... blah*. As I said earlier, starting off with a sales pitch puts you in a weak position, because the buzzwords that make up your value proposition are instantly commoditized. They sound just like what any of your competitors would say, or has already said. Furthermore, if you want prospects to have more than one reason to buy from you, then you will want to uncover multiple implications of the problem, thereby giving you multiple opportunities to provide value. In other words, when a prospect says, "I've got water in the basement," we want to steer the conversation into a more in-depth discovery of what that means to them. What are their specific hot buttons?

Be careful with your questions, however. Just because you want to uncover a prospect's hot buttons doesn't mean they want to be probed. For example, if a prospect says, *"I've got a flooded basement,"* an inexperienced salesperson trying to uncover implications might be tempted to ask, *"Why is flooding in your basement a problem?"*

What do you think happens to this salesperson's credibility? No doubt the prospect wonders why they are being asked such an obviously rhetorical question. They are probably thinking, *"Huh? Are you kidding me?"*

Prospects are always forming impressions, so asking valueless questions will quickly reduce your credibility. Asking overly rhetorical questions is a common mistake that can cost you an opportunity. To avoid this scenario, I use a simple technique that ensures a more robust conversation. Let's revisit the scenario.

Knock-knock. Door opens.

Salesperson: *"Hi! My name is Tom Freese, and I'm from XYZ Water Pump Company. How can we help you?"*

Prospect: *"Thanks for coming. I've got a flooded basement."*

Salesperson: *"Okay. Can I ask, besides the obvious goal of getting the water out of your basement, what specifically are you most concerned about?"*

A non-rhetorical question like this one will invariably cause prospects to pause, think a moment, and start naming specific implications—perhaps concerns about structural damage, damage to personal property, or potential health risks. That's because probing beyond the obvious goal encourages the potential buyer to think in terms of the specific hot buttons that are causing them the greatest concerns.

What are the chances that the prospect will rattle off a list of ten or twelve implications that mirror the list we created in our strategy meeting? The chances are slim. In fact, most prospects will only name one or two implications, and every once in a while, three. If that's true, who's going to bring up the rest? Hint…if it's not you, then you leave the door wide open for one of your competitors to be seen as a more valuable resource.

This concept of being proactive in the sales process applies to virtually every value-driven sale. When I sold technology, for example, it was fashionable to run around talking to customers about issues like downtime, growth, system manageability, and support. But these issues would rarely justify a purchase all by themselves. Instead, it was the implications of downtime, growth, system manageability, and support that increased the prospect's sense of urgency and caused them to move forward with a decision. That's why I always looked for opportunities to ask more thought-provoking questions like: *"When your computer system goes down, besides the obvious issue of getting the system back on-line, what are your biggest concerns?"* Questions like this one cause prospects to focus on the underlying implications of computer downtime, which gives you an opportunity to understand how a system outage might cost their company $10,000 per hour or how, without the computer, they are unable to properly service their customers. Once again, the one problem of system downtime creates a whole series of potential implications related to the system being unavailable. This logic applies whether you sell technology, medical supplies, financial services, or manufacturing equipment. Raising potential implications with prospects and customers creates one of the greatest opportunities for salespeople to establish credibility early in the sales process.

> **Secret #134**   Raising potential implications creates one of the greatest opportunities for sellers to establish credibility early in the sales process.

Raising Implications Increases Your Value

My recommendation back in chapter 2 was to prepare an actual list of potential implications in advance to put yourself in a strong position to have more productive sales conversations. Now you have to use that list. Rather than endlessly probing to try to get prospects to articulate their own needs, however, you can significantly increase your value by bringing potential implications to the forefront in the conversation. Let me show you what I mean using the previous example.

To guide the conversation and identify more potential implications, I suggested that you could ask, *"Besides the obvious goal of getting the water out of your basement, what specifically are you most concerned about?"* Suppose the prospect responds by saying that he is concerned about two things, *cost* and *structural damage.* Rather than jumping ahead into your sales pitch (S), you now have a wonderful opportunity to raise additional implications (P) by asking questions like, "What about personal property? Do you have any personal items in the basement that could be damaged by the water?"

If the implications you raise are relevant to the prospect's situation, as in this case, you are likely to hear, *"Yes, we do have some things stored in the basement that we would like to protect."* Bingo! You have just uncovered another opportunity to add value. You have also earned the right to probe for additional implications.

Using this technique, you can create all kinds of opportunities to add value by asking implication questions like:

Seller: *"Is the flooding problem affecting any other systems in the house like a downstairs furnace, water heater, air conditioner, or electrical circuits (P)?"*

"Are you starting to sense any odor or mildew issues (P)?"

"What about safety? Do you have any kids or pets (P)?"

Guess what happens to a salesperson's credibility every time they bring up a relevant implication to a qualified prospect? You guessed it. Their credibility goes up. Way up! The reason is simple. You bond with prospects on their problems (P), not on your sales pitch (S). And the more successful you are in expanding their problems (via implications), the more opportunities you will have to add value when it's time to position your solutions. Essentially, when you use this technique you make the (P) bigger.

Something else happens when you bond with prospects on their problems. Back in chapter 8 we talked about the fact that salespeople start the sales process with near-zero credibility. Buyers are skeptical, but as soon as they begin to form the impression that, *"Hey, this salesperson might be able to help me,"* they start helping you help them.

> **Secret #135** When prospective customers form the impression that you might be able to help them, they lower their defenses and start helping you to help them.

For salespeople, this is a huge point! Herein lies the difference between potential buyers who are cautious and standoffish and who hold salespeople at arm's length, and those who choose to engage in mutually beneficial business relationships. You simply cannot succeed in making a sale until a customer helps you to help them. That's what we are doing here, executing a strategy where prospects want to engage in more productive conversations.

Position Away the Competition

Bonding with prospects on their problems creates opportunities for salespeople to offer potential solutions. Of course, once you accomplish some bonding it's natural for sellers to want to jump ahead into their sales presentations (S). But once again, jumping ahead with the SPA approach isn't the most productive way to increase your probability of success.

Instead, the most productive way to position the value of your product or service begins with a discussion of possible alternatives—the (A) in PAS—and why they might not offer the best solution.

We talked about the fallacies of starting with the traditional elevator pitch already. When it comes to positioning alternatives, you have to be ready to talk about your competition. Sellers can be tentative when it comes to discussing the competition. They sometimes avoid the issue entirely until customers start asking tough questions. Don't try to avoid these comparisons. If you do, you'll forfeit a wonderful opportunity to differentiate your value.

One way to add value in your sales conversations is by helping customers identify needs. Earlier we discussed how you accomplish this by bonding with prospects on their problems (P) and respective implications. But, we can also add value when positioning our solutions against possible alternatives. Guide the prospect through the possible decision options. Helping them conclude that yours is indeed the best solution is still helping, right?

That's why I favor the PAS model we discussed earlier in the chapter. But we're enhancing the (P) here. We are making the problem bigger by identifying potential implications, and then proactively raising potential alternatives (A), in order to position them away as *not* the most effective. To succeed in making a sale, your prospects must conclude that because they have problems (P), that won't be addressed as effectively by competing alternatives (A), they would be better off choosing your solution (S). In Question Based Selling, this is the PAS positioning model, which is much different than traditional SPA selling methods.

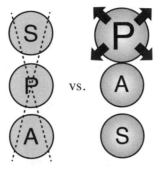

Secret #136   Your value proposition gets stronger if you can successfully
position away other alternatives as *not* the best solution.

Think about it this way. Positioning away competing alternatives opens the door for you to provide greater value. How does this work in real life? Let me show you by going back to my conference call with the vice president of sales from IBM. If you remember, I opened the dialogue by asking a series of short-answer diagnostic questions to establish credibility and kick off the discovery process. Next, I bonded with him on his problems (P) by asking:

TF:	*"Do you have salespeople out in the field trying to penetrate new accounts, picking up the telephone, leaving lots of voice-mail messages, and not being called back?"*
VP:	*"We sure do."*
TF:	*"What about new hires? Do some people ramp up in a relatively short time frame, while others struggle along and sometimes never make it over the hump?"*
VP:	*"Yes (again)."*
TF:	*"QBS solves that, too."*

I could have jumped right into a presentation of the QBS Methodology, but I didn't, because I wanted to first differentiate Question Based Selling from other sales training alternatives (A). You will see how I did that as we pick up the conversation.

TF: *"As you know, Mr. Vice President, there are a couple of ways to roll sales training out to your salespeople. One approach is to hire a motivational speaker, someone who will come in and tell stories and funny anecdotes in the hopes of energizing your sales teams. The problem is, if your salespeople return to their desks and gravitate back to the same old habits, they are likely to get the same results—as hype tends to wear off relatively quickly (A).*

"Another approach to training is to implement a sales process that requires sellers to fill out massive spreadsheets that document every nuance in their accounts. While reporting is important, just because you give a salesperson a blank spreadsheet to fill, doesn't mean their prospects and customers will want to share information with them (A).

"That's why at Question Based Selling, we take a different approach—one that will differentiate your salespeople from the rest of the masses (S)."

Did you recognize the (A)? If you noticed, I don't bad-mouth other training programs or engage in any kind of mudslinging. That's because putting someone else down makes you sound defensive and insecure. Instead, the technique of positioning away your competition in the PAS model is called *subtly poisoning.* Essentially, the strategy is to gently (but proactively) poison other alternatives in the prospect's mind, in order to position them away as *not* the best alternative.

Critics of PAS might argue it is better just to focus on your solutions and wait for prospects to investigate alternatives on their own. I disagree for two reasons. First, what if the prospect waits until the end of the conversation (or sales presentation) to ask how your solution compares with other potential alternatives? Do you really want to spend the last few minutes of your sales call or presentation talking with them about someone else's product? Second, since most of your prospects are going to consider various alternatives anyway,

I would argue that if you don't help them compare your solution to others, your competitors will.

Positioning away the competition is not a complex process. When prospects consider alternatives (other than yours), they basically have three options. They could choose to do nothing, thereby maintaining the status quo. Frankly, the decision to do nothing is often one of your toughest competitors. Another option is for prospects to try to solve their problems by themselves. Lastly, they can choose to purchase a competitive product or service from someone else. With a proactive effort on your part, any of these alternatives can be positioned away early in the sale, thus clearing the way for you to differentiate your solution and more effectively address their needs.

Go back to our water pump analogy. If you're talking to a prospect with a flooded basement, once you have initially bonded with them on the problem, you could easily poison the alternative of doing nothing (for example) by saying something like: *"Mr. Prospect, one option you have is to do nothing and put off your decision until later. The problem is issues like potential structural damage, mildew, and safety risks typically don't go away by themselves. If anything, they tend to get worse and increase the extent of the problem."*

If you were selling computer software, and you suddenly found yourself in a meeting where the key decision makers of a Fortune 500 company were considering the option of installing your software themselves, you could subtly poison this alternative by saying: *"Mr. Prospect, you certainly have the option to install this software yourself. The challenge is most of the customers we work with already have more responsibility than they can handle. As a result, they're trying to make their to-do lists shorter, not longer. That's why they partner with us, to leverage our expertise with this software, so they can focus on other important projects."*

When customers are considering proposals from other vendors, you can position these alternatives away using the same techniques I used in my conversation with the VP of sales. In any case you consider, our objective is the same. We want prospects to recognize that their problems (P) are not going to be addressed as effectively by other alternatives (A). Therefore, they would be much better off choosing our proposed solution (S).

Be Ready to Present Your Solutions

As I've said many times, salespeople cannot offer value to customers, at any time, until the customer recognizes the existence of a need. Whose job is it to uncover needs? It's the salesperson's job, of course. Once you have identified the prospect's needs and have positioned other alternatives away as not the most effective, then you are in a strong position to communicate the benefits of your proposed solution.

Finally, you're ready to tell them what you can offer. So, what benefits does your solution offer? Oddly enough, the answer may not be as obvious as you think.

Companies spend millions of dollars trying to craft value messages that will differentiate their products and services. Sales teams are then pumped full of detailed benefits and told to take these value messages out into their respective territories. If we take a closer look at these benefits, we might discover that the salesperson's perspective on what is valuable is very different from what a prospect thinks.

To illustrate, I am going to refer to the water pump analogy one more time. Remember when we were strategizing in advance of the call? Well, after we developed the need (P) and thought about how to position away other alternatives (A), it would be time to strategize about benefits (S). Therefore, let's take a moment now to do just that, by asking ourselves, *"What are the benefits that our proposed water pump offers?"*

The natural tendency for sellers is to point out benefits like the speed of the pump, or the fact that the product is quiet, and its excellent service record after the sale. The problem is, these features aren't necessarily beneficial to the customer. Your solution may be fast, quiet, and serviceable, but that's not why people buy water pumps. People buy water pumps because of the implications of having a flooded basement. Remember? Implications like structural damage, damage to personal property, potential health risks, mildew, odor issues, and the resulting monetary expense. These are ultimately what cause potential buyers to move forward with a water pump purchase.

What does this mean for salespeople? It simply means that the real value you offer should be a reflection of the implications uncovered during the *Discovery* stage of your sales conversations.

> **Secret #137** The real value you offer is a reflection of the implications identified during the *Discovery* stage of your sales conversations.

In another one of the examples we referred to earlier, computer downtime was the issue (P). For salespeople, it's tempting to jump into a benefits presentation when they hear prospects talk about issues like downtime. But if you take the time to drill down and identify different implications of a straightforward problem like downtime, you can create multiple opportunities to convey value. Examples of implications caused by system downtime include reduced revenue, customer dissatisfaction, scheduling delays, end-user complaints, and a negative reputation in the marketplace. Consequences like these are the true buying motivations behind every purchase. Therefore, salespeople must recognize that the real benefits they offer should be a reflection of these implications—they are what ultimately drive the decision.

There is a hidden advantage here for salespeople who want to differentiate themselves and their solutions. Virtually every decision issue can be broken down into multiple implications—at least ten, as we discussed earlier. Just ask yourself, "Why might this issue be important to the customer?" For those who are analytically inclined, look at the mathematical significance. Identifying multiple implications for every issue gives sellers exponentially more opportunities to add value and gives prospects more reasons to buy from you. When we talk about closing strategies later in the book, uncovering more needs also helps support your prospect's efforts to cost-justify a favorable decision for your product or service. Everybody wins.

Summary

The message to take away from this chapter is simple—don't start your sales conversations with an elevator pitch! This is a point I emphatically make when speaking to live audiences all over the globe. I am not against talking about your solutions. I just believe that in today's increasingly competitive marketplace, the traditional SPA approach commoditizes your value proposition with generic-sounding claims of greatness. Instead, re-engineering the elevator pitch by using the PAS model to bond with prospects on their problems puts you in a strong position to identify more needs, position away the competition, and then convey greater value.

Chapter 15

BUILDING VALUE IN THE QBS PRESENTATION

Phase II of the QBS sales process is the sales presentation. Once you generate enough interest to motivate prospects to want to engage further, the presentation is your opportunity to convey the value of your products and services.

This chapter isn't about pure presentation skills, however, like using voice inflection, or how not to walk in front of the slide projector, or the proper way to point with a laser pointer. Instead, what we will focus on are the more strategic aspects of the sales presentation—like how to leverage curiosity, credibility, and momentum to differentiate yourself and your solutions.

After you have successfully generated a good amount of interest and identified needs in Phase I of the sales process, the logical next step is educating prospects on the value of your product or service. This is usually done in the context of a sales presentation—where sellers have an opportunity to match the benefits of their solutions to the prospect's specific needs.

Back in chapter 11, we introduced the three phases of the QBS sales process. In Phase I, our objective was generating enough interest to motivate qualified prospects to move forward into Phase II. Now that we have made it to the presentation, there are three strategic objectives we want to accomplish in Phase II. First, we want to communicate enough value in our solutions to justify a favorable

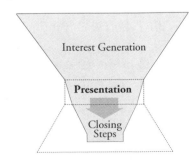

Phase II: Presentation

purchase decision. Second, we want to increase the prospect's sense of urgency so they will want to move forward with a purchase decision for our solution sooner rather than later. Lastly, the sales presentation provides sellers with an excellent opportunity to identify and cultivate potential champions who can be groomed to carry our flag if the decision needs management's approval.

The sales presentation also gives you an opportunity to teach qualified prospects the three *hows* of QBS: *how to buy*, *how to sell*, and *how it works*. Some prospects will have a clear picture of the criteria they want to use when evaluating potential solutions. Other prospects won't have any idea what to look for, or how to choose between competing vendors. Rather than let decision makers fend for themselves, the QBS salesperson takes a proactive role in the presentation, not only to educate prospects about their offerings, but also to teach them *how to buy*. This means working with prospects to establish decision criteria, as well as coaching them on what to look for in a potential solution—presumably using criteria that will lead them to your product or service.

QBS recommends you should also take a proactive role in teaching your prospects *how to sell*. If the presentation goes well, you want the people who attended to promote your proposal to others in the organization who also need to sign off on the recommended solution. The sales presentation is an excellent opportunity to teach these people *how* to position the value of your offering to others.

The third *how* is teaching your prospects *how it works*. This is the main thrust of the sales presentation—educating people about all the features and benefits your solution provides.

> **Secret #138**   The value you build in the sales presentation is what ulti-
> mately justifies a favorable purchase decision.

The format of a sales presentation can vary dramatically depending on the product you sell and the audience you're selling to. In smaller sales, where your first call is typically face-to-face, the Phase II presentation is often an extension of the initial sales call. If you sell pharmaceutical supplies to doctors, for example, and you've waited ninety minutes to be seen, you had better be ready to deliver a presentation right then and there. If you sell life insurance, brokerage services, or advertising space, prospects expect the initial sales call to lead directly into a presentation of value. Frankly, with some prospects, you may not get a second chance.

When selling to individual buyers, the presentation phase of the sales process tends to be less formal and more relaxed. That's okay, because in a one-on-one sale, we want prospects to feel comfortable in an environment where they can freely ask questions. This way, you can tailor your value messages to the unique needs of each specific buyer.

> **Secret #139**   When selling to individual buyers, the presentation phase of the sales process tends to be less formal and more relaxed.

For larger corporate sales, the Phase II presentation is much more strategic. It's also significantly more complex. Once you pique the interest of someone in the account, whether it's on the phone or in a face-to-face meeting, the presentation is generally scheduled as a separate event. This gives everyone who will be involved in the decision, or who needs to know about your product or service, a chance to participate. Managing this level of complexity will be our focus throughout the rest of the chapter.

Essentially, we want everyone who will be involved in the purchase to attend the presentation. As we said earlier, it's our premise in Question Based Selling that everyone who does not understand the value of your solution will ultimately vote against it. But your success in the presentation isn't as simple as convening an audience and telling them about the value you offer. In addition to having good content, you must also secure the audience's time and attention, and you must overcome some of the same credibility issues you faced in the initial sales call.

Challenges Salespeople Face in the Presentation

At the beginning of the sales process, salespeople start with near-zero credibility. When we first pick up the telephone to initiate contact with a new account, we inherit all the negative biases and prejudices prospects have formed as the result of having to fend off a steady stream of pushy and overzealous salespeople. Again, salespeople are perceived as valueless until proven otherwise.

These same prejudices carry over into Phase II of the sales presentation. While you may have already established some good contacts in the account, other people who show up at your presentation might be meeting you for the very first time—in which case, they're likely to see you as just another salesperson who has little credibility.

To illustrate the challenge, let's suppose that you sell manufacturing equipment to large corporations, and along comes a promising new prospect. Carol Williams, the director of operations, was so impressed with your product that she invited you to come in and present at next month's project committee meeting. It's a wonderful opportunity, because they have a very specific need and you have a terrific solution.

Like any good salesperson, you understand that preparation is the key to success; therefore, you go into reconnaissance mode. Using your network of industry contacts, you find out who will be in the audience, what their various hot buttons are, and what questions might get raised. Essentially, you want to be ready so you can avoid being blindsided in the presentation by something you're not prepared to address.

Then comes the actual event. Your champion in the account (Carol) says a few words to introduce the presentation, and suddenly it's your show. It's do or die. Unfortunately, this is where many sellers make a costly mistake. They assume that because they have come to make a presentation, they should jump right into an explanation of their product features and benefits. For the same reasons we recommended against jumping ahead in Phase I, we advise you not to jump ahead in your sales presentations either.

In chapter 6, we made the point that in order to present solutions, you must first accomplish certain prerequisite steps. These were outlined in QBS's Conversational Layering Model. The same is true in a sales presentation. Here, the prerequisites for success include piquing the audience's curiosity, establishing your own credibility, and uncovering needs that will justify your solution. If you press on with the presentation without first accomplishing these prerequisites, you are setting yourself up for failure.

Conversational Layering

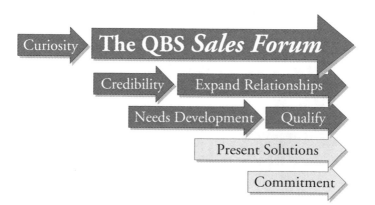

Going back to our example, Carol Williams may be the only person in your audience who is ready for you to jump into an explanation of how your product works. She wants to hear more about your offerings because she has already formed a positive impression of you, and she is curious to find out how your solutions can satisfy her needs.

Contrast Ms. Williams's level of readiness with that of the rest of the attendees. Everyone else comes into your presentation cold. They don't know you from Adam—meaning, they aren't necessarily curious, you aren't credible in their eyes, and they may or may not recognize the existence of a need. In fact, many of them could just sit there with their arms folded against their chests, glaring at you as if to say, *"Can we get this over with? I've got more important things to do."*

Can you blame them? If yours is the fifth, tenth, or twentieth sales presentation they've had to sit through so far this month, their patience has already been tested. Moreover, the odds that they'll be impressed by yours are stacked against you, because only a small fraction of sales presentations ever generate value for the attendees. Most prospects say they only get something out of 15 to 20 percent of the presentations they attend, which means the other 80 to 85 percent they sit through are just wastes of time. No wonder some people are biased against you before the meeting even starts.

> **Secret #140**   Just like the initial sales call, sellers begin the presentation with *near-zero credibility.*

With the exception of the person who sponsored the presentation, everyone is starting from scratch. You haven't yet piqued their interest, you have near-zero credibility, and you inherit all the negative baggage from other salespeople who have preceded you. You may have experienced this yourself—ever been in the middle of your presentation and realized only a few people were nodding in agreement and everyone else was just sitting there with a glazed look? The truth is, just because you've been invited to present doesn't mean everyone in your audience is ready to listen. And if they aren't yet ready to listen, plowing forward with your presentation is not only a bad strategy—it's a recipe for disaster.

In Question Based Selling, we want everyone who is going to be involved in the decision to attend the presentation. We also want them to listen attentively. For this to occur, we must adopt a more strategic approach in Phase II of the sales process. That means it is crucial to accomplish each of the prerequisite steps in the Conversational Layering Model before you start positioning the value of your product or service.

Breaking the Ice

The beginning of a presentation sets the tone for the rest of the event. That means it's particularly important for your sales presentations to get off to a good start. Audience participants will form their impressions quickly, and you want their first impression to be a good one.

When I present, I want people in my presentation audience to feel comfortable; but more importantly, I want them to be mentally engaged and emotionally involved. This doesn't happen by itself. Given the hectic pace of today's business environment, people are bound to have other things on their minds, and if they aren't thinking about a previous meeting, they're thinking about their next one. Now that everyone has an iPhone, there's a good chance your audience's minds are somewhere else, like viewing email, or texting their secretary, or even on Twitter. That's why one of my foremost objectives at the beginning of a sales presentation is breaking the ice—getting the audience to focus their attention on what I'm about to present, and stop thinking about everything else.

To successfully break the ice in your sales presentations, QBS suggests a four-step approach that consists of introducing the presenter and the audience, delivering an interactive opener, identifying the objectives in the presentation, and managing audience expectations.

Introduce the Presenter and the Audience

If you are presenting to a committee, it's always better to be introduced by someone from the audience than to walk up and introduce yourself. But don't leave this to chance. If your contact in the account doesn't offer, you should ask them if they would be willing to kick the event off with some brief introductory words that explain why the meeting was called, and summarize the objectives of the presentation.

A well-planned introduction can significantly enhance your credibility. Since your contact in the account has a built-in incentive to make you look good, a little bit of advance coaching can make them sound like one of your best references. Using your contacts can be a terrific way to kick off your sales presentations.

> **Secret #141** Your champions in the account have a built-in incentive to make you (the presenter) look good.

In addition to introducing *you* as the presenter, ask your champion to introduce the audience as well. Unless the size of the presentation audience is prohibitive, having someone (other than you) go around the room and attach names with faces offers a number of strategic advantages.

First, it reduces your risk. To be effective, sellers need to know who's in the audience. The problem is, it sometimes feels hokey or uncomfortable to ask people to introduce themselves. So let the person who kicked things off handle this function. They are usually happy to do so, and it reduces any risk of creating an awkward first impression.

Secondly, introducing the audience tends to create instant interaction. As people go around the room giving their "name, rank, and serial number," you can interject comments or ask specific questions about their areas of responsibility. This gives you an opportunity to bond with people in the audience before the presentation begins. In addition to increasing the number of "friendly faces" in the room, this technique makes it easy to emphasize key points and target your remarks during the actual presentation.

Lastly, fostering interaction at the beginning of a sales presentation is likely to yield some valuable information about how the decision will be made. If you want to know who the decision makers, influencers, and potential anti-champions are, then listen carefully. The politics of a decision will generally unfold before your eyes during the pre-presentation banter.

Deliver an Interactive Opener

After the introductions, it's show time. Interestingly, there are as many opinions for how to begin a presentation as there are presenters. Some presenters like to kick off with a joke or a funny story. Others choose a more serious approach and dive right into the key issues. In QBS, we favor an interactive approach—where the salesperson gains control of the audience, kicks off the event, and points the presentation in the right direction. To illustrate, here's an example of what I might say to deliver an interactive opener:

Seller:	*"Hello, everybody, and welcome. I appreciate your making the time to join us today. My name is Tom Freese, and I started QBS Research, Inc., the company that developed and delivers the Question Based Selling methodology. For years, we've been working with some of the world's leading sales organizations, including IBM, General Electric, Lanier Worldwide, AT&T, Motorola, Cisco Systems, and Hewlett Packard (just to name a few), teaching their salespeople how to leverage the most powerful tool in business to double their sales results.*

> *"To prepare for this presentation, I've talked at length with Carol Williams (vice president of sales), and I have become somewhat familiar with your operation. But rather than assume I already know everything about your business, it might be better to ask: What would you like me to accomplish in this presentation today?"*

Then I pause and listen carefully. If I give them time, the audience will begin to talk to me.

The effectiveness of this approach is buried in its subtlety. In just a few sentences, I have let the audience know I am prepared, and I have a degree of knowledge about their company because of my discussions with Carol Williams. But I also gain a significant advantage by inviting them to participate in setting the direction for the presentation.

I could have opened with the traditional, *"My name is …, and here's my agenda for the presentation,"* but I intentionally shy away from such a canned opening. The reason is because phrases like "my agenda" are easily mismatched, and can sound self-serving. Prospects do want to know you are prepared, but they may not be ready to buy into hearing what *you* think is important, or even what Steve Johnson thinks is important. In fact, the only way to know what the audience actually wants or needs is to invite them to give input at the beginning of the presentation, rather than just plow ahead with your own agenda.

In the sample dialogue above, you will notice that I start by thanking the audience. Right off the bat, I want them to know I understand that their time is valuable, and that I intend to make their participation a worthwhile experience. It's a courtesy…so be gracious, but don't go overboard. There's no need to thank the audience profusely as if they're doing you a favor by attending. After all, if you truly provide value, they have as much to gain from your presentation as you do.

Next, I introduced myself (again). Even if your contact or champion within the account has formally introduced you, you should always make it a point to introduce yourself, your company, and anyone else you may have brought with you for the presentation. This allows you to set a more personal tone for the meeting and gives audiences a taste of your personality and style.

Secret #142 When prospects identify with you personally, they're more likely to identify with your presentation and your solutions.

The opening of the sales presentation is also a great time to leverage momentum. In QBS, that means using the Herd Theory to rattle off a robust list of "herd" references. This gives audiences a sense of confidence and reassurance that other companies have tested, utilized, and are already benefiting from the solutions you are about to present.

"What Would You Like Me to Accomplish?"

At the end of my sample opening, I do the unthinkable. After admitting to the audience that I do know something about their business (but not everything), I ask, *"What would you like me to accomplish in this presentation today?"*

Some salespeople are hesitant to ask this question, but you shouldn't be. This is a great question. More importantly, it's a wonderful diffusion strategy. If we assume that most audiences are naturally skeptical of salespeople, then asking what *they* would like to accomplish in the presentation is a huge deviation from the "standard" sales pitch. You might even be surprised at how much this one question will make prospects perk up in their seats.

Of course, there are people who would argue that asking the audience for input at the very beginning of a sales presentation increases your risk. What if they bring something up that you're not prepared to cover? Good point. But if someone in the audience wants to bring up an issue during the presentation, they will. The only question is, would you rather know about any potential obstacles upfront or be surprised later on in the presentation?

The truth is, being fully prepared and still asking for input at the beginning of your sales presentations can enhance your value to the audience. It demonstrates a great deal of confidence and expertise on your part, and also lets prospects know that it's important to you to tailor your comments to make the best use of their time.

Secret #143   An interactive opener lets prospects know that you plan to tailor *your* presentation to make good use of *their* time.

Depending on your relationship with the prospect, this may be enough to get your presentation off to a good start. But one other key component that will help break the ice and point your presentation in the right direction is managing your audience's expectations.

Managing Audience Expectations

After years of presenting to all kinds of sales audiences, I have adopted a simple formula that sums up the relationship between the audience's expectations and your delivery. Happiness (H) is the difference between expectations (E) and reality (R). To put this formula in mathematical terms: $H = R - E$. When a sales presentation falters, it's usually because the presenter fails to live up to the expectations of his or her audience. Although we can't always control reality in the overall sales process, we should have an opportunity to manage the audience's expectations in the presentation portion. In fact, managing expectations is critical to your success in Phase II.

> **Secret #144** Happiness is the difference between expectations and reality. In QBS, we put this into a simple formula: $H = R - E$.

One of the best ways to manage audience expectations is to use presentation qualifiers. What's that, you ask? It's a positioning question designed to secure the audience's buy-in, so you can get off to a good start in your sales presentations. For example, if you want to start off talking about the prospect's business issues in order to set the stage for the benefits you offer, you can manage the audience's expectations and secure their buy-in by saying:

Seller: *"Because some people in the audience are more familiar with our product than others, we usually start off by overviewing the issues our product solves, and then talk more specifically about how the product works. Would that make sense for this group?"*

Most people will say, *"That's fine."* It's a predictable response. When your audience consists of people with different levels of expertise (which is usually the case when you are presenting to a group of people), it's easy to get them to agree that it *does* make sense to start off covering the bigger picture—in this case, talking about the prospect's needs.

Another qualifier you can use to point your presentations in the right direction is:

Seller: *"Would you rather have a canned sales pitch, or would it make more sense to focus on your specific business issues?"*

You and I already know I'm going to tailor the presentation, but asking the question sets up my next move in the meeting. We also already know what the audience's answer is going to be. Of course prospects would much rather focus on their specific issues than sit through another generic sales pitch. When the audience tells me that they would rather focus on their specific business issues, I have suddenly earned the right to ask specific questions that will establish my credibility and uncover their needs.

Use Diagnostic Questions to Establish Credibility

No matter how you slice it, credibility sells. Credibility raises the intrinsic value of the material being presented, and gives the salesperson tremendous leverage in guiding the audience toward a favorable decision. But as we pointed out earlier, sellers must establish credibility first in order to uncover needs and communicate the value of their product or service.

> **Secret #145** The greater your credibility, the more value prospects will attach to the information, ideas, and solutions you present.

What's the best way to establish credibility at the beginning of a sales presentation? Unfortunately, too many presenters attempt to "claim" their own credibility by *telling* audiences how great their company or product is. In QBS, we do just the opposite. We establish credibility by asking questions. Using the same strategy we outlined earlier in chapter 8, we recommend *narrowing the scope* of your questions to demonstrate a higher level of competence and value.

After breaking the ice in your presentation, you can easily transition into a series of short-answer, diagnostic questions. In many cases, I ask the same questions I asked earlier in Phase I—only now, I am posing those questions to the audience. Just like before, when you demonstrate an ability to ask relevant and intelligent questions, you raise the prospect's perception of your credibility.

The difference is, the diagnostic questions you ask at the beginning of the presentation will often confirm or verify information that you already have. Though you are going to ask for information, the way in which you ask gives people in the audience the impression that you've done your homework in advance. To illustrate, in the earlier example where you were selling manufacturing equipment to large corporations, you could start off your sales presentation by verifying information you have by asking a series of diagnostic questions like:

Seller:	*"Your company produces between twenty-five hundred and three thousand widgets each year, depending on demand, right?"*
Audience:	*"Yes."*

Seller:	*"And your current system runs on an IBM mainframe system that was originally installed in…2005, yes?"*
Audience:	*"Yes, a nineteen-month installation was completed in fall of 2005."*
Seller:	*"And how many end users does the system support?"*
Audience:	*"Approximately 265."*
Seller:	*"Is your software home-grown or turnkey?"*
Audience:	*"We purchased most of our current software packages, but we usually integrate them ourselves."*

If you are appropriately prepared, you probably know the answers to these questions. But this is not an exercise in playing dumb. Dumb doesn't sell! Rather, these questions are part of a technique that allows you to convey a higher level of credibility with the larger audience. They also help to validate the information you have. In some cases, you might find out that the information you collected earlier was incomplete or incorrect. To be successful you want to have complete and accurate information before the presentation begins.

Generally, you should ask enough diagnostic questions to establish your credibility (usually five or six), and then move on. Move on to what? If you remember from chapter 8, establishing credibility (first) earns you the right to *broaden the scope* of your questions—to uncover prospect needs. These needs will ultimately serve as the foundation for every successful sales presentation.

Without Needs…There Are No Solutions

The presentation is the salesperson's opportunity to educate prospects on the value of their solutions. But there's a catch. In order to build value in the presentation, the audience must first recognize the existence of a need. If they perceive a need, then you have an opportunity to deliver value. If they don't recognize their own needs, however, they will find very little value in the solutions you present. Seems reasonable, doesn't it?

To maximize the impact of your presentation, you want prospects to have multiple needs so they will feel a greater sense of urgency to have these needs addressed. By identifying more needs, you also give yourself an opportunity to present greater value. (Chapters 9 and 14 talked about increasing needs to escalate the prospect's sense of urgency.) Suffice it to say, if you can satisfy nine or ten needs in your presentation, then you give your prospects nine or ten reasons to make a favorable buying decision. In that way, you are also making it easier for them to cost-justify a purchase.

> **Secret #146** The greater the prospect's need, the more value you will be able to deliver in the presentation.

Realize, too, that different people in your presentation audience have different goals, objectives, priorities, and needs. Whenever people with differing responsibilities come together for a presentation, it's safe to assume there will be a variety of issues and concerns. This variety creates an interesting challenge for salespeople. If you want everyone to be on the same page with respect to your presentation, then you must get everyone to buy into a common agenda—one that will address the individuals' needs as well as satisfying the audience as a whole. That's exactly what you'll accomplish by creating a *Mutual Agenda*.

Building a Mutual Agenda

Every sales presentation needs an agenda. The agenda serves as a road map for matching potential solutions against the prospect's needs. The question is, whose agenda should you follow—yours, or the audience's?

There's an old adage about presentations that says you should start by telling the audience what you plan to say, say it, and then summarize by telling them what you've said. Presentation skills courses have been teaching this technique for decades. As a result, salespeople are quick to whip out their pre-planned agendas and "tell" audiences what they are going to say.

There is an inherent problem with this approach, however. Opening a sales presentation with a canned agenda greatly increases your risk. Your champion in the account might nod in agreement because they were included in previous discussions and they already buy into the points you plan to cover. In a sense, they are emotionally ready to hear the solutions you want to present. But what about everyone else? Do they even recognize the existence of a need? Do they have the same issues? If not, then your prefab agenda will miss the mark before the presentation even starts.

> **Secret #147** Just because you know where you want to go in the presentation, doesn't mean the rest of your audience will want to go there.

My experience at NetFrame Systems taught me a lot about how best to position a sales presentation. At the time, very few prospects had ever heard of NetFrame, and even fewer knew what a Superserver was, so I was starting from ground zero when educating most audiences. The standard NetFrame product pitch was a two-hour affair, complete with eighty slides and a detailed chalk-talk discussion about how the product worked.

In layman's terms, NetFrame's product was a mainframe-type computer that was designed to drive large local area networks. It was a great product, able to solve a number of important business issues that large corporations had been wrestling with for years. Issues like:

- Growth/Scalability
- Data Integrity
- Maximum Uptime
- Network Management

- Cost Effectiveness
- Upgradability
- Better Support
- Increased Performance

Our success hinged on getting audiences to buy into this list of business issues. If the audience *did* agree that growth, data integrity, uptime, etc., were indeed important to their business, then building value in our presentations was relatively easy. If they did not agree these issues were important, it didn't matter how robust or well-priced our product was—they weren't going to buy.

The challenge was securing their buy-in. As in many other companies, NetFrame salespeople (including myself) were getting up and trying to tell audiences that *our* list of issues was critical to *their* business. We even attempted to strengthen our case using countless slides, charts, and testimonials to prove the issues we solved should be important to them.

Ironically, the more emphatically we tried to "tell" prospects what their issues were, the more they resisted. *"How can anyone refute the importance of issues like growth, uptime, or data integrity?"* I wondered. Nonetheless, they resisted. Whenever I tried to explain why a certain issue should be critical to their business, they would argue that their situation was unique, or that my suppositions didn't necessarily apply to them. In fact, the harder I pushed (to secure their buy-in on my list of business issues), the more prospects and customers would push back. As you can imagine, that kind of resistance does not get sales presentations off to a good start.

> **Secret #148**   Telling prospects why an issue is important often causes them to *mismatch*, and tell you why it's not.

The problem is, whenever salespeople try to *tell* audiences what their issues are, audiences tend to mismatch. They think to themselves, *"Who are you to tell us what's important?"* As a result, sellers often have difficulty securing the audience's buy-in that the issues they plan to cover in the presentation are, in fact, relevant to their business. In QBS, we solve this problem by simply asking instead of telling.

Ask and Ye Shall Receive

Prior to the actual presentation, most salespeople already know what the key issues are. They've met with various contacts in the account and have encouraged them to share their thoughts, feelings, and concerns. But we want the entire audience to buy into these issues, not just the people who already know us. This is easily accomplished by escalating the *focus* of your questions prior to jumping in.

After you break the ice in your presentations and establish credibility by asking a series of diagnostic questions, you simply transition using the same Issue Questions that we introduced in chapter 9, asking:

Presenter (to audience):   *"To what extent is _____ important?"*

Now, just fill in the blank with one of the key issues you plan to address in your presentation and you'll be shocked at how quickly your audience will come alive. By giving them an opportunity to participate in defining the problems that need to be addressed, your audience develops a sense of ownership with respect to your presentation.

> **Secret #149**   When a presentation audience helps to define the problem, it's easier to get them to buy into your solution.

Asking "to what extent" not only confirms the importance of the issues being raised, but also expands the discussion by allowing you to probe further and identify specific implications of these issues. Moreover, asking "to what extent" prevents your questions from sounding rhetorical.

Building a Road Map for Success

Your presentation may already have an agenda that's designed to go down a certain path. If not, focusing on the issues of growth and change is a good starting topic to secure consensus from the audience and start building the actual agenda for the presentation. You simply ask, "To what extent is your network environment growing or changing?"

What happens next is critically important. If your audience responds by agreeing that network change is prevalent (which they will, because you will have done your homework in the account), then you turn to the flip chart and write the word "Growth." By writing it down, you confirm that the audience *does* think growth is indeed an important issue—one that needs to be addressed in your presentation. Growth becomes the first item on the agenda. Then you simply move on to the next issue you plan to cover, asking:

Presenter:	*"What about data integrity? If something were to corrupt your data, to what extent would that be a problem?"*
Audience:	*"That would be a huge problem!"*

You can make the issues that get raised even bigger by asking Implication Questions to help people in the audience visualize scenarios that would dictate a need for your product or service. The goal is to emotionally involve each of the participants in some way, so be spontaneous and broaden the conversation when you can. For example, you might say:

Presenter:	*"When you said corrupting your data would be a huge problem, what specifically did you mean?"*
Jim:	*"Losing data would cripple the entire marketing department."*
Presenter:	*"Susan, how would data problems affect the accounting department?"*
Susan:	*"We would completely lose track of our assets and liabilities."*

Now that you have identified another need to build value against in your presentation, walk over to the flip chart and write down "Data Integrity." Once again, writing it down confirms that *data integrity* is an important issue, and one that needs to be addressed in the presentation. Data Integrity becomes the second item on your agenda.

If you repeat this exercise for each of the issues you plan to cover in your presentation, you end up with a flip chart filled with all the issues your product or service addresses, arranged in the order you plan to present them. I usually complete this process by pointing at the flip chart, and asking, *"Is there anything else you would like me to add to this agenda?"* If you are on target with your questioning, your list will be a comprehensive one.

Congratulations! You have just created an agenda for your presentation. But, whose agenda is it? Well, that's the beauty of this technique. The list of issues that you have compiled represents the audience's agenda because they are the ones who validated the importance of each decision issue raised.

But guess what? This list of issues also represents your agenda for the presentation—after all, you chose

> *Growth*
> *Data Integrity*
> *Uptime*
> *Network Mgt.*
> *Cost eff.*
> *Upgradability*
> *Support*
> *Performance*

which issues to ask about and in what order. That's why we at QBS call it a Mutual Agenda. You get to present issues that are important to you, and the audience gets to hear about issues that are important to them. This is a far cry from projecting a canned agenda onto the wall and announcing to the audience, *"This is what I plan to cover today."*

> **Secret #150** The Mutual Agenda is your strategic road map for building value in the Phase II sales presentation.

If you use the Mutual Agenda as a road map for your presentations, you are more likely to get audiences excited about the solutions you present. They will perceive that you are responding to their specific needs as opposed to focusing only on those things that are most important to you.

It's Time to Knock Their Socks Off

After you have developed a Mutual Agenda for your presentation, it's time to knock the audience's socks off by matching your solutions to their specific business and personal needs. This is essentially the meat of your presentation, where your ability to educate will supplement the interest generated in Phase I with an even greater sense of value in Phase II.

It's impossible for me to script out your actual sales presentation in this book. I have no way of knowing what specific value points you have to offer, and I can only hypothesize about what your prospects need. What I can do, however, is identify and outline five specific strategies you can use to deliver more effective question based sales presentations. These five strategies are outlined below.

Divide and Conquer

The Mutual Agenda is a divide-and-conquer strategy. Since we want prospects to have multiple reasons to buy our products and services, we want them to credit us with having accomplished a number of different objectives in the presentation, rather than just one or two. By compiling each of the issues you plan to cover onto a written Mutual Agenda, you will expand the prospect's needs and in so doing, increase their sense of urgency for finding a solution.

A divide-and-conquer strategy also helps to break the larger, more complex decision down into smaller component parts. It's easier to educate people when you can focus on the individual aspects of a decision. Plus, it's easier to accumulate value when you address and conquer each of the prospect's issues separately.

When you apply this divide-and-conquer strategy to your own sales presentations, be aware that different people in your audience will gravitate to different issues on the Mutual Agenda. We talked about this back in chapter 4 when we introduced the idea that people have different buying motivations. If your Mutual Agenda is comprehensive enough to include something for everyone, you may find your audience ends up arguing about the many different reasons they like your product or service.

Stories Get Remembered Long after the Presentation Ends

Your ability to relate to a presentation audience is critical to your success in Phase II. In addition to gaining their buy-in on the key points you make during the actual presentation, you want your messages to leave a lasting impression. How can you give presentations that audiences will remember? By using related stories, anecdotes, and parables to support your value proposition.

Stories are remembered long after your presentation ends. Think about it this way. What do you remember from the seventh grade? Do you remember what was actually taught in the classroom, or are you more likely to remember that Bobby Schmitt was sent to the principal's office for pulling the fire alarm during study hall? If you're like me, you remember the stories.

I mention this for two reasons. First, your competitors in the account will have an opportunity to present their solutions to the same audience at some point in the process. Your value messages need to stay fresh in the prospect's mind or your probability of success will be significantly reduced. Secondly, strategic purchases often require people in your presentation audience to go out and "sell" others on the idea of buying your solution. Their ability to recall the information you present will most likely determine your success in the sale.

Stories about other prospects and customers are particularly powerful. This is another application of the Herd Theory from chapter 5. During the presentation, be sure to let audiences know how excited other companies are about your offering. That means rattling off a few marquee customer names like Texas Instruments, General Mills, Nike, Owens Corning, Pfizer, IBM, Monsanto, and General Electric. You may also find it valuable to cite stories about prospects that suffered negative consequences because they elected not to purchase your solution.

Position Gold Medals and German Shepherds

Back in chapter 4, QBS changed the paradigm for positioning benefits by expanding on the motivations behind why customers buy. In presentations, prospects will see value in different ways. So instead of trying to get potential buyers excited about all the wonderful things your product or service offers, you can more effectively motivate prospects if you position your product in terms of both *Gold Medals* and *German Shepherds*. Remember: *While some people are motivated to run fast toward Gold Medals, many others run even faster from German Shepherds.* While some prospects will be motivated by positive reward, others will be motivated more by negative aversion.

To maximize your effectiveness in the Phase II presentation, you'll want to satisfy both. This means positioning each of your value points both ways—as a *Gold Medal* and also as a *German Shepherd*. Be sure to let prospects know, for example, that your warranty is the best in the industry (*Gold Medal*), which will prevent all those nagging support problems they've been experiencing with their current system (*German Shepherd*).

Ask Confirmation Questions

Just because you have the floor in a presentation doesn't mean that everyone in your audience is totally engaged and constantly listening. The truth is, it's difficult to get the prospect's attention, and it's sometimes even harder to keep it for any length of time. This shouldn't surprise us; prospects do have other things on their minds, and if they are not captivated by your presentation, their thoughts will surely drift elsewhere. How can you hold the audience's attention throughout your presentation? One way is by asking *Confirmation Questions*.

A Confirmation Question is a conversational tool presenters use to ensure that everyone is following along with the discussion. I learned this technique from John Van Siclen—one of my early sales mentors.

John was smart enough to recognize that prospects who are responsive in the presentation are more emotionally engaged. So when John gives a presentation, whether in a formal setting or one-on-one, he regularly asks confirmation questions to maintain an emotional connection. He isn't looking for tons of feedback, he is just seeking a subtle reassurance that the presentation audience is following along. *"Does that make sense?"*

Soliciting feedback from your audience is also an effective way to control the pace of a presentation. Since we know that prospects process information differently, going too fast can be just as detrimental as going too slow. Therefore, a few well-placed Confirmation Questions during the presentation give people in your audience a chance to absorb key points before you move on. *"Are you with me?"*

A side benefit of asking Confirmation Questions happens when you cause gray cells to move. What does this mean? When people in your audience are busy thinking about the questions you are asking, they won't be thinking about something else. They'll be focused on you and your material. As a result, Confirmation Questions not only solicit the audience's feedback on key points, but also help recapture the audience's time and attention for your material, which has the added benefit of increasing their retention rate. *Do you have any questions?*

If You Take the Time to Say It, Take the Time to Explain It

One of the best pieces of sales advice I ever received came from another one of my mentors, Barry Gillman. Barry used to say: *If you take the time to say it, then take the time to explain it.* This is critical in the QBS presentation.

As salespeople, we talk about the same set of issues every day. We are very familiar with how our products provide value and the typical problems prospects face. We're so close to our own solutions that we sometimes fail to recognize the audience doesn't share the same level of awareness or knowledge. Have you ever sat through a presentation where the presenter used an acronym you didn't understand? What about buzzwords? While some audience members might ask questions to clarify what the presenter is saying, most will remain silent, not wanting to draw attention to themselves. Fortunately, this problem is easy to fix if you, the presenter, are willing to both say it and explain it.

Secret #151   If you take the time to say it, then take the time to explain it.

Closing Your Sales Presentations

In the QBS model, the end of Phase II (*Presentation*) is also the beginning of Phase III (*Closing Steps*). This is where qualified potential buyers will either want to move forward to investigate the details of a purchase transaction, or they will choose to disengage.

Some people say that the end of a sales presentation is where the real selling begins. To a large extent, they are right. The end of your sales presentation is your opportunity to summarize how well your product or service matches up to each of the items listed on the Mutual Agenda, and it's also an opportunity for you to start positioning the sale for closure. Consequently, how your presentation ends is just as important as how it begins.

> **Secret #152**   How your sales presentation ends is important because the last impression typically leaves a lasting impression.

In smaller sales, where you are presenting to an individual decision maker, the entire sales process can occur within a single sales call. After you understand the prospect's needs, and you have educated them on the value of your solutions, it's time to close. Why wait? If the buyer is on an emotional high from your presentation, you should go ahead and ask for the order—they might just say, "*Yes.*"

Larger sales are more complex, and the timing rarely works the same way. Decision makers, influencers, and executive sponsors all have to weigh the alternatives and come to some kind of consensus before a decision can be made. With larger sales, the end of a presentation is typically *not* a good time to ask for the order. Thus, putting your audience on the spot as you conclude your presentation usually elicits a standoffish response, which can make people uncomfortable when it is time to close.

The end of a sales presentation is also not a good time to ask questions like:

Presenter: *"So…what do you think?"*

This vague request for feedback is likely to produce a weak response. People who are not ready to make a commitment, are unlikely to share what they actually think. Instead, they're more likely to say:

Spokesman: *"Thank you for presenting your company's solutions. After we have a chance to carefully consider your proposal, we will get back to you with a decision."*

The value of this response is hardly worth the oxygen required to speak the words. It sounds more like what an unqualified job candidate might hear at the end of a bad interview. Therefore, asking questions like *What do you think?* usually doesn't cause prospects to share what they really thought of your presentation or help you know what to do next.

That doesn't mean you shouldn't ask questions at the end of your presentations. Quite the contrary. But if you want to move prospects forward in the sales process, you might try asking a question that will actually let you know where you stand in the opportunity.

"Do You Like It?"

Here's how I close my sales presentations. First, I summarize each of the points made during the presentation. This gives me a chance to reiterate the benefits of my product and show how well we have addressed the issues that were on the Mutual Agenda. Then, I simply say to the audience:

> **Seller:**   *"That's pretty much what we had planned to cover today. The question now is, do you like it?"*

Asking audiences if they *like* your solution is a refreshing change from the "same old same old" closer. Instead of asking for a commitment or a dissertation on how they feel about your solution, you are simply asking for their gut reaction. For the presenter, this accomplishes two things. First, it encourages people to put aside the details and focus on how comfortable they are with your solution. Second, if the prospect responds favorably and acknowledges that they do, in fact, "like" what they heard in your presentation, you can easily transition the opportunity into the third phase of the QBS sales process.

There are lots of reasons why prospects might like your solution. Some people will like your product because it's versatile. Other people will like it because it can be upgraded over time, or because they think your solution will increase their productivity and bolster their bottom line. Still others will like your solution because the price can be amortized over the life of the product. Whatever the reason, if prospects like the solution you've just articulated, then they will want more information about the details of a purchase—starting with how much it costs. This is your ticket into Phase III.

Your Ticket into Phase III

The transition from the Phase II presentation to the close in Phase III can feel as awkward as having to walk across the dance floor to ask that special someone to dance. It's the moment of truth where sellers find out if the prospect wishes to continue the relationship.

The good news is the transition between Phase II and Phase III doesn't have to feel awkward. In fact, QBS makes it downright comfortable by making the transition seamless. Rather than finishing your presentation and then trying to figure out how to move the opportunity forward, we suggest asking transition questions that will make the shift from Phase II to Phase III logical and seemingly automatic. Let me show you how this works.

Once the prospect acknowledges that they do *like* what they've just seen in your presentation, you can easily secure the appropriate next steps in the sales process by asking questions like:

Salesperson:	*"Would you like me to prepare a detailed proposal that outlines the cost of our solutions?"*
Prospect:	*"Yes, please."*
Salesperson:	*"Can we schedule a technical meeting so my engineer can assess your existing configuration?"*
Prospect:	*"That would be good, too."*

I always end my presentations by asking the prospect if they would like to know how much it costs. How can they refuse? If they "liked" your solution, why wouldn't they want to know how much it costs?

In smaller sales, you may have the pricing at your fingertips, but I would still recommend asking the question, because it helps transition your conversation without the usual awkwardness. In larger sales, preparing a detailed proposal often creates the need for additional events—in this case, perhaps a technical meeting to assess the prospect's existing configuration. It might also make sense to schedule a follow-up meeting to review your proposal.

Some sellers avoid talking about price until the very last minute. QBS says bring it up at the end of the presentation. Besides securing the option for additional events, the best time to cost-justify a purchase is right after the presentation, when the value of your offering is fresh in the mind of your prospects. Personally, I want the price to be on the table at the beginning of Phase III because I'd like to know sooner rather than later if price is going to be an obstacle in the sale. This gives me time to overcome objections, and it might spare some wasted effort if the prospect isn't as qualified as I once thought.

> **Secret #153** Rather than avoid a discussion about price, QBS recommends using price to transition the sale into Phase III.

If the prospect likes your presentation enough to request a proposal, you *earn the right* to suggest all kinds of follow-up events—including site surveys, technical meetings, on-site product demonstrations, executive overviews, even reconvening the committee to review your proposal. Now, you have successfully transitioned the sale into Phase III—*Closing Steps.*

Summary

In the QBS sales presentation, the goal is building enough value to justify a favorable purchase decision. This requires audiences to recognize the existence of a need and listen attentively to the solutions being offered. Presentation skills like voice inflection, facial expressions, and gesturing are definitely important. But even more important is your ability to accomplish the strategic objectives of the presentation and move the opportunity forward into the third and final phase of the QBS sales process. That's what we will focus on next in chapter 16—understanding what must happen to close more sales…faster.

CLOSING MORE SALES...FASTER

With Question Based Selling, closing the sale is just a logical extension of the sales process. Once you have successfully uncovered prospect needs, qualified the opportunity, and presented your solution, it's time to wrap up the business transaction.

You don't have to use high-pressure tactics to be a successful closer, however. QBS simplifies the process by identifying the five prerequisites for closing. Then we focus on the four keys that will enable you to close more sales...in less time.

The third and final phase of the QBS sales process is appropriately called Closing Steps. As you can see in the diagram, Phase III is represented by the bottom of the sales funnel. This is where all your selling efforts to date will culminate to transform qualified prospect opportunities into valuable customer accounts.

As you saw in the presentation (Phase II), your actual closing steps will depend on the product you sell and the audience you are selling to. In smaller sales, where you are face-to-face with a single decision maker, all three phases of the sales process can occur within a single sales call. In this situation, the presentation is followed immediately by the close. After summarizing the value offered by your product or service, you wrap up the sale by securing the prospect's commitment to purchase.

With larger, more strategic sales, however, closing is significantly more complex. Ironically, the reason is simple. When multiple players are involved in a buying

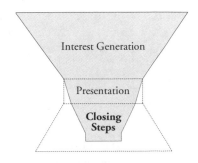

Phase III: Closing Steps

decision, it's more difficult to secure the consensus needed to pull the trigger on a decision. Each person involved forms their own impressions about the solutions being offered; and while some people on the committee will favor your offering, others will support an alternate solution. Some might even gravitate to the path of least resistance—wanting to maintain the status quo. So, here's your challenge. To close a sale, you must succeed in bringing all these people together to make a consensus decision that favors your product or service.

Moving Away from the Old School

Most prospects are nervous in the final stages of a sale. It's a natural reaction—people get nervous whenever they have to make a commitment. We get nervous when we are about to buy a new car; we get nervous when we are about to sign the contract to buy a new house; and many of us have experienced the nervous butterflies that appear on the day of the big wedding. It's understandable then that our prospects may be nervous about making a commitment to purchase our product or service. What if they make a mistake? What if they make the wrong decision?

The old school of selling tends to view closing as a series of tricks, gimmicks, and schemes designed to manipulate potential buyers into saying yes. QBS doesn't rely on gimmicks. I think prospective customers are smarter and more sophisticated today than ever before, and while most people love to buy, they don't want to be *sold*. Prospects are no longer willing to be pushed, pressured, or otherwise harassed into making a purchase, so there's no point in trying to force a decision. As we pointed out earlier, the harder you push, the harder your prospects and customers will push back.

Closing should not be a one-sided affair. If you offer valuable solutions at a reasonable price, then you shouldn't have to *dupe* your prospects into buying. Instead, the decision to buy should be a win-win scenario—where the salesperson accomplishes his or her goal of completing the sale, and the customer satisfies his or her own objectives by acquiring a valuable solution.

> **Secret #154** Closing isn't something you do *to* somebody; rather, it's a mutual experience you have *with* them.

QBS's approach to closing sales is an intentional departure from the "old school." Rather than pressing prospects to force a decision, QBS focuses on leading them (via questions) to the desired result. We believe that the key to closing sales is getting buyers to value your product so much that they will *want to* move forward with a purchase.

Closing is by no means easy, however. Phase III of the sales process is filled with risk. Potential buyers are nervous about making a commitment, and salespeople are equally nervous about asking for one. As most of us already know, asking for the order is another one of those moments of truth in the sales process where the seller finds out whether their efforts will result in a successful sale or a missed opportunity.

Hope Is Not a Method

Back in high school, my tenth grade sex education teacher used to tell us, "Hope is not a method." Of course, he was talking about family planning and birth control. Oddly enough, hope is not a method when it comes to closing sales either.

Some sellers try to avoid the risk of being rejected by plowing forward with a variety of events, activities, and action items, *hoping* that their extra effort will move potential buyers toward a favorable decision. This "hopefulness" can be detrimental to your sales efforts, however. The following story illustrates this point with an important lesson about closing.

A few years ago during the holiday season, I headed off to the mall to do some Christmas shopping. My first stop was Macy's Department Store, where I wanted to purchase some perfume for my wife, Laura. If you have never been to Macy's at Christmastime, you have missed quite a spectacle. The displays are beautifully decorated with all the holiday trappings, and the aisles are bustling with people. I headed straight for the cosmetics department, where I noticed several other men who were on similar missions, trying to find that perfect gift for someone special.

When I reached the perfume counter, the number of options from which to choose overwhelmed me. There were perfumes, colognes, powders, bath beads, body lotions, and eau de toilette (whatever that is). All kinds of fragrances were on display, from every brand name you could think of. Most of the items were sold separately, but some were also available in holiday gift sets, which seemed like a good option.

One perfume in particular caught my eye, a fragrance by Alfred Sung. I remembered Laura had mentioned this one by name, which reduced my risk of making a bad decision. It smelled nice too. My search was over.

Some People Will Do Anything to Make a Sale

I flagged down one of Macy's finest to complete the transaction—but first, I had a question. I had noticed that Alfred Sung didn't come in a holiday gift set, which was really what I wanted. I shared this concern with the Macy's clerk, and she offered, *"Would you like me to create a custom gift set by bundling a few items together into a nice basket?"*

"That would be great," I replied.

The Macy's clerk promptly ducked down behind the counter. When she popped back up, she was holding two small bottles; one was a cologne and the other was a scented lotion. She explained that if I bought both, she could include the Alfred Sung body powder at no additional cost.

"That would be wonderful," I said. Then, more out of ignorance than strategy, I asked, *"Can you include anything else?"*

"I'll see what I can do," she said. Once again, she ducked down behind the counter. In twenty or thirty seconds, she popped back up and said, *"I can throw in a freshening kit—two smaller fragrance items that would easily fit inside your wife's purse or in a glove compartment."*

"Thank you," I said. Sensing that I was on a roll, I asked, *"What else?"*

She smiled and once again ducked down behind the counter. This time she popped up with a cute little carrying case to add to the pile.

"You're doing a great job!" I said. *"What else?"*

This time, she ducked behind the counter and came back up with a handful of fragrance samplers. *"These make great stocking stuffers."*

To my surprise, we had established a routine. Every time I asked, *"What else?"* my new friend, the Macy's clerk, sweetened the deal. So I continued asking, *"What else?"*

"Hmmm," she said as she disappeared into the back room. After a few moments, she came out holding a neatly wrapped box. *"How about a set of champagne glasses? These were being offered as part of another promotion, but if you like, I can throw them in too."*

"That's terrific…and thank you once again," I said. Even though I sensed the end was drawing near, my curiosity forced me to see just how far this salesperson was willing to go to make a sale. So, once again, I asked, *"What else?"*

After a pause, she smiled and said, *"Isn't that enough?"* I smiled back and nodded. Frankly, it was enough three trips ago, but as long as the clerk was willing to keep making my wife's Christmas present better and better, I had to keep asking, *"What else?"* When I walked out of Macy's that day, I had a shopping bag full of perfume and accessories, all for the price of the first two items. Even though that was several years ago, I think we're still knee-deep in Alfred Sung.

An Important Lesson about Closing

I'm not criticizing Macy's department store. Macy's provides excellent value and their customer service has always been exceptional. That's why I've been a loyal customer for many years. Nonetheless, this scenario does illustrate a valuable lesson about closing—or should I say, how *not* to close.

The Macy's clerk in this story was certainly pleasant, and she provided terrific customer service, but her closing strategy left something to be desired. She made the mistake of assuming that the more value she threw into the deal, the closer she got to consummating a sale. Her assumption had two problems. First, the only way a salesperson can exceed the customer's expectations is to understand what those expectations are. If the Macy's clerk had simply asked, *"Mr. Freese, if we wrap these three items into a holiday gift set, will that work for you?"* I would have said, "Sure," and the sale would have been over. Furthermore, this salesperson's willingness to give away more than was actually required to close the sale was counterproductive. In addition to reducing the company's profit on the transaction, this person's commitment to customer service was actually encouraging me (the buyer) to keep asking for more. In a sense, she was too customer-service oriented—trying to sweeten the deal in the hopes of achieving the desired result. But the more value she was willing to offer, the more my expectations changed, which in this case, actually moved the salesperson further away from closing the sale.

> **Secret #155** Giving away too much isn't mutually beneficial. Sellers have to know when to add value...and when to stop.

The "kill 'em with customer service" closing mentality isn't restricted to department store clerks. It's alive and well in large-account corporate sales, insurance sales, medical sales, technology sales, and many other types of selling. Instead of identifying obstacles in the sale and then addressing the outstanding deficiencies, too many sellers try to close by asking questions like, *"What else can I do?"* This encourages prospects to think up objections or additional action steps to keep you occupied. In Question Based Selling, we want to be effective, not just busy. Good intentions and extra effort are only part of the puzzle. If you really want to close more sales, then you must accomplish each of the five prerequisites for closing.

Five Prerequisites for Closing

It's natural to assume that the most productive salespeople are also the best closers—after all, aren't they the ones who close the most sales? Yes, but there's a catch. Productive salespeople are not successful because they have a secret formula for closing deals. They're successful because they know how to get prospects *ready* to be closed. This is an important distinction.

> **Secret #156**   Success in selling hinges less on your ability to close, and more on your ability to get prospects *ready* to be closed.

I have always believed if the sales process is executed properly, the actual close should be an anticlimactic event. In reality, there are no magical closing phrases that can force a prospect to buy a product or service they don't really want. And if the potential buyer *does* want the solution you offer, you won't need magic to close the sale.

The only trick is getting your prospects "ready" to be closed, which means satisfying each of the prerequisites for the sale. What do we mean by prerequisites? Just as credibility was a prerequisite for building relationships (in the Conversational Layering Model), there are five prerequisite conditions that must be satisfied before potential buyers will purchase your product or service. These five prerequisites are as follows:

Five Prerequisites to Closing Sales

1. **A Recognized Need**
2. **A Viable Solution**
3. **Value Must Justify the Cost**
4. **A Sense of Urgency**
5. **The Authority to Buy**

Your ability to satisfy each of these prerequisites in Phase III is largely dependent on what happened in Phases I and II of the QBS sales process. For example, prospective customers should recognize needs long before you try to close the sale in Phase III. In fact, by the time you move into the *Closing Steps* phase of the sales process, much of the groundwork for the sale should already be in place. To show you what I mean, let's review each of the prerequisites for closing.

Prerequisite #1: A Recognized Need

Every purchase decision represents a buyer's attempt to satisfy a need. Their needs are what initially motivate them to investigate potential solutions, and needs are what ultimately motivates them to buy. Prospects will only want to buy your product or service if they recognize a need for it. Of course, the more needs you uncover in the sales process, the more reasons they have to make a favorable decision when it's time to close.

Prerequisite #2: A Viable Solution

Once the existence of a need causes prospects to recognize that it's time to change the status quo, the discovery of a viable solution is what motivates them to move forward toward a decision. The best opportunity to showcase the viability of your solution occurs in the Phase II presentation. That's when you get an opportunity to match the benefits of your product or service against the prospect's specific needs.

Prerequisite #3: Value Must Justify the Cost

Cost justification is the basis for every strategic decision. It's also a prerequisite for closure. By itself, the existence of a need is never enough to justify a purchase. Likewise, just because you offer a viable solution doesn't mean prospects can justify the expense. To purchase your product or service, the perceived value of your solution must exceed its cost. Keep in mind that the greater the value, the easier it is to cost-justify a purchase.

Prerequisite #4: A Sense of Urgency

Without a compelling and discernible reason to make a decision, it's always easier to maintain the status quo. You've heard the phrase *if it ain't broke, don't fix it*. Well, this phrase applies to closing sales. Until your prospect feels a sense of urgency, he or she is not likely to buy your product or service.

Creating a sense of urgency is different than cost-justification, however. Even if the value of your solution justifies its cost, some people still won't pull the trigger until they are ready to make an emotional commitment.

Prerequisite #5: The Authority to Buy

Needs, solutions, justification, and a sense of urgency, all rolled together, still aren't enough to get prospects off the dime. Your prospect must also have the authority to make a buying decision. Imagine how rich you would be if you had a nickel for every proposal that was left stranded at the end of the sales process because the prospect did not have the authority to make a decision.

I've said it before, and I'll say it again. Qualifying the opportunity is critical to your success. This includes knowing who will make the actual buying decision. In addition to doing the right things, you also have to be dealing with the right people—those who will influence or make the decision.

QBS Makes Closing Easy

If all five of the prerequisites for closing have been completely satisfied, meaning the prospective buyer recognizes the existence of a need *and* the viability
of your solution, they have the authority to make a decision *and* the sense of
urgency to move forward, *and* the value of your product or service is great
enough to justify its cost, then closing the sale should be a breeze. At that point,
all you have to do is offer encouragement and ask for the order.

If one or more of these prerequisite conditions is not in place, however, then
the opportunity is not *ready* to be closed. That's when sellers must either push
prospects to try to force a sale or step back and figure out how to address any outstanding issues. As you might guess, the rest of this chapter is based on the latter.

The Four Keys to Closing More Sales

Some people think the act of closing is a combination of two things: asking
prospects for the business and overcoming their objections. That's what the
"old school" has been teaching for years—that sellers must be bold enough
to ask for the order and aggressive enough to conquer objections when the
prospect says no. Essentially, the thinking has always been that a seller's ability
to *push* must exceed the prospect's ability to *resist*.

QBS's approach to closing sales is much less pushy and far more productive. Instead of beating potential buyers over the head in the hopes of closing a
sale, we base our strategy on mutual benefit and the prevention of conflict. We
want prospects to *want* to move forward. That's why QBS focuses our closing
efforts on the four keys to closing more sales.

Key #1: Know the Status of the Opportunity

Knowing the status of an opportunity is critical when you are trying to close
a sale. Does your buyer like the proposed solution? How does it compare to
other solutions? When do they plan to make a decision? How much are they
willing to pay? What are their outstanding concerns? The answers to these and
other questions are pivotal to understanding the status of your opportunities,
and knowing how best to proceed toward completing a sale.

This is an area where sales managers in particular get very frustrated. They
know that in order to have an effective strategy for closing a sale, you have
to know where you stand in the account. If all five prerequisites for closing
have been fully satisfied, then you have a "green light" to ask for the order
and wrap up the transaction. Everybody wins. But if the prospect is not ready
to be closed, it's critical that you know exactly where you stand, so you can
determine what else needs to occur to secure a favorable decision.

Having a complete and accurate status of your prospect opportunities also reduces your risk. Throughout this book we have introduced and discussed a myriad of techniques that enable sellers to find out where the prospect stands before asking for a commitment. This is very different from the traditional risky method of sticking your neck out and hoping that it doesn't get chopped off.

> **Secret #157**   Soliciting feedback is important, but it's even more important to solicit complete and accurate feedback.

The real challenge in closing is having a complete and accurate status of the sale. We've acknowledged that most prospects are naturally cautious of salespeople. Experience has taught them to play it close to the vest, so they are often reluctant to share their thoughts, feelings, or concerns. This creates somewhat of a dichotomy—where sellers, who want to know where they stand in their sales opportunities, are facing off against prospects who may not be willing to openly share. Can you see the dilemma?

To Find Out if They're Ready, Ask for the Order

Wayne Gretzky, arguably one of the greatest professional hockey players of all time, once said, *"You will miss 100 percent of the shots you never take."* The same is true in professional sales—you won't close many sales unless you're willing to ask for the order. It's the only real way to find out if a sale is *ready* to be closed.

But asking for the order is a high-risk proposition. What if the prospect says no? Then your sale, along with all the resources and effort you've invested thus far, would be lost. Unfortunately, the fear of receiving a negative response causes many salespeople to gravitate to the idea that *if I don't ask, the prospect can't say no.*

With Question Based Selling, we believe that asking for the order actually reduces your risk. That's because asking for the order isn't the end of the closing process. Rather, it's the beginning. If the prospect *is* indeed ready to move forward, then you simply wrap up the details of the transaction. If they are *not* ready, however, then you still have taken a valuable step forward because your closing question will help smoke out any obstacles that stand in the way of a deal. If you've satisfied the prerequisites for closing, being upfront reduces your risk because you can only overcome those problems and objections that you know about.

To Keep It Simple, Use the Direct Approach

Just as there's more than one way to skin a cat, there's also more than one way to ask for the order. Many salespeople like the direct approach. After each of the prerequisite conditions has been satisfied, they come right out and ask, *"Mr. Prospect, are you ready to make a decision?"* or *"Is there anything that would prevent you from moving forward on this proposal?"* Note that even the direct approach has a certain softness, with the salesperson asking if they are "ready" to move forward, as opposed to going for the jugular and asking for the actual transition.

The direct approach is remarkably effective, particularly if you have invested the time to develop personal relationships with your prospects and customers.

Up Close and Personal

People love to give advice and they love to be asked for their opinion. Since one of our objectives in Phase III is finding out how the prospect feels about your offering, why not get up close and personal to find out where you stand in the sale? Asking for someone's opinion is a terrific way to solicit feedback. Here are some examples of up close and personal questions you might ask:

Seller:	*"Ms. Prospect, what are your thoughts about…?"*
	"How do you feel about the current status of…?"
	"Since you have lots of experience, how would you handle…?"

One note: some prospects are cautious about revealing their intentions. This can be a challenge for sellers because cautious prospects tend to limit the quantity and the quality of the information they share. For prospects that are particularly standoffish, try taking your conversations *off the record*. This is a wonderful technique for getting overly prudent prospects to open up. For example, you might ask: *"Mr. Prospect, can I ask you something—off the record? How does your management really feel about the proposal we submitted?"*

> **Secret #158** It's amazing how many people will suddenly open up when their comments are considered "off the record."

In addition to knowing how a prospect feels, it's also important to know what they are expecting. For example, suppose one of your prospects raises the issue of cost, saying, *"The price in your proposal seems a little high."* Many sellers hear this and launch into objection-handling mode. Not so in QBS. We believe that in order to successfully handle an objection, you must first understand the prospect's expectations. Therefore, we encourage sellers to refrain from objection handling until they probe the issue further—in this case, by saying:

Seller: *"Really? How much were you expecting to pay?"*

If you probe an objection and listen carefully to the prospect's response, you will not only know where you stand in the sale, you will also find out what the prospect was expecting.

Another way to ferret out a prospect's expectations is to switch places in the conversation. Ask your prospects what *they* would do if they were in your shoes. Since everyone loves to give advice, this is a good way for prospects to help themselves by helping you.

Seller: *"Mr. Prospect, if you were in my shoes, how would you handle...?"*

                 "If you were the salesperson on this account, what would you propose to management?"

                 "If our roles were reversed, what would you be doing differently?"

Your prospect's insight is a wonderful source of information and ideas. What better way to navigate the sales process than to leverage the experience of those people closest to the decision? In fact, most advice is free for the asking... so ask away!

Trial Closing Strategies

If you're uncomfortable with the direct approach, you can still uncover the status of an opportunity by using *trial closes*. Trial closing reduces your risk even further because it allows you to test the waters (to find out if the prospect is ready to be closed), before you jump in with both feet. Here are a few of my favorite question-based trial closes.

Alternate Choice

The alternate choice close is a popular technique. It's also a very effective closing strategy. Rather than directly asking prospects if they are ready to move forward, you ask them to choose between two viable alternatives…hence the name *alternate choice*. Here are a few examples.

Seller:	*"Would you rather have a cash discount or attractive financing?"*
	"Are you interested in the standard service agreement, or would you like the extended warranty?"
	"Is regular mail acceptable, or would you prefer over-night delivery?"

If the prospect chooses either option, they are essentially telling you that they are ready to move forward—after all, why would anyone select financial terms, a service agreement, or a delivery preference unless they were planning to purchase your product or service?

Asking about Smaller Components of the Larger Sale

Big decisions are sometimes difficult for prospects to swallow. With larger commitments comes greater risk. This is an emotional hurdle that can stymie the strategic sale. One way to avoid this is by asking questions that cause prospects to focus on smaller components of the larger sale.

Seller:	*"Where do you plan to warehouse the product once it arrives?"*
	"Have you already talked to your bank about financing?"
	"Have you thought about when you'd like to take delivery?"

A real estate agent, for example, might ask a prospective home-buyer, *"Have you thought about how you would furnish this house?"* If they have, then there's a good chance the prospect is getting ready to make a buying decision.

The Impending Event Close

Some prospects waffle and delay until they are literally forced to make a decision. But rather than allow them to wait until the eleventh hour, I recommend using the impending event close to create a sense of urgency that gives the prospect a reason to move forward.

What's an impending event? It's something that is going to happen in the near future that will impact the price, performance, serviceability, or availability of your goods and services. For example, if your company is planning a price increase on January 1, you have an opportunity to save customers money and pull in orders by leveraging the impending event. To encourage your prospects to focus on completing their business by this date, you might ask:

Seller: *"Mr. Prospect, does it make sense to try to wrap this sale up by year-end so you can take advantage of our lower price?"*

"If so, what needs to happen between now and then?"

Rather than pressuring prospects to close a sale, the salesperson in this example is simply letting the prospect know there is a significant benefit to be gained by moving forward prior to the impending event. The beauty of this approach is if a prospect wants to take advantage of the benefit, then they will put pressure on themselves to wrap up the sale.

Neutralize the Disposition of Your Closing Questions
One of the best ways to find out where you stand in the sale is to neutralize the disposition of your questions. We introduced this idea in chapter 10. When it's time to close, sellers start to feel the risk of rejection. As a result, they ask positive questions in the hopes of generating a more positive response. This behavior is counterproductive, however. Prospects tend to mismatch the hopefulness of positive questions, in which case, salespeople end up receiving cautious, reluctant, or even negative responses.

In Question Based Selling, we want prospects to respond openly, honestly, and accurately to our closing questions. If there's bad news lurking somewhere in the deal, we want to know about it so we have a chance to address it. Conversely, if there's good news, we want to know about that too. You can easily accomplish this by neutralizing the disposition of your closing questions.

Seller: *"Ms. Prospect, you look concerned. Something's not right, is it?"*

"Are we in good shape to get the deal, or do you think we're at risk?"

> *"If there was a problem lurking, one that would neg-
> atively impact your decision, would you be willing to
> share it with me?"*

By inserting "the negative" into your trial closes, you will be rewarded with more open, honest, and accurate responses. Some sales traditionalists might argue that neutralizing the disposition of your questions gives prospects an easy out. As before, I would argue that prospects already have an out. They don't *have* to buy from you—and many won't, without ever sharing the reason why not.

You Might Even Try Being Honest

Buyers understand that salespeople have goals and objectives. In fact, most are smart enough to recognize that you probably report to someone who's just as intense and demanding as their boss. This puts you (the salesperson) in a unique position to ask:

Seller:	*"Mr. Prospect, can I ask your advice on something? I'm supposed to have a conference call with my sales manager tomorrow morning. I was originally fore-casting this opportunity to close in September, but I would rather be accurate than optimistic. Do you think September is still a reasonable target, or should I tell my boss something different?"*

This is a sincere and honest request for help. It reinforces the fact that you are willing to put accuracy and the prospect's needs ahead of your own goals. If you have established a decent amount of credibility with the prospect, and you have provided value in the sales process thus far, they are usually happy to reciprocate by helping you. If the prospect reassures you that your forecast is indeed accurate, your probability of closing the sale increases significantly. On the other hand, if they inform you that your forecasted time frames are not realistic, that's your signal to ask additional questions to better understand where you stand in the sale.

Key #2: Tit-for-Tat

When an opportunity is not yet ready to be closed, more selling needs to occur. So salespeople invest additional time, effort, and resources to influence the outcome of the decision. When the opportunity still isn't ready, sellers invest even more effort. After investing even more effort, some opportunities still are not ready to be closed. This can go on and on in what seems like an endless chase. Some people call it the closing dance.

To avoid falling into this trap, you must realize that a sale represents a mutual exchange of value. The key word here is *mutual*. In a mutual exchange, both parties succeed in accomplishing their own goals. The seller wins because he or she completes the sale. The buyer wins because he or she receives the equivalent value in products or services. Both parties win.

Tit-for-tat is actually a negotiation strategy that adheres to one simple principle. If you are going to expend time, effort, and resources working on a sale, then you should expect something in return—a commitment, or at least a gesture that lets you know your efforts are accomplishing mutual goals. Every effective closing strategy is based on tit-for-tat.

Secret #159 Salespeople who expend effort and provide value should expect to get something in return.

In the Macy's story, the clerk kept throwing more and more value into the deal in the hopes of closing a sale. But that wasn't mutually beneficial. She should have secured a commitment from me (the customer) first, by saying, "*If I create a holiday gift set with these three items, will that work for you?*" This one question would have ended the negotiation, and I would have been a satisfied consumer.

Ask Prospects for a Commitment

Asking for a commitment is actually easier than it sounds. Rather than be intimidated by the possibility that a potential buyer will say no, sellers can use hypothetical questions to facilitate this concept of tit-for-tat. For example, a salesperson might ask, "*Ms. Prospect, if we do this or that...would you be willing to agree to move forward with a purchase?*"

A hypothetical question like this one will prompt one of two responses. Either the prospect *will* agree to purchase your product or service, or she will back off. If she backs off, then some other obstacle is preventing the sale.

Let's not get hung up on the word *commitment*, however. With a tit-for-tat strategy, you aren't looking for an absolute guarantee that the prospect will buy, just some indication that your sales efforts will yield a mutual benefit. Using a variation of this technique, you could also ask, "*After we do this or that... what happens next?*" Depending on how the prospect responds, you would then decide how best to proceed.

QBS's tit-for-tat principle applies even when you're not dealing directly with the decision maker. Whether it's a champion, coach, or some other person in the account who doesn't have authority to make a commitment, you can still ask for reciprocal effort. For example, you might say, *"Mr. Champion, if we do this or that…would you be willing to recommend our solution to the rest of the committee?"* Notice that we're still asking for mutual effort.

Is the Business Worth Chasing?

Once you know exactly where the prospect stands, you have a decision to make: is the business even worth chasing? If the prospect's expectations are reasonable, and the rewards from the sale are worth the invested effort, then it makes sense to continue working toward the sale. But there will be cases where the prospect's expectations are not reasonable. After they ask for the world, they will want you to throw in the moon and the stars. When you are in these situations, and you know you cannot accommodate their requests, you must decide whether to continue chasing the deal or refocus your efforts on other more qualified accounts.

> **Secret #160** Just because your product or service adds value doesn't mean every deal is worth chasing.

What should you do when a prospect's expectations are unreasonable? Should you ignore their requests and risk losing the sale, or should you give in to every demand under the theory that the customer is always right?

The answer is neither. Success in today's business environment is based on win-win relationships, and everything is negotiable. Therefore, a request that is unreasonable under one set of conditions might be quite acceptable if those conditions were to change. For example, let's say one of your prospects asked for an extra 10 percent discount off your best price. Should you get upset or indignant and take the position that the customer was being unreasonable? I wouldn't. Instead, it might be wiser to let the customer know what set of conditions would allow you to honor their request. You might say, *"We would be happy to give you an extra 10 percent discount…if you would be willing to double the size of your order."* How's that for a win-win scenario?

Tit-for-tat protects you from having to be the bad guy—the one who ultimately refuses the prospect's request. In that regard, it's a risk reduction strategy. Best of all, you can use tit-for-tat to negotiate just about anything. Here's a little anecdote that illustrates how tit-for-tat can change your perspective.

One night in the middle of supper, Ben Jenkins, a five-year-old boy, turned to his mother and asked, "Can I have a treat?"

Noticing that Ben hadn't eaten very much, his mother said, *"No, you may not have a treat until you clean your plate."* Not surprisingly, Ben didn't particularly like his mother's response, so he kicked, pouted, and fussed. Even though his mother was doing the proper thing under the circumstances, she was suddenly the bad guy—the one standing in the way of Ben's request for a treat.

This same behavior continued, night after night. Ben would eat a fraction of his dinner and then ask for a treat. And night after night, Mrs. Jenkins stuck to her guns and would not allow Ben to have a treat until he finished his supper. As you might guess, Ben became increasingly rebellious and difficult at dinner.

Finally, after more than a week of internal strife, Mr. Jenkins had had enough. He consulted his QBS materials and decided it was time to invoke a little tit-for-tat negotiating strategy. From now on, if Ben asked for a treat before finishing his dinner, the husband and wife agreed that Mr. Jenkins would handle the request.

Sure enough, the very next night, Ben had only eaten a portion of his supper when he turned to his mother and asked, *"Mom, can I have a treat?"*

"Tonight you need to ask your father," Mrs. Jenkins countered.

Slowly, Ben turned to his father and said, *"Dad, can I have a treat?"*

"Sure," Mr. Jenkins said. *"You may absolutely have a treat...just as soon as you finish your dinner."*

Ben's parents were in total agreement on principle, but the way they responded to their son's request was very different. The mother responded based on the current set of conditions. Ben hadn't finished his dinner; therefore, he wasn't entitled to a treat. The father, using our tit-for-tat philosophy, put Ben in control of his own destiny by assuring that he could "absolutely" have a treat as soon as he met the conditions that made his request a reasonable one. The moral to this story is the next time one of your customers asks for something, rather than dig your heels in and say no, let them know the conditions that would make their request mutually beneficial.

Tit-for-tat is especially valuable once we realize that buyers have been conditioned to ask for more than they actually expect. It's all part of the closing dance. But that certainly doesn't mean you have to bend over backward to close a sale.

Key #3: Reiterate Your Value Proposition

Phase III of the QBS funnel is also a good time for review. It's an opportunity for salespeople to help prospects organize their thoughts, and an opportunity to summarize the key points that have been made thus far in the sales process.

Ultimately, you want the sale to crescendo and peak just as prospects are getting ready to make their decision. You want them to be in touch with their own needs and register value in the solutions that were presented. You also want them to feel a sense of urgency. This requires an active effort on your part to summarize needs and reiterate value.

Secret #161   Effectively representing a product or service requires salespeople to *re-present* its value prior to closing.

Whether the sales cycle lasts two months or two years, it's easy to assume that if something has already been covered, there's no need to go over it again. *"We've already covered that,"* salespeople sometimes think to themselves. And it's true—through diligence and hard work, they probably have.

Unfortunately, salespeople sometimes fail to recognize that just because something has already been covered doesn't mean prospects will remember the most salient points. Particularly in larger sales, prospective buyers are asked to assimilate lots of information, so by the end of the sales process much of the material that was originally presented has faded over time. This creates a problem. If the information that justifies your solution fades, then the prerequisites for closing that were once satisfied may no longer be intact.

In the early 1900s, scientists began studying nuclear particles. During this research, they discovered that the radioactivity in nuclear substances dissipates naturally over time. They began measuring this phenomenon in units of *half-life*—the time required for half of the radioactivity contained in a nuclear material to dissipate naturally over time. Some nuclear substances have a half-life of many years, while others lose half their radiation in a matter of hours.

A similar phenomenon happens in sales. Although we would like to think our prospects and customers remember everything we present, much of the information that gets covered during the sales process also dissipates naturally over time. Case in point, what's the half-life of your typical sales presentation? In other words, how long does it take for someone in your audience to forget a significant portion of what they've heard? Two or three days? Or, perhaps only two or three hours?

The human memory is a limited resource—so when fresh information comes in, older information tends to get pushed to the background. Accordingly, some portion of what was originally stored in memory is lost. For example, say you went to a party one night, and soon after the party ended you were asked to name the people you met there. You would probably remember most of whom you talked with and what you talked about. But a few weeks later, you would likely only recall some fraction of the guest list, and only snippets of your conversations. After a few months, you would remember even less...and so on.

> **Secret #162** *Half-life* impacts your sales efforts because it causes information that was once fully intact to fade over time.

During the course of a sale, salespeople provide lots of information to communicate the value of their product or service offering. But as you might expect, some of the points made early in the process are subject to this phenomenon of intellectual erosion. What that means to you is, when the end of the sale comes and it's time to close, certain prerequisites that were once intact may no longer be satisfied; the prospect will *not* be ready to be closed. That's why one of the keys to closing more sales is reiteration—helping prospects revisit both the problems you solve and the value you bring to the table. As time passes during the sales process, you will need to remind the prospect of several key issues, impacts, and solutions.

If you want prospects to make a decision in your favor, the perceived value of your solution must be great enough to justify its cost. That's one of the prerequisites for closing.

Justification starts with needs. Their needs are what originally motivate prospects to investigate potential solutions, and needs will ultimately motivate them to buy. But just like anything else, needs are also subject to this concept of half-life, where a prospect who once had many reasons to buy may only recall some fraction of those needs by the end of the sale.

To rekindle your prospect's sense of urgency, it's always a good idea to revisit the Mutual Agenda—the one you created in Phase II. As a compilation of the prospect's needs, the Mutual Agenda served as a wonderful road map for building value in the presentation. It can also be used to help close the sale. Reviewing each of the items on the Mutual Agenda is an excellent way to bring the prospect's needs back to the forefront of the decision.

> **Secret #163** As a prospect's hot buttons get hotter, the corresponding value of your solutions will increase significantly.

In addition to revisiting the prospect's needs, you should also reiterate the value of your product or service. But since people are motivated differently, be sure to revisit your *Gold Medal* and *German Shepherd* benefits. Since reward and aversion can each weigh heavily on a purchase decision, QBS recommends that you reiterate both.

This brings us to an interesting point about cost justification. Most sellers try to cost-justify the purchase with *Gold Medal* benefits—by pointing out all the wonderful benefits the prospect will get from choosing their solution. But, what about considering the cost of *not* selecting your solution? Perhaps we should take a lesson from Charlie Simms, one of the largest contractors in the southeast.

Whenever Charlie is asked to provide a price estimate on a roofing job, for example, he inspects the job site and then gives the homeowner a two-part quote. At the top of the quote, he details the specifications for the job—square footage, estimated materials, and labor. These line items are subtotaled into a cost estimate for installing a new roof.

The bottom of the estimate is reserved for a second quote. There, Charlie details how much the job will cost if the homeowner chooses to ignore the current problems, and the existing roof is exposed to further weather damage, leakage, or rot. Essentially, he gives prospective customers a chance to realize that while fixing the current problem isn't cheap, it's significantly less expensive than choosing to do nothing and let the problem get progressively worse.

Charlie is an excellent salesman, and his two-part quote has helped him close lots of business. This same concept can be applied in almost any sale. For example, what's the cost of *not* having life insurance in the event of an untimely death? What's the cost of *not* keeping pace with technology or *not* updating the service contract? What's the cost of downtime for the typical Fortune 500 Company? With a little effort on your part, you can help prospects realize that *not* buying your product or service might be their most expensive option.

> **Secret #164**   For prospects with pressing needs, not buying your product or service might be their most expensive option.

Key #4: Emotional Reassurance

The fourth and final key to closing more sales is providing emotional reassurance. Most purchases are highly emotional. After the analysis has been completed and the committee has issued its recommendation, the actual decision usually boils down to how the decision maker *feels* about the solution being offered, and whether they are comfortable enough to pull the trigger on a purchase.

Consequently, decision-making is very subjective. It's also laced with a tremendous amount of uncertainty and risk. On one hand, decision makers want to choose the right option for themselves and the organizations they represent. On the other hand, they want to avoid making a mistake. They get particularly nervous as the end of the sale approaches; as I've said before, the larger the purchase, the greater their risk.

To offset this risk, sellers must offer support at the end of the sales process—analytical support to justify the cost of the decision, and emotional reassurance to make prospects feel more comfortable.

> **Secret #165** Spending a few minutes to make customers feel special is more significant than spending hours to make them feel average.

There are lots of ways to reassure your prospects. Some of this might be common sense, but much of it is strategic positioning. In either case, the net effect is the same. The more comfortable your prospects are, the more likely they are to make a favorable buying decision.

When a prospect is facing the pressure of a difficult decision, they don't need to be pushed. Once you've challenged their thinking, what they really need now is a friend—someone who can empathize with the challenges of the decision, rather than caring only about the status of the sale. Your ability to show this kind of emotional support will help you bond with prospects and close more sales. Here are some sample questions sellers can use to empathize with their prospects.

Seller: *"I understand this is a difficult decision. How can I help?"*

"Obviously you've been thinking long and hard about this decision. Would you feel better if...?"

"Are you comfortable with...?"

Another way to empathize with a prospective buyer is to walk a mile in their shoes. This is accomplished by offering to participate in the decision. You simply adjust your questions by replacing the word "you" with the more inclusive pronoun "we." Here are some examples.

Seller: *"What can we do to convince the rest of the committee?"*

"How should we position this proposal to your vice president?"

"Is there anything we should be doing differently?"

Sincere empathy is very reassuring to a prospect who is about to make a buying decision. It shows that you appreciate the importance of the purchase and lets them know that you are interested in their success.

Safety in Numbers

The Herd Theory is a powerful strategy for engaging new prospects in productive sales conversation. But it's also a good technique for making prospects feel more comfortable at the end of the sales process. Knowing that "everyone else" seems to be moving in the same direction is very reassuring to prospects. That inclusiveness lets them know that they are indeed making a good decision. You can use this sense of momentum to bolster the prospect's confidence as an opportunity moves closer to closing. If your prospect raises a question or concern about price, for example, you can easily leverage the rest of the herd by saying:

Seller:	*"Mr. Prospect, I'm not surprised to hear you ask about price. Do you know why? It's because I've had this same discussion with Westinghouse, Southern Company, Bank of America, General Motors, United Healthcare, Hewlett Packard, AT&T, British Telecom…and many others. Would you like to know what finally solidified their decision?"*

The Herd Theory is not only a momentum builder, it's also an effective objection-handling strategy. By giving potential buyers the sense that other customers have already blazed the trail to success, you increase your own credibility while reducing the prospect's risk. Everybody wins!

In decisions that involve multiple players, salespeople can gain tremendous leverage from an internal champion who is willing to "go to bat" for their product or service. Particularly in large corporate sales, you probably won't have the luxury of personally engaging every person who will influence the decision. That's why it's so important to develop internal champions—people who are willing to carry your flag when you can't.

Secret #166   A champion who understands *how to sell* your product or service is worth their weight in commission checks.

For an internal champion to be effective, they must be emotionally involved. They must *like* what you are selling and they must be willing to tell others why they should like it too. You can help develop these internal champions, and their sense of loyalty, by asking *Solution Questions*.

We first talked about Solution Questions in chapter 9, when we were expanding the needs development conversation. Now, as we near the end of the sale, these same questions are excellent tools for grooming potential champions, and making sure they know how to effectively position the value of your product or service. To find out how effective your internal champions are, you should make it a point to ask questions like:

Seller: *"Mr. Champion, how do you think this product will benefit your specific environment?"*

"How would you compare our solution to other alternatives?"

"What will you do if your boss, or someone on the committee, objects to this proposal?"

Prospects who can thoughtfully articulate the benefits of your solution will respond by "selling you" on why their needs are important and how your solutions add value. This gives you an opportunity to listen and coach them if they need help or cheer them on if they can articulate a robust message.

Summary: Wrapping Up the Sale

Once the prerequisites for closing have been satisfied, it's time to wrap up the business transaction. That means working through the details of the purchase and providing prompt and excellent customer service. Once again, if the sales process is executed properly, the actual close should be an anticlimactic event.

But there's a larger lesson to be learned. If you want to close more sales, then you need to have more opportunities coming into the top of the sales funnel. This means using the Question Based Selling methodology to penetrate more new accounts, uncover more needs, present more value, and differentiate yourself from your competition. At the end of the day, there is no substitute for hard work. If you are committed to excellence, and you can challenge the customer's thinking by first challenging your own, you will accomplish the larger objective of significantly increasing your sales results.

EPILOGUE

FOR SALES MANAGERS ONLY

Salespeople who read *The Secrets of Question Based Selling* are trying to increase their own sales effectiveness. They want to penetrate more new accounts, uncover more needs, create a greater sense of urgency, and move qualified opportunities forward toward closure. Sales managers, on the other hand, are tasked with increasing the effectiveness of the sales team as a whole.

Sales managers definitely have the bigger challenge. They have to deal with many different selling styles and personalities, in addition to managing a broad range of sales experience. Salespeople who are just starting out often need lots of attention, and they often ask for it. But experienced sellers need attention too, even if it's just a kick in the pants to fix some bad habits that have crept into their daily routine. Ultimately, sales managers want to boost productivity by getting the entire sales organization to execute on a consistent and proven strategy.

Implementing a strategic sales methodology is *not* as easy as it sounds, however. With so many different philosophies to choose from, sales managers are discovering that some sales methods are overly simplistic, while others are so incredibly complex that their implementation in the real world is impractical.

Hype is another problem. A super-enthusiastic approach to selling may succeed in making some salespeople more excited, but it has been my experience that being "ultra-positive" rarely makes up for having poor technique. High-pressure sales tactics are equally ineffective, as today's prospects are no longer willing to endure the constant hammering from a steady stream of over-zealous salespeople.

Not surprisingly, salespeople and sales managers have grown tired of the same old sales training. Experienced sellers have heard it all before, and brand-new salespeople are applying traditional methods with limited success. What they want is something different—something that works.

> **Secret #167** In today's business culture, there is an *overwhelming* demand for proven sales talent, but there is an *underwhelming* infrastructure for teaching salespeople how to succeed.

Question Based Selling is a refreshing change from traditional sales methods. We don't use "hype" to get salespeople excited in the hopes they will sell more. Instead, we show them how to become more effective, knowing that salespeople who are more effective will be more successful. They will naturally get excited. It's fun to win, and you win by getting your prospects and customers excited about the value you bring to the table.

Question Based Selling is easy to implement so salespeople no longer have to wait weeks or months to see results. Results come immediately. The realization that buyers are motivated by *Gold Medals* and *German Shepherds*, for example, will instantly double the number of benefits your salespeople can present. It will also double the number of needs they can identify. Salespeople will receive similarly impressive results when they implement the Conversational Layering Model, the Herd Theory, the Lukewarm Calling template, and the Mutual Agenda. They will also discover how to leverage the most powerful tool in sales as they learn how to effectively manage the *Scope*, *Focus*, and *Disposition* of their questions. Each of the QBS strategies and techniques outlined in this book is designed to be implemented right away, perhaps in your very next sales opportunity.

This brings us to a very important question. What's the best way to introduce Question Based Selling to your sales organization? Actually, there are several ways. Each sales organization has different needs, and every Question Based Selling client is unique; therefore, we offer a variety of options from which you can choose to implement the QBS methodology.

This Book

The new *Secrets of Question Based Selling* is a unique book because it was written with a dual purpose. In addition to upgrading the QBS methodology, this book also serves as a reference guide salespeople can use again and again. Whether people read the book from cover to cover or go directly to those sections that speak to their specific needs, salespeople will learn how positioning themselves differently will identify more needs, communicate more value, and significantly increase their sales results.

This book is not just for salespeople, however. It's for everyone who touches the sales process, including product specialists, sales engineers, managers, marketing, telesales, and customer service personnel. Ultimately, selling is about positioning, and QBS is ultimately a positioning strategy. In the best-case scenario, everyone should be on the same page, which is easy with QBS.

QBS Methodology Training

QBS Research, Inc. offers a complete menu of sales training programs that focus on every aspect of the strategic sale. In our two- and three-day QBS Methodology Training courses, sellers learn how to more effectively penetrate new accounts, move opportunities forward in the sales process, overcome objections, justify the proposed solution, and close more sales. QBS training is a highly interactive experience, and the content for each program is customized to meet the specific needs of the client. We encourage clients to broaden the scope of their training audience to include telesales, sales engineers, product managers, and marketing—basically everyone who impacts the positioning of your product or service.

QBS Virtual Online Training

QBS Research, Inc. has partnered with Lightspeed VT to deliver a full menu of virtual training options in conjunction with our books, CDs, and customized on-site training options. The virtual training is our newest option and will enable students to have 24/7 access to QBS Training modules. Subscriptions can be set up for individual users, or a "roof plan" can be implemented to allow unlimited client access for a fixed monthly fee. Now our clients can bring new salespeople up to speed at their own pace, and reinforce the methodology with online interactive learning.

QBS Sales Talk

Salespeople who are highly motivated tend to be more productive. And one of the best ways to motivate your sales team is by giving them a dose of Question Based Selling at your next regional or national sales meeting. Using the QBS methodology as a backdrop, the author, or one of our other certified QBS instructors, can deliver a powerful sales talk that will inspire your salespeople by transforming a speaking engagement into a real learning experience. QBS sales talks can range from one to four hours in length and cover a variety of strategic topics.

One-Day QBS Training "Blitz"

The One-Day QBS Sales Training "Blitz" is a hybrid solution. Some clients want more than a sales talk, but they can only carve a single day out of their sales meeting for strategic training. For these clients, we have created a condensed version of the full QBS sales training. In a single day, we cover large portions of the QBS methodology at an aggressive pace. While many salespeople are accustomed to getting only one or two things out of a full day of sales training, the One-Day QBS "Blitz" offers a thought-provoking program packed with new ideas and strategic techniques.

QBS Continuing Education

Some sales training sessions are a one-shot deal. You educate the sales force, and then hope they remember enough to successfully implement the material. To maximize our client's return on investment, QBS Research, Inc. offers several options for ongoing training. Once your salespeople understand the methodology, QBS virtual training and/or periodic refresher courses can be scheduled to reinforce the original training as well as fine-tune specific skill sets. Popular topics include curiosity building, credibility strategies, objection handling, presentation skills, and closing.

Train the Trainers

Salespeople who implement Question Based Selling can also learn how to teach it. "Train the trainers" and coaching are concepts that have been in practice for a long time, and have proven themselves to be very effective. Any major roll-out of the QBS methodology can be significantly enhanced by developing in-house trainers and coaches. A QBS affiliate can help you accomplish this.

Contact Information

If you enjoyed reading *The Secrets of Question Based Selling*, then you will really enjoy putting the QBS methodology to work in your business. Success is contagious, and selling is exciting when prospective buyers *want* to hear more about the solutions you offer. To get started with QBS, all you need is a commitment to excellence and a willingness to challenge yourself to step outside the box of traditional sales thinking. Please let us know how we can help.

For more information about QBS Research, Inc., or QBS Sales Training Programs, please contact:

QBS Research, Inc.
Atlanta, Georgia
Office: (770) 840-7640
Fax: (770) 840-7642
Email: tfreese@QBSresearch.com
Website: www.QBSresearch.com

Notes

Index

origination, 30–32

pain vs. desire, 31–32, 34, 35, 37, 38, 55

presentations, 148–149, 248, 260, 261, 272–279, 283, 284

recognition, 29–30, 32–44, 154, 162, 163, 292–293

repository, 40–43, 250, 254–255

sales process, 99, 100, 101–103, 109, 192, 197, 199, 266–267

SPA vs. PAS positioning, 244–261

strategic process, 153–158

See also diagnostic questions; focus; implications

negative aversion. *See* German Shepherds

negative dispositioning, 92, 176–177, 180–183, 211–212

negative responses. *See* mismatching; rejection

negative selling, 54

negotiation, 300–303

NetFrame Systems, 48–49, 50, 92–93, 142–143, 149–150, 151, 158, 235, 276

neutralization of questions, 92, 175–176, 179–180, 183, 299–300

newness, 115–116, 131–132

Northwestern Mutual Life, 208

numbers game, xvi, 190–191, 201–202

O

objection handling, 75–76, 89, 199, 236, 285, 291, 294, 295, 296–297, 300–302, 308

office furniture sales, 145, 213

"off the record" conversations, 296

Olympics analogy, 49–50

one-upmanship, 85–86

online training, 313

open-ended questions, 101–102, 139–140, 141, 144, 151–152, 153–154, 159, 160, 216–219, 274, 278

order, asking for. *See* commitment requests

P

pain, 31–32, 34, 35, 37, 55

paradigm shift, 103

partial information, 127–129

PAS vs. SPA positioning, 244–261

perception of value, 5–10, 32–35, 38–40

perfect solutions, 169

persistence, 105, 190, 203

personal endorsements, 69, 138, 208

personalities, 4, 47–48, 52

politeness, 113–114, 117, 211, 212, 214, 217, 270

popcorn credibility, 72–75

positive attitude, 4, 46–47, 311

positive dispositioning, 4, 172–174, 180, 183, 289–291, 299

positive rewards. *See* gold medals

power, 197–198

presentation-centered model, 189

presentation qualifiers, 272–273

presentations, 263–286

   breaking the ice, 268–273

   chart, 263

   closing, 283–286, 293, 305

   credibility, 148–149, 265–267, 268, 273–274, 277

   effective delivery strategies, 280–283

About the Author

The first time Tom Freese oversold his sales quota by 200 percent, everyone thought it was a fluke. When he did it again, they assumed it was just some sort of freak accident. Over and over for seven consecutive years, Tom not only exceeded his sales quota, he doubled it. Suddenly, his success in selling was more than a trend. It was a business phenomenon!

With more than seventeen years' experience in the corporate sales and management trenches, Tom packaged his unique approach into a highly proven strategic sales methodology called Question Based Selling. Now, he works with sales organizations all over the world to show salespeople how a question-based approach can significantly increase their sales results. As founder and president of QBS Research, Inc., Tom is considered one of the foremost authorities on sales methodology, buyer motivation, and business strategy.

Tom Freese lives in Atlanta, Georgia, with his wife and two daughters. Between training engagements, Tom is busy working on his next book—a collection of strategic tools and selling techniques that will give salespeople the edge they need to compete in an increasingly tumultuous sales marketplace.

"As a salesperson, I was bored with traditional methods. I had been through all the standard 101 training, and I had already endured all the hype I could stand. What I really wanted was a methodology that would increase my effectiveness and differentiate my value in every aspect of the sales process. That's why I created Question Based Selling."

—Thomas A. Freese, President, QBS Research, Inc.

QBS Audio Program

Cassettes/CDs

Repetition is a critical success factor in any implementation. That's why QBS is now available on Audio Tapes and CDs. If you don't have the time or patience to read books, and you spend lots of time in your car or in front of an exercise machine, then this audio program is for you!

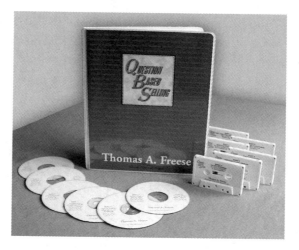

Order Your Books, Tapes or CDs Today!

Qty Description

___Audio CDs (Retail $99.95, plus S&H)

___Secrets of QBS (Retail $16.99, plus S&H)

___It Only Takes 1%... (Retail $16.95, plus S&H)

*Discounts available for quantity orders.

**Shipping and handling: $6.95 for first item; $2.50 for
additional items. International orders are additional.

QBS Research, Inc. • P.O. Box 922933
Atlanta, GA 30010-2933
www.QBSresearch.com